Mastering Java for Data Science

Building data science applications in Java

Alexey Grigorev

BIRMINGHAM - MUMBAI

Mastering Java for Data Science

First published: April 2017

Production reference: 1250417

Published by Packt Publishing Ltd.
Livery Place
35 Livery Street
Birmingham
B3 2PB, UK.

ISBN 978-1-78217-427-1

www.packtpub.com

Credits

Author
Alexey Grigorev

Reviewers
Stanislav Bashkyrtsev
Luca Massaron
Prashant Verma

Commissioning Editor
Veena Pagare

Acquisition Editor
Manish Nainani

Content Development Editor
Amrita Noronha

Technical Editor
Akash Patel
Deepti Tuscano

Copy Editor
Laxmi Subramanian

Project Coordinator
Shweta H Birwatkar

Proofreader
Safis Editing

Indexer
Aishwarya Gangawane

Graphics
Tania Dutta

Production Coordinator
Nilesh Mohite

About the Author

Alexey Grigorev is a skilled data scientist, machine learning engineer, and software developer with more than 7 years of professional experience.

He started his career as a Java developer working at a number of large and small companies, but after a while he switched to data science. Right now, Alexey works as a data scientist at Searchmetrics, where, in his day-to-day job, he actively uses Java and Python for data cleaning, data analysis, and modeling.

His areas of expertise are machine learning and text mining, but he also enjoys working on a broad set of problems, which is why he often participates in data science competitions on platforms such as kaggle.com.

You can connect with Alexey on LinkedIn at `https://de.linkedin.com/in/agrigorev`.

I would like to thank my wife, Larisa, and my son, Arkadij, for their patience and support while I was working on the book.

About the Reviewers

Stanislav Bashkyrtsev has been working with Java for the last 9 years. Last years were focused on automation and optimization of development processes.

Luca Massaron is a data scientist and a marketing research director specialized in multivariate statistical analysis, machine learning, and customer insight with over a decade of experience in solving real-world problems and in generating value for stakeholders by applying reasoning, statistics, data mining, and algorithms. From being a pioneer of Web audience analysis in Italy to achieving the rank of top ten Kaggler, he has always been passionate about everything regarding data and analysis and about demonstrating the potentiality of data-driven knowledge discovery to both experts and nonexperts. Favoring simplicity over unnecessary sophistication, he believes that a lot can be achieved in data science just by doing the essential. He is the coauthor of five recently published books and he is just working on the sixth. For Packt Publishing he contributed as an author to *Python Data Science Essentials* (both 1st and 2nd editions), *Regression Analysis with Python,* and *Large Scale Machine Learning with Python*.

You can find him on LinkedIn at `https://it.linkedin.com/in/lmassaron`.

Prashant Verma started his IT carrier in 2011 as a Java developer in Ericsson working in telecom domain. After a couple of years of JAVA EE experience, he moved into big data domain, and has worked on almost all the popular big data technologies such as Hadoop, Spark, Flume, Mongo, Cassandra, and so on. He has also played with Scala. Currently, he works with QA Infotech as lead data engineer, working on solving e-learning domain problems using analytics and machine learning.

Prashant has worked for many companies such as Ericsson and QA Infotech, with domain knowledge of telecom and e-learning. Prashant has also been working as a freelance consultant in his free time.

I want to thank Packt Publishing for giving me the chance to review the book as well as my employer and my family for their patience while I was busy working on this book.

www.PacktPub.com

For support files and downloads related to your book, please visit www.PacktPub.com.

Did you know that Packt offers eBook versions of every book published, with PDF and ePub files available? You can upgrade to the eBook version at www.PacktPub.com and as a print book customer, you are entitled to a discount on the eBook copy. Get in touch with us at service@packtpub.com for more details.

At www.PacktPub.com, you can also read a collection of free technical articles, sign up for a range of free newsletters and receive exclusive discounts and offers on Packt books and eBooks.

https://www.packtpub.com/mapt

Get the most in-demand software skills with Mapt. Mapt gives you full access to all Packt books and video courses, as well as industry-leading tools to help you plan your personal development and advance your career.

Why subscribe?

- Fully searchable across every book published by Packt
- Copy and paste, print, and bookmark content
- On demand and accessible via a web browser

Customer Feedback

Thanks for purchasing this Packt book. At Packt, quality is at the heart of our editorial process. To help us improve, please leave us an honest review on this book's Amazon page at `https://www.amazon.com/dp/1782174273`.

If you'd like to join our team of regular reviewers, you can e-mail us at `customerreviews@packtpub.com`. We award our regular reviewers with free eBooks and videos in exchange for their valuable feedback. Help us be relentless in improving our products!

Table of Contents

Preface	1
Chapter 1: Data Science Using Java	7
Data science	8
Machine learning	9
Supervised learning	10
Unsupervised learning	11
Clustering	11
Dimensionality reduction	11
Natural Language Processing	12
Data science process models	13
CRISP-DM	13
A running example	15
Data science in Java	16
Data science libraries	17
Data processing libraries	17
Math and stats libraries	19
Machine learning and data mining libraries	19
Text processing	20
Summary	21
Chapter 2: Data Processing Toolbox	23
Standard Java library	23
Collections	24
Input/Output	25
Reading input data	25
Writing ouput data	27
Streaming API	28
Extensions to the standard library	31
Apache Commons	31
Commons Lang	31
Commons IO	32
Commons Collections	33
Other commons modules	33
Google Guava	34
AOL Cyclops React	38
Accessing data	39
Text data and CSV	39

Web and HTML   41
JSON   44
Databases   46
DataFrames   49
Search engine - preparing data   51
Summary   55

Chapter 3: Exploratory Data Analysis   57

Exploratory data analysis in Java   57
Search engine datasets   58
Apache Commons Math   59
Joinery   62
Interactive Exploratory Data Analysis in Java   64
JVM languages   64
Interactive Java   65
Joinery shell   66
Summary   71

Chapter 4: Supervised Learning - Classification and Regression   73

Classification   74
Binary classification models   74
Smile   75
JSAT   77
LIBSVM and LIBLINEAR   79
Encog   86
Evaluation   87
Accuracy   88
Precision, recall, and F1   89
ROC and AU ROC (AUC)   91
Result validation   94
K-fold cross-validation   97
Training, validation, and testing   99
Case study - page prediction   101
Regression   105
Machine learning libraries for regression   106
Smile   106
JSAT   107
Other libraries   108
Evaluation   108
MSE   108
MAE   109
Case study - hardware performance   109
Summary   115

Chapter 5: Unsupervised Learning - Clustering and Dimensionality Reduction   117
   Dimensionality reduction   118
     Unsupervised dimensionality reduction   118
     Principal Component Analysis   119
     Truncated SVD   123
     Truncated SVD for categorical and sparse data   126
       Random projection   132
   Cluster analysis   135
     Hierarchical methods   136
     K-means   143
       Choosing K in K-Means   144
       DBSCAN   146
     Clustering for supervised learning   147
       Clusters as features   147
       Clustering as dimensionality reduction   148
       Supervised learning via clustering   151
     Evaluation   152
       Manual evaluation   152
       Supervised evaluation   153
       Unsupervised Evaluation   155
   Summary   156
Chapter 6: Working with Text - Natural Language Processing and Information Retrieval   157
   Natural Language Processing and information retrieval   158
     Vector Space Model - Bag of Words and TF-IDF   158
       Vector space model implementation   161
     Indexing and Apache Lucene   167
     Natural Language Processing tools   171
       Stanford CoreNLP   171
     Customizing Apache Lucene   175
   Machine learning for texts   177
     Unsupervised learning for texts   177
       Latent Semantic Analysis   177
       Text clustering   181
       Word embeddings   183
     Supervised learning for texts   192
     Text classification   193
     Learning to rank for information retrieval   196
       Reranking with Lucene   201
   Summary   204

Chapter 7: Extreme Gradient Boosting   205

Gradient Boosting Machines and XGBoost   205
  Installing XGBoost   206
XGBoost in practice   209
  XGBoost for classification   209
    Parameter tuning   216
    Text features   218
    Feature importance   219
  XGBoost for regression   220
  XGBoost for learning to rank   224
Summary   229

Chapter 8: Deep Learning with DeepLearning4J   231

Neural Networks and DeepLearning4J   231
  ND4J - N-dimensional arrays for Java   232
  Neural networks in DeepLearning4J   235
  Convolutional Neural Networks   245
Deep learning for cats versus dogs   251
  Reading the data   252
  Creating the model   255
  Monitoring the performance   259
  Data augmentation   266
  Running DeepLearning4J on GPU   269
Summary   274

Chapter 9: Scaling Data Science   275

Apache Hadoop   276
  Hadoop MapReduce   276
  Common Crawl   277
Apache Spark   287
Link prediction   290
  Reading the DBLP graph   291
  Extracting features from the graph   293
  Node features   295
  Negative sampling   299
  Edge features   304
  Link Prediction with MLlib and XGBoost   309
  Link suggestion   314
Summary   319

Chapter 10: Deploying Data Science Models   321

Microservices   322
    Spring Boot   322
    Search engine service   323
Online evaluation   333
    A/B testing   333
    Multi-armed bandits   338
Summary   341

Index   343

Preface

Data science has become a quite important tool for organizations nowadays: they have collected large amounts of data, and to be able to put it into good use, they need data science--the discipline about methods for extracting knowledge from data. Every day more and more companies realize that they can benefit from data science and utilize the data that they produce more effectively and more profitably.

It is especially true for IT companies, they already have the systems and the infrastructure for generating and processing the data. These systems are often written in Java--the language of choice for many large and small companies across the world. It is not a surprise, Java offers a very solid and mature ecosystem of libraries that are time proven and reliable, so many people trust Java and use it for creating their applications.

Thus, it is also a natural choice for many data processing applications. Since the existing systems are already in Java, it makes sense to use the same technology stack for data science, and integrate the machine learning model directly in the application's production code base.

This book will cover exactly that. We will first see how we can utilize Java's toolbox for processing small and large datasets, then look into doing initial exploration data analysis. Next, we will review the Java libraries that implement common Machine Learning models for classification, regression, clustering, and dimensionality reduction problems. Then we will get into more advanced techniques and discuss Information Retrieval and Natural Language Processing, XGBoost, deep learning, and large scale tools for processing big datasets such as Apache Hadoop and Apache Spark. Finally, we will also have a look at how to evaluate and deploy the produced models such that the other services can use them.

We hope you will enjoy the book. Happy reading!

What this book covers

Chapter 1, *Data Science Using Java*, provides the overview of the existing tools available in Java as well and introduces the methodology for approaching Data Science projects, CRISP-DM. In this chapter, we also introduce our running example, building a search engine.

Chapter 2, *Data Processing Toolbox*, reviews the standard Java library: the Collection API for storing the data in memory, the IO API for reading and writing the data, and the Streaming API for a convenient way of organizing data processing pipelines. We will look at the extensions to the standard libraries such as Apache Commons Lang, Apache Commons IO, Google Guava, and AOL Cyclops React. Then, we will cover most common ways of storing the data--text and CSV files, HTML, JSON, and SQL Databases, and discuss how we can get the data from these data sources. We will finish this chapter by talking about the ways we can collect the data for the running example--the search engine, and how we prepare the data for that.

Chapter 3, *Exploratory Data Analysis*, performs the initial analysis of data with Java: we look at how to calculate common statistics such as the minimal and maximal values, the average value, and the standard deviation. We also talk a bit about interactive analysis and see what are the tools that allow us to visually inspect the data before building models. For the illustration in this chapter, we use the data we collect for the search engine.

Chapter 4, *Supervised Learning - Classification and Regression*, starts with Machine Learning, and then looks at the models for performing supervised learning in Java. Among others, we look at how to use the following libraries--Smile, JSAT, LIBSVM, LIBLINEAR, and Encog, and we see how we can use these libraries to solve the classification and regression problems. We use two examples here, first, we use the search engine data for predicting whether a URL will appear on the first page of results or not, which we use for illustrating the classification problem. Second, we predict how much time it takes to multiply two matrices on certain hardware given its characteristics, and we illustrate the regression problem with this example.

Chapter 5, *Unsupervised Learning – Clustering and Dimensionality Reduction*, explores the methods for Dimensionality Reduction available in Java, and we will learn how to apply PCA and Random Projection to reduce the dimensionality of this data. This is illustrated with the hardware performance dataset from the previous chapter. We also look at different ways to cluster data, including Agglomerative Clustering, K-Means, and DBSCAN, and we use the dataset with customer complaints as an example.

Chapter 6, *Working with Text – Natural Language Processing and Information Retrieval*, looks at how to use text in Data Science applications, and we learn how to extract more useful features for our search engine. We also look at Apache Lucene, a library for full-text indexing and searching, and Stanford CoreNLP, a library for performing Natural Language Processing. Next, we look at how we can represent words as vectors, and we learn how to build such embeddings from co-occurrence matrices and how to use existing ones like GloVe. We also look at how we can use machine learning for texts, and we illustrate it with a sentiment analysis problem where we apply LIBLINEAR to classify if a review is positive or negative.

Chapter 7, *Extreme Gradient Boosting*, covers how to use XGBoost in Java and tries to apply it to two problems we had previously, classifying whether the URL appears on the first page and predicting the time to multiply two matrices. Additionally, we look at how to solve the learning-to-rank problem with XGBoost and again use our search engine example as illustration.

Chapter 8, *Deep Learning with DeepLearning4j*, covers Deep Neural Networks and DeepLearning4j, a library for building and training these networks in Java. In particular, we talk about Convolutional Neural Nets and see how we can use them for image recognition--predicting whether it is a picture of a dog or a cat. Additionally, we discuss data augmentation--the way to generate more data, and also mention how we can speed up the training using GPUs. We finish the chapter by describing how to rent a GPU server on Amazon AWS.

Chapter 9, *Scaling Data Science*, talks about big data tools available in Java, Apache Hadoop, and Apache Spark. We illustrate it by looking at how we can process Common Crawl--the copy of the Internet, and calculate TF-IDF of each document there. Additionally, we look at the graph processing tools available in Apache Spark and build a recommendation system for scientists, we recommend a coauthor for the next possible paper.

Chapter 10, *Deploying Data Science Models*, looks at how we can expose the models to the rest of the world in such a way they are usable. Here we cover Spring Boot and talk how we can use the search engine model we developed to rank the articles from Common Crawl. We finish by discussing the ways to evaluate the performance of the models in the online settings and talk about A/B tests and Multi-Armed Bandits.

What you need for this book

You need to have any latest system with at least 2GB RAM and a Windows 7 /Ubuntu 14.04/Mac OS X operating system. Further, you will need to have Java 1.8.0 or above and Maven 3.0.0 or above installed.

Who this book is for

This book is intended for software engineers who are comfortable with developing Java applications and are familiar with the basic concepts of data science. Additionally, it will also be useful for data scientists who do not yet know Java, but want or need to learn it.

Conventions

In this book, you will find a number of text styles that distinguish between different kinds of information. Here are some examples of these styles and an explanation of their meaning.

Code words in text, database table names, folder names, filenames, file extensions, pathnames, dummy URLs, user input, and Twitter handles are shown as follows: "Here, we create `SummaryStatistics` objects and add all body content lengths."

A block of code is set as follows:

```
SummaryStatistics statistics = new SummaryStatistics();
data.stream().mapToDouble(RankedPage::getBodyContentLength)
    .forEach(statistics::addValue);
System.out.println(statistics.getSummary());
```

Any command-line input or output is written as follows:

```
mvn dependency:copy-dependencies -DoutputDirectory=lib
mvn compile
```

New terms and **important words** are shown in bold. Words that you see on the screen, for example, in menus or dialog boxes, appear in the text like this: "If, instead, our model outputs some score such that the higher the values of the score the more likely the item is to be positive, then the binary classifier is called a **ranking classifier**."

Warnings or important notes appear in a box like this.

Tips and tricks appear like this.

Reader feedback

Feedback from our readers is always welcome. Let us know what you think about this book-what you liked or disliked. Reader feedback is important for us as it helps us develop titles that you will really get the most out of.

To send us general feedback, simply e-mail `feedback@packtpub.com`, and mention the book's title in the subject of your message.

If there is a topic that you have expertise in and you are interested in either writing or contributing to a book, see our author guide at `www.packtpub.com/authors`.

Customer support

Now that you are the proud owner of a Packt book, we have a number of things to help you to get the most from your purchase.

Downloading the example code

You can download the example code files for this book from your account at `http://www.packtpub.com`. If you purchased this book elsewhere, you can visit `http://www.packtpub.com/support` and register to have the files e-mailed directly to you.

You can download the code files by following these steps:

1. Log in or register to our website using your e-mail address and password.
2. Hover the mouse pointer on the **SUPPORT** tab at the top.
3. Click on **Code Downloads & Errata**.
4. Enter the name of the book in the **Search** box.
5. Select the book for which you're looking to download the code files.
6. Choose from the drop-down menu where you purchased this book from.
7. Click on **Code Download**.

Once the file is downloaded, please make sure that you unzip or extract the folder using the latest version of:

- WinRAR / 7-Zip for Windows
- Zipeg / iZip / UnRarX for Mac
- 7-Zip / PeaZip for Linux

The code bundle for the book is also hosted on GitHub at `https://github.com/PacktPublishing/Mastering-Java-for-Data-Science`. We also have other code bundles from our rich catalog of books and videos available at `https://github.com/PacktPublishing/`. Check them out!

Downloading the color images of this book

We also provide you with a PDF file that has color images of the screenshots/diagrams used in this book. The color images will help you better understand the changes in the output.

You can download this file from `https://www.packtpub.com/sites/default/files/down` `loads/MasteringJavaforDataScience_ColorImages.pdf`.

Errata

Although we have taken every care to ensure the accuracy of our content, mistakes do happen. If you find a mistake in one of our books-maybe a mistake in the text or the code-we would be grateful if you could report this to us. By doing so, you can save other readers from frustration and help us improve subsequent versions of this book. If you find any errata, please report them by visiting `http://www.packtpub.com/submit-errata`, selecting your book, clicking on the **Errata Submission Form** link, and entering the details of your errata. Once your errata are verified, your submission will be accepted and the errata will be uploaded to our website or added to any list of existing errata under the Errata section of that title.

To view the previously submitted errata, go to `https://www.packtpub.com/books/conten` `t/support` and enter the name of the book in the search field. The required information will appear under the **Errata** section.

Piracy

Piracy of copyrighted material on the Internet is an ongoing problem across all media. At Packt, we take the protection of our copyright and licenses very seriously. If you come across any illegal copies of our works in any form on the Internet, please provide us with the location address or website name immediately so that we can pursue a remedy.

Please contact us at `copyright@packtpub.com` with a link to the suspected pirated material.

We appreciate your help in protecting our authors and our ability to bring you valuable content.

Questions

If you have a problem with any aspect of this book, you can contact us at `questions@packtpub.com`, and we will do our best to address the problem.

1

Data Science Using Java

This book is about building data science applications using the Java language. In this book, we will cover all the aspects of implementing projects from data preparation to model deployment.

The readers of this book are assumed to have some previous exposure to Java and data science, and the book will help to take this knowledge to the next level. This means learning how to effectively tackle a specific data science problem and get the most out of the available data.

This is an introductory chapter where we will prepare the foundation for all the other chapters. Here we will cover the following topics:

- What is machine learning and data science?
- **Cross Industry Standard Process for Data Mining (CRIPS-DM)**, a methodology for doing data science projects
- Machine learning libraries in Java for medium and large-scale data science applications

By the end of this chapter, you will know how to approach a data science project and what Java libraries to use to do that.

Data science

Data science is the discipline of extracting actionable knowledge from data of various forms. The name **data science** emerged quite recently--it was invented by DJ Patil and Jeff Hammerbacher and popularized in the article *Data Scientist: The Sexiest Job of the 21st Century* in 2012. But the discipline itself had existed before for quite a while and previously was known by other names such as **data mining** or **predictive analytics**. Data science, like its predecessors, is built on statistics and machine learning algorithms for knowledge extraction and model building.

The **science** part of the term **data science** is no coincidence--if we look up **science**, its definition can be summarized to *systematic organization of knowledge in terms testable explanations and predictions*. This is exactly what data scientists do, by extracting patterns from available data, they can make predictions about future unseen data, and they make sure the predictions are validated beforehand.

Nowadays, data science is used across many fields, including (but not limited to):

- **Banking**: Risk management (for example, credit scoring), fraud detection, trading
- **Insurance**: Claims management (for example, accelerating claim approval), risk and losses estimation, also fraud detection
- **Health care**: Predicting diseases (such as strokes, diabetes, cancer) and relapses
- **Retail and e-commerce**: Market basket analysis (identifying product that go well together), recommendation engines, product categorization, and personalized searches

This book covers the following practical use cases:

- Predicting whether an URL is likely to appear on the first page of a search engine
- Predicting how fast an operation will be completed given the hardware specifications
- Ranking text documents for a search engine
- Checking whether there is a cat or a dog on a picture
- Recommending friends in a social network
- Processing large-scale textual data on a cluster of computers

In all these cases, we will use data science to learn from data and use the learned knowledge to solve a particular business problem.

We will also use a running example throughout the book, building a search engine. We will use it to illustrate many data science concepts such as, supervised machine learning, dimensionality reduction, text mining, and learning to rank models.

Machine learning

Machine learning is a part of computer science, and it is at the core of data science. The data itself, especially in big volumes, is hardly useful, but inside it hides highly valuable patterns. With the help of machine learning, we can recognize these hidden patterns, extract them, and then apply the learned information to the new unseen items.

For example, given the image of an animal, a machine learning algorithm can say whether the picture is a dog or a cat; or, given the history of a bank client, it will say how likely the client is to default, that is, to fail to pay the debt.

Often, machine learning models are seen as black boxes that take in a data point and output a prediction for it. In this book, we will look at what is inside these black boxes and see how and when it is best to use them.

The typical problems that machine learning solves can be categorized in the following groups:

- **Supervised learning**: For each data point, we have a *label*--extra information that describes the outcome that we want to learn. In the cats versus dogs case, the data point is an image of the animal; the label describes whether it's a dog or a cat.
- **Unsupervised learning**: We only have raw data points and no label information is available. For example, we have a collection of e-mails and we would like to group them based on how similar they are. There is no explicit label associated with the e-mails, which makes this problem unsupervised.
- **Semi-supervised learning**: Labels are given only for a part of the data.
- **Reinforcement learning**: Instead of labels, we have a *reward*; something the model gets by interacting with the *environment* it runs in. Based on the reward, it can adapt and maximize it. For example, a model that learns how to play chess gets a positive reward each time it eats a figure of the opponent, and gets a negative reward each time it loses a figure; and the reward is proportional to the value of the figure.

Supervised learning

As we discussed previously, for supervised learning we have some information attached to each data point, the label, and we can train a model to use it and to learn from it. For example, if we want to build a model that tells us whether there is a dog or a cat on a picture, then the picture is the data point and the information whether it is a dog or a cat is the label. Another example is predicting the price of a house--the description of a house is the data point, and the price is the label.

We can group the algorithms of supervised learning into classification and regression algorithms based on the nature of this information.

In **classification** problems, the labels come from some fixed finite set of classes, such as {cat, dog}, {default, not default}, or {office, food, entertainment, home}. Depending on the number of classes, the classification problem can be **binary** (only two possible classes) or **multi-class** (several classes).

Examples of classification algorithms are Naive Bayes, logistic regression, perceptron, **Support Vector Machine** (**SVM**), and many others. We will discuss classification algorithms in more detail in the first part of Chapter 4, *Supervised Learning - Classification and Regression*.

In **regression** problems, the labels are real numbers. For example, a person can have a salary in the range from $0 per year to several billions per year. Hence, predicting the salary is a regression problem.

Examples of regression algorithms are linear regression, LASSO, **Support Vector Regression** (**SVR**), and others. These algorithms will be described in more detail in the second part of Chapter 4, *Supervised Learning - Classification and Regression*.

Some of the supervised learning methods are universal and can be applied to both classification and regression problems. For example, decision trees, random forest, and other tree-based methods can tackle both types. We will discuss one such algorithm, gradient boosting machines in Chapter 7, *Extreme Gradient Boosting*.

Neural networks can also deal with both classification and regression problems, and we will talk about them in Chapter 8, *Deep Learning with DeepLearning4J*.

Unsupervised learning

Unsupervised learning covers the cases where we have no labels available, but still want to find some patterns hidden in the data. There are several types of unsupervised learning, and we will look into cluster analysis, or clustering and unsupervised dimensionality reduction.

Clustering

Typically, when people talk about unsupervised learning, they talk about **cluster analysis** or **clustering**. A cluster analysis algorithm takes a set of data points and tries to categorize them into groups such that similar items belong to the same group, and different items do not. There are many ways where it can be used, for example, in customer segmentation or text categorization.

Customer segmentation is an example of clustering. Given some description of customers, we try to put them into groups such that the customers in one group have similar profiles and behave in a similar way. This information can be used to understand what do the people in these groups want, and this can be used to target them with better advertisements and other promotional messages.

Another example is **text categorization**. Given a collection of texts, we would like to find common topics among these texts and arrange the texts according to these topics. For example, given a set of complaints in an e-commerce store, we may want to put ones that talk about similar things together, and this should help the users of the system navigate through the complaints easier.

Examples of cluster analysis algorithms are hierarchical clustering, k-means, **density-based spatial clustering of applications with noise** (**DBSCAN**), and many others. We will talk about clustering in detail in the first part of `Chapter 5`, *Unsupervised Learning - Clustering and Dimensionality Reduction*.

Dimensionality reduction

Another group of unsupervised learning algorithms is **dimensionality reduction** algorithms. This group of algorithms *compresses* the dataset, keeping only the most useful information. If our dataset has too much information, it can be hard for a machine learning algorithm to use all of it at the same time. It may just take too long for the algorithm to process all the data and we would like to compress the data, so processing it takes less time.

There are multiple algorithms that can reduce the dimensionality of the data, including **Principal Component Analysis** (**PCA**), Locally linear embedding, and t-SNE. All these algorithms are examples of unsupervised dimensionality reduction techniques.

Not all dimensionality reduction algorithms are unsupervised; some of them can use labels to reduce the dimensionality better. For example, many feature selection algorithms rely on labels to see what features are useful and what are not.

We will talk more about this in Chapter 5, *Unsupervised Learning - Clustering and Dimensionality Reduction.*

Natural Language Processing

Processing natural language texts is very complex, they are not very well structured and require a lot of cleaning and normalizing. Yet the amount of textual information around us is tremendous: a lot of text data is generated every minute, and it is very hard to retrieve useful information from them. Using data science and machine learning is very helpful for text problems as well; they allow us to find the right text, process it, and extract the valuable bits of information.

There are multiple ways we can use the text information. One example is information retrieval, or, simply, text search--given a user query and a collection of documents, we want to find what are the most relevant documents in the corpus with respect to the query, and present them to the user. Other applications include sentiment analysis--predicting whether a product review is positive, neutral or negative, or grouping the reviews according to how they talk about the products.

We will talk more about information retrieval, **Natural Language Processing** (**NLP**) and working with texts in Chapter 6, *Working with Text - Natural Language Processing and Information Retrieval*. Additionally, we will see how to process large amounts of text data in Chapter 9, *Scaling Data Science*.

The methods we can use for machine learning and data science are very important. What is equally important is the the way we create them and then put them to use in production systems. Data science process models help us make it more organized and systematic, which is why we will talk about them next.

Data science process models

Applying data science is much more than just selecting a suitable machine learning algorithm and using it on the data. It is always good to keep in mind that machine learning is only a small part of the project; there are other parts such as understanding the problem, collecting the data, testing the solution and deploying to the production.

When working on any project, not just data science ones, it is beneficial to break it down into smaller manageable pieces and complete them one-by-one. For data science, there are best practices that describe how to do it the best way, and they are called **process models**. There are multiple models, including CRISP-DM and OSEMN.

In this chapter, CRISP-DM is explained as **Obtain, Scrub, Explore, Model, and iNterpret (OSEMN)**, which is more suitable for data analysis tasks and addresses many important steps to a lesser extent.

CRISP-DM

Cross Industry Standard Process for Data Mining (CRISP-DM) is a process methodology for developing data mining applications. It was created before the term *data science* became popular, it's reliable and time-tested by several generations of analytics. These practices are still useful nowadays and describe the high-level steps of any analytical project quite well.

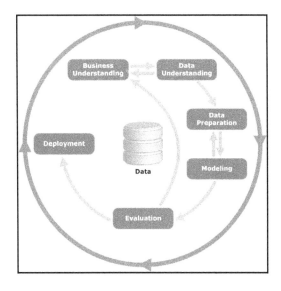

Image source: https://en.wikipedia.org/wiki/File:CRISP-DM_Process_Diagram.png

The CRISP-DM methodology breaks down a project into the following steps:

- Business understanding
- Data understanding
- Data preparation
- Modeling
- Evaluation
- Deployment

The methodology itself defines much more than just these steps, but typically knowing what the steps are and what happens at each step is enough for a successful data science project. Let's look at each of these steps separately.

The first step is **Business Understanding**. This step aims at learning what kinds of problems the business has and what they want to achieve by solving these problems. To be successful, a data science application must be useful for the business. The result of this step is the formulation of a problem which we want to solve and what is the desired outcome of the project.

The second step is **Data Understanding**. In this step, we try to find out what data can be used to solve the problem. We also need to find out if we already have the data; if not, we need to think how we can we get it. Depending on what data we find (or do not find), we may want to alter the original goal.

When the data is collected, we need to explore it. The process of reviewing the data is often called **Exploratory Data Analysis** and it is an integral part of any data science project. it helps to understand the processes that created the data, and can already suggest approaches for tackling the problem. The result of this step is the knowledge about which data sources are needed to solve the problem. We will talk more about this step in Chapter 3, *Exploratory Data Analysis*.

The third step of CRISP-DM is **Data Preparation**. For a dataset to be useful, it needs to be cleaned and transformed to a tabular form. The tabular form means that each row corresponds to exactly one observation. If our data is not in this shape, it cannot be used by most of the machine learning algorithms. Thus, we need to prepare the data such that it eventually can be converted to a matrix form and fed to a model.

Also, there could be different datasets that contain the needed information, and they may not be homogenous. What this means is that we need to convert these datasets to some common format, which can be read by the model.

This step also includes **Feature Engineering**--the process of creating features that are most informative for the problem and describe the data in the best way.

Many data scientists say that they spend most of their time on this step when building Data Science applications. We will talk about this step in Chapter 2, *Data Processing Toolbox* and throughout the book.

The fourth step is **Modeling**. In this step, the data is already in the right shape and we feed it to different Machine Learning algorithms. This step also includes parameter tuning, feature selection, and selecting the best model.

Evaluation of the quality of the models from the machine learning point of view happens during this step. The most important thing to check is the ability to generalize, and this is typically done via cross validation. In this step, we also may want to go back to the previous step and do extra cleaning and feature engineering. The outcome is a model that is potentially useful for solving the problem defined in Step 1.

The fifth step is **Evaluation**. It includes evaluating the model from the business perspective--not from the machine learning perspective. This means that we need to perform a critical review of the results so far and plan the next steps. Does the model achieve what we want? Additionally, some of the findings may lead to reconsidering the initial question. After this step, we can go to the deployment step or re-iterate the process.

The, final, sixth step is **Model Deployment**. During this step, the produced model is added to the production, so the result is the model integrated to the live system. We will cover this step in Chapter 10, *Deploying Data Science Models*.

Often, evaluation is hard because it is not always possible to say whether the model achieves the desired result or not. In these cases, the evaluation and deployment steps can be combined into one, the model is deployed and applied only to a part of users, and then the data for evaluating the model is collected. We will also briefly cover the ways of doing them, such as A/B testing and multi-armed bandits, in the last chapter of the book.

A running example

There will be many practical use cases throughout the book, sometimes a couple in each chapter. But we will also have a running example, building a search engine. This problem is interesting for a number of reasons:

- It is fun
- Business in almost any domain can benefit from a search engine

- Many businesses already have text data; often it is not used effectively, and its use can be improved
- Processing text requires a lot of effort, and it is useful to learn to do this effectively

We will try to keep it simple, yet, with this example, we will touch on all the technical parts of the data science process throughout the book:

- **Data Understanding**: Which data can be useful for the problem? How can we obtain this data?
- **Data Preparation**: Once the data is obtained, how can we process it? If it is HTML, how do we extract text from it? How do we extract individual sentences and words from the text?
- **Modeling**: Ranking documents by their relevance with respect to a query is a data science problem and we will discuss how it can be approached.
- **Evaluation**: The search engine can be tested to see if it is useful for solving the business problem or not.
- **Deployment**: Finally, the engine can be deployed as a REST service or integrated directly to the live system.

We will obtain and prepare the data in Chapter 2, *Data Processing Toolbox*, understand the data in Chapter 3, *Exploratory Data Analysis*, build simple models and evaluate them in Chapter 4, *Supervised Machine Learning - Classification and Regression*, look at how to process text in Chapter 6, *Working with Text - Natural Language Processing and Information Retrieval*, see how to apply it to millions of webpages in Chapter 9, *Scaling Data Science*, and, finally, learn how we can deploy it in Chapter 10, *Deploying Data Science Models*.

Data science in Java

In this book, we will use Java for doing data science projects. Java might not seem a good choice for data science at first glance, unlike Python or R, it has fewer data science and machine learning libraries, it is more verbose and lacks interactivity. On the other hand, it has a lot of upsides as follows:

- Java is a statically typed language, which makes it easier to maintain the code base and harder to make silly mistakes--the compiler can detect some of them.
- The standard library for data processing is very rich, and there are even richer external libraries.

- Java code is typically faster than the code in scripting languages that are usually used for data science (such as R or Python).
- Maven, the de-facto standard for dependency management in the Java world, makes it very easy to add new libraries to the project and avoid version conflicts.
- Most of big data frameworks for scalable data processing are written in either Java or JVM languages, such as Apache Hadoop, Apache Spark, or Apache Flink.
- Very often production systems are written in Java and building models in other languages adds unnecessary levels of complexity. Creating the models in Java makes it easier to integrate them to the product.

Next, we will look at the data science libraries available in Java.

Data science libraries

While there are not as many data science libraries in Java compared to R, there are quite a few. Additionally, it is often possible to use machine learning and data mining libraries written in other JVM languages, such as Scala, Groovy, or Clojure. Because these languages share the runtime environment, it makes it very easy to import libraries written in Scala and use them directly in Java code.

We can divide the libraries into the following categories:

- Data processing libraries
- Math and stats libraries
- Machine learning and data mining libraries
- Text processing libraries

Now we will see each of them in detail.

Data processing libraries

The standard Java library is very rich and offers a lot of tools for data processing, such as collections, I/O tools, data streams, and means of parallel task execution.

There are very powerful extensions to the standard library such as:

- Google Guava (`https://github.com/google/guava`) and Apache Common Collections (`https://commons.apache.org/collections/`) for richer collections

- Apache Commons IO (`https://commons.apache.org/io/`) for simplified I/O
- AOL Cyclops-React (`https://github.com/aol/cyclops-react`) for richer functional-way parallel streaming

We will cover both the standard API for data processing and its extensions in `Chapter 2`, *Data Processing Toolbox*. In this book, we will use Maven for including external libraries such as Google Guava or Apache Commons IO. It is a dependency management tool and allows to specify the external dependencies with a few lines of XML code. For example, to add Google Guava, it is enough to declare the following dependency in `pom.xml`:

```
<dependency>
 <groupId>com.google.guava</groupId>
 <artifactId>guava</artifactId>
 <version>19.0</version>
</dependency>
```

When we do it, Maven will go to the Maven Central repository and download the dependency of the specified version. The best way to find the dependency snippets for `pom.xml` (such as the previous one) is to use the search at `https://mvnrepository.com` or your favorite search engine.

Java gives an easy way to access databases through **Java Database Connectivity** (**JDBC**)--a unified database access protocol. JDBC makes it possible to connect virtually any relational database that supports SQL, such as MySQL, MS SQL, Oracle, PostgreSQL, and many others. This allows moving the data manipulation from Java to the database side.

When it is not possible to use a database for handling tabular data, then we can use DataFrame libraries for doing it directly in Java. The DataFrame is a data structure that originally comes from R and it allows to easily manipulate textual data in the program, without resorting to external database.

For example, with DataFrames it is possible to filter rows based on some condition, apply the same operation to each element of a column, group by some condition or join with another DataFrame. Additionally, some data frame libraries make it easy to convert tabular data to a matrix form so that the data can be used by machine learning algorithms.

There are a few data frame libraries available in Java. Some of them are as follows:

- Joinery (`https://cardillo.github.io/joinery/`)
- Tablesaw (`https://github.com/lwhite1/tablesaw`)
- Saddle (`https://saddle.github.io/`) a data frame library for Scala
- Apache Spark DataFrames (`http://spark.apache.org/`)

We will also cover databases and data frames in `Chapter 2`, *Data Processing Toolbox* and we will use DataFrames throughout the book.

There are more complex data processing libraries such as Spring Batch (`http://projects.spring.io/spring-batch/`). They allow creating complex data pipelines (called ETLs from Extract-Transform-Load) and manage their execution.

Additionally, there are libraries for distributed data processing such as:

- Apache Hadoop (`http://hadoop.apache.org/`)
- Apache Spark (`http://spark.apache.org/`)
- Apache Flink (`https://flink.apache.org/`)

We will talk about distributed data processing in `Chapter 9`, *Scaling Data Science*.

Math and stats libraries

The math support in the standard Java library is quite limited, and only includes methods such as `log` for computing the logarithm, `exp` for computing the exponent and other basic methods.

There are external libraries with richer support of mathematics. For example:

- Apache Commons Math (`http://commons.apache.org/math/`) for statistics, optimization, and linear algebra
- Apache Mahout (`http://mahout.apache.org/`) for linear algebra, also includes a module for distributed linear algebra and machine learning
- JBlas (`http://jblas.org/`) optimized and very fast linear algebra package that uses the BLAS library

Also, many machine learning libraries come with some extra math functionality, often linear algebra, stats, and optimization.

Machine learning and data mining libraries

There are quite a few machine learning and data mining libraries available for Java and other JVM languages. Some of them are as follows:

- Weka (`http://www.cs.waikato.ac.nz/ml/weka/`) is probably the most famous data mining library in Java, contains a lot of algorithms and has many extensions.

- JavaML (`http://java-ml.sourceforge.net/`) is quite an old and reliable ML library, but unfortunately not updated anymore
- Smile (`http://haifengl.github.io/smile/`) is a promising ML library that is under active development at the moment and a lot of new methods are being added there.
- JSAT (`https://github.com/EdwardRaff/JSAT`) contains quite an impressive list of machine learning algorithms.
- H2O (`http://www.h2o.ai/`) is a framework for distributed ML written in Java, but is available for multiple languages, including Scala, R, and Python.
- Apache Mahout (`http://mahout.apache.org/`) is used for in-core (one machine) and distributed machine learning. The Mahout Samsara framework allows writing the code in a framework-independent way and then executes it on Spark, Flink, or H2O.

There are several libraries that specialize solely on neural networks:

- Encog (`http://www.heatonresearch.com/encog/`)
- DeepLearning4j (`http://deeplearning4j.org/`)

We will cover some of these libraries throughout the book.

Text processing

It is possible to do simple text processing using only the standard Java library with classes such as `StringTokenizer`, the `java.text` package, or the regular expressions.

In addition to that, there is a big variety of text processing frameworks available for Java as follows:

- Apache Lucene (`https://lucene.apache.org/`) is a library that is used for information retrieval
- Stanford CoreNLP (`http://stanfordnlp.github.io/CoreNLP/`)
- Apache OpenNLP (`https://opennlp.apache.org/`)
- LingPipe (`http://alias-i.com/lingpipe/`)
- GATE (`https://gate.ac.uk/`)
- MALLET (`http://mallet.cs.umass.edu/`)
- Smile (`http://haifengl.github.io/smile/`) also has some algorithms for NLP

Most NLP libraries have very similar functionality and coverage of algorithms, which is why selecting which one to use is usually a matter of habit or taste. They all typically have tokenization, parsing, part-of-speech tagging, named entity recognition, and other algorithms for text processing. Some of them (such as StanfordNLP) support multiple languages, and some support only English.

We will cover some of these libraries in `Chapter 6`, *Working with Text - Natural Language Processing and Information Retrival.*

Summary

In this chapter, we briefly discussed data science and what role machine learning plays in it. Then we talked about doing a data science project, and what methodologies are useful for it. We discussed one of them, CRISP-DM, the steps it defines, how these steps are related and the outcome of each step.

Finally, we spoke about why doing a data science project in Java is a good idea, it is statically compiled, it's fast, and often the existing production systems already run in Java. We also mentioned libraries and frameworks one can use to successfully accomplish a data science project using the Java language.

With this foundation, we will now go to the most important (and most time-consuming) step in a data science project--Data Preparation.

2
Data Processing Toolbox

In the previous chapter, we discussed the best practices for approaching data science problems. We looked at CRISP-DM, which is the methodology for dealing with data mining projects, and one of the first steps there is data preprocessing. In this chapter, we will take a closer look at how to do this in Java.

Specifically, we will cover the following topics:

- Standard Java library
- Extensions to the standard library
- Reading data from different sources such as text, HTML, JSON, and databases
- DataFrames for manipulating tabular data

In the end, we will put everything together to prepare the data for the search engine.

By the end of this chapter, you will be able to process data such that it can be used for machine learning and further analysis.

Standard Java library

The standard Java library is very rich and offers a lot of tools for data manipulation, including:

- Collections for organizing data in memory
- I/O for reading and writing data
- Streaming APIs for making data transformations easy

In this chapter, we will look at all these tools in detail.

Collections

Data is the most important part of data science. When dealing with data, it needs to be efficiently stored and processed, and for this we use data structures. A data structure describes a way to store data efficiently to solve a specific problem, and the Java Collection API is the standard Java API for data structures. This API offers a wide variety of implementations that are useful in practical data science applications.

We will not describe the collection API in full detail, but concentrate on the most useful and important ones--list, set, and map interfaces.

Lists are collections where each element can be accessed by its index. The g0-to implementation of the `List` interface is `ArrayList`, which should be used in 99% of cases and it can be used as follows:

```
List<String> list = new ArrayList<>();
list.add("alpha");
list.add("beta");
list.add("beta");
list.add("gamma");
System.out.println(list);
```

There are other implementations of the `List` interface, `LinkedList` or `CopyOnWriteArrayList`, but they are rarely needed.

Set is another interface in the Collections API, and it describes a collection which allows no duplicates. The go-to implementation is `HashSet`, if the order in which we insert elements does not matter, or `LinkedHashSet`, if the order matters. We can use it as follows:

```
Set<String> set = new HashSet<>();
set.add("alpha");
set.add("beta");
set.add("beta");
set.add("gamma");
System.out.println(set);
```

`List` and `Set` both implement the `Iterable` interface, which makes it possible to use the `for-each` loop with them:

```
for (String el : set) {
    System.out.println(el);
}
```

The `Map` interface allows mapping keys to values, and is sometimes called as dictionary or associative array in other languages. The g0-to implementation is `HashMap`:

```
Map<String, String> map = new HashMap<>();
map.put("alpha", "α");
map.put("beta", "β");
map.put("gamma", "γ");
System.out.println(map);
```

If you need to keep the insertion order, you can use `LinkedHashMap`; if you know that the `map` interface will be accessed from multiple threads, use `ConcurrentHashMap`.

The `Collections` class provides several helper methods for dealing with collections such as sorting, or extracting the `max` or `min` elements:

```
String min = Collections.min(list);
String max = Collections.max(list);
System.out.println("min: " + min + ", max: " + max);
Collections.sort(list);
Collections.shuffle(list);
```

There are other collections such as `Queue`, `Deque`, `Stack`, thread-safe collections, and some others. They are less frequently used and not very important for data science.

Input/Output

Data scientists often work with files and other data sources. I/O is needed for reading from the data sources and writing the results back. The Java I/O API provides two main types of abstraction for this:

- `InputStream`, `OutputStream` for binary data
- `Reader`, `Writer` for text data

Typical data science applications deal with text rather than raw binary data--the data is often stored in TXT, CSV, JSON, and other similar text formats. This is why we will concentrate on the second part.

Reading input data

Being able to read data is the most important skill for a data scientist, and this data is usually in text format, be it TXT, CSV, or any other format. In Java I/O API, the subclasses of the `Reader` classes deal with reading text files.

Suppose we have a `text.txt` file with some sentences (which may or may not make sense):

- My dog also likes eating sausage
- The motor accepts beside a surplus
- Every capable slash succeeds with a worldwide blame
- The continued task coughs around the guilty kiss

If you need to read the whole file as a list of strings, the usual Java I/O way of doing this is using `BufferedReader`:

```
List<String> lines = new ArrayList<>();

try (InputStream is = new FileInputStream("data/text.txt")) {
    try (InputStreamReader isReader = new InputStreamReader(is,
            StandardCharsets.UTF_8)) {
        try (BufferedReader reader = new BufferedReader(isReader)) {
            while (true) {
                String line = reader.readLine();
                if (line == null) {
                    break;
                }
                lines.add(line);
            }

            isReader.close();
        }
    }
}
```

 It is important to provide character encoding--this way, the `Reader` knows how to translate the sequence of bytes into a proper `String` object. Apart from UTF-8, there are UTF-16, ISO-8859 (which is ASCII-based text encoding for English), and many others.

There is a shortcut to get `BufferedReader` for a file directly:

```
Path path = Paths.get("data/text.txt");
try (BufferedReader reader = Files.newBufferedReader(path,
        StandardCharsets.UTF_8)) {
    // read line-by-line
}
```

Even with this shortcut, you can see that this is quite verbose for such a simple task as reading a list of lines from a file. You can wrap this in a helper function, or instead use the Java NIO API, which gives some helper methods to make this task easier:

```
Path path = Paths.get("data/text.txt");
List<String> lines = Files.readAllLines(path, StandardCharsets.UTF_8);
System.out.println(lines);
```

 The Java NIO shortcuts work only for files. Later, we will talk about shortcuts that work for any InputStream objects, not just files.

Writing ouput data

After the data is read and processed, we often want to put it back on disk. For text, this is usually done using the `Writer` objects.

Suppose we read the sentences from `text.txt` and we need to convert each line to uppercase and write them back to a new file `output.txt`; the most convenient way of writing the text data is via the `PrintWriter` class:

```
try (PrintWriter writer = new PrintWriter("output.txt", "UTF-8")) {
    for (String line : lines) {
        String upperCase = line.toUpperCase(Locale.US);
        writer.println(upperCase);
    }
}
```

In Java NIO API, it would look like this:

```
Path output = Paths.get("output.txt");
try (BufferedWriter writer = Files.newBufferedWriter(output,
        StandardCharsets.UTF_8)) {
    for (String line : lines) {
        String upperCase = line.toUpperCase(Locale.US);
        writer.write(upperCase);
        writer.newLine();
    }
}
```

Both ways are correct and you should select the one that you prefer. However, it is important to remember to always include the encoding; otherwise, it may use some default values which are platform-dependent and sometimes arbitrary.

Streaming API

Java 8 was a big step forward in the history of the Java language. Among other features, there were two important things--Streams and Lambda expressions.

In Java, a stream is a sequence of objects, and the Streams API provides functional-style operations to transform these sequences, such as map, filter, and reduce. The sources for streams can be anything that contain elements, for example, arrays, collections, or files.

For example, let's create a simple `Word` class, which contains a token and its part of speech:

```
public class Word {
    private final String token;
    private final String pos;
    // constructor and getters are omitted
}
```

For brevity, we will always omit constructors and getters for such data classes, but indicate that with a comment.

Now, let's consider a sentence *My dog also likes eating sausage*. Using this class, we can represent it as follows:

```
Word[] array = { new Word("My", "RPR"), new Word("dog", "NN"),
    new Word("also", "RB"), new Word("likes", "VB"),
    new Word("eating", "VB"), new Word("sausage", "NN"),
    new Word(".", ".") };
```

Here, we use the Penn Treebank POS notation, where `NN` represents a noun or `VB` represents a verb.

Now, we can convert this array to a stream using the `Arrays.stream` utility method:

```
Stream<Word> stream = Arrays.stream(array);
```

Streams can be created from collections using the `stream` method:

```
List<Word> list = Arrays.asList(array);
Stream<Word> stream = list.stream();
```

The operations on streams are chained together and form nice and readable data processing pipelines. The most common operations on streams are the map and filter operations:

- Map applies the same transformer function to each element
- Filter, given a predicate function, filters out elements that do not satisfy it

At the end of the pipeline, you collect the results using a collector. The `Collectors` class provides several implementations such as `toList`, `toSet`, `toMap`, and others.

Suppose we want to keep only tokens which are nouns. With the Streams API, we can do it as follows:

```
List<String> nouns = list.stream()
        .filter(w -> "NN".equals(w.getPos()))
        .map(Word::getToken)
        .collect(Collectors.toList());
System.out.println(nouns);
```

Alternatively, we may want to check how many unique POS tags there are in the stream. For this, we can use the `toSet` collector:

```
Set<String> pos = list.stream()
        .map(Word::getPos)
        .collect(Collectors.toSet());
System.out.println(pos);
```

When dealing with texts, we may sometimes want to join a sequence of strings together:

```
String rawSentence = list.stream()
        .map(Word::getToken)
        .collect(Collectors.joining(" "));
System.out.println(rawSentence);
```

Alternatively, we can group words by their POS tag:

```
Map<String, List<Word>> groupByPos = list.stream()
        .collect(Collectors.groupingBy(Word::getPos));
System.out.println(groupByPos.get("VB"));
System.out.println(groupByPos.get("NN"));
```

Also, there is a useful `toMap` collector that can index a collection using some fields. For example, if we want to get a map from tokens to the `Word` objects, it can be achieved using the following code:

```
Map<String, Word> tokenToWord = list.stream()
        .collect(Collectors.toMap(Word::getToken, Function.identity()));
System.out.println(tokenToWord.get("sausage"));
```

Apart from object streams, the Streams API provides primitive streams--streams of ints, doubles, and other primitives. These streams have useful methods for statistical calculations such as `sum`, `max`, `min`, or `average`. A usual stream can be converted to a primitive stream using functions such as `mapToInt` or `mapToDouble`.

For example, this is how we can find the maximum length across all words in our sentence:

```
int maxTokenLength = list.stream()
        .mapToInt(w -> w.getToken().length())
        .max().getAsInt();
System.out.println(maxTokenLength);
```

Stream operations are easy to parallelize; they are applied to each item separately, and therefore multiple threads can do that without interfering with one another. So, it is possible to make these operations a lot faster by splitting the work across multiple processors and execute all the tasks in parallel.

Java leverages that and provides an easy and expressive way to create parallel code; for collections, you just need to call the `parallelStream` method:

```
int[] firstLengths = list.parallelStream()
        .filter(w -> w.getToken().length() % 2 == 0)
        .map(Word::getToken)
        .mapToInt(String::length)
        .sequential()
        .sorted()
        .limit(2)
        .toArray();
System.out.println(Arrays.toString(firstLengths));
```

In this example, the filtering and mapping is done in parallel, but then the stream is converted to a sequential stream, sorted, and the top two elements are extracted to an array. While the example is not very meaningful, it shows how much it is possible to do with streams.

Finally, the standard Java I/O library offers some convenience methods. For example, it is possible to represent a text file as a stream of lines using the `Files.lines` method:

```
Path path = Paths.get("text.txt");
try (Stream<String> lines = Files.lines(path, StandardCharsets.UTF_8)) {
    double average = lines
        .flatMap(line -> Arrays.stream(line.split(" ")))
        .map(String::toLowerCase)
        .mapToInt(String::length)
        .average().getAsDouble();
    System.out.println("average token length: " + average);
}
```

Streams are an expressive and powerful way to process data and mastering this API is very helpful for doing data science in Java. Later on, we will often use the Stream API, so you will see more examples of how to use it.

Extensions to the standard library

The standard Java library is quite powerful, but some things take a long time to write using it or they are simply missing. There are a number of extensions to the standard library, and the most prominent libraries are Apache Commons (a collection of libraries) and Google Guava. They make it easier to use the standard API or extend it, for example, by adding new collections or implementations.

To begin with, we will briefly go over the most relevant parts of these libraries, and later on we will see how they are used in practice.

Apache Commons

Apache Commons is a collection of open source libraries for Java, with the goal of creating reusable Java components. There are quite a few of them, including Apache Commons Lang, Apache Commons IO, Apache Commons Collections, and many others.

Commons Lang

Apache Commons Lang is a set of utility classes that extend the `java.util` package and they make the life of a Java developer a lot easier by providing many little methods that solve common problems and save a lot of time.

To include external libraries in Java, we usually use Maven, which makes it very easy to manage dependencies. With Maven, the Apache Commons Lang library can be included using this `dependency` snippet:

```
<dependency>
  <groupId>org.apache.commons</groupId>
  <artifactId>commons-lang3</artifactId>
  <version>3.4</version>
</dependency>
```

The library contains a lot of methods useful for general-purpose Java programming, such as making it easier to implement the `equals` and `hashCode` methods for objects, serialization helpers and others. In general, they are not very specific to data science, but there are a few helper functions that are quite useful. For example,

- `RandomUtils` and `RandomStringUtils` for generating data
- `StringEscapeUtils` and `LookupTranslator` for escaping and un-escaping strings

- `EqualsBuilder` and `HashCodeBuilder` for the fast implementation of `equals` and `hashCode` methods
- `StringUtils` and `WordUtils` for useful string manipulation methods
- the `Pair` class

For more information, you can read the documentation at `https://commons.apache.org/l ang`.

 The best way to see what is available is to download the package and see the code available there. Every Java developer will find a lot of useful things.

Commons IO

Like Apache Commons Lang extends the `java.util` standard package, Apache Commons IO extends `java.io`; it is a Java library of utilities to assist with I/O in Java, which, as we previously learned, can be quite verbose.

To include the library in your project, add the `dependency` snippet to the `pom.xml` file:

```
<dependency>
  <groupId>commons-io</groupId>
  <artifactId>commons-io</artifactId>
  <version>2.5</version>
</dependency>
```

We already learned about `Files.lines` from Java NIO. While it is handy, we do not always work with files, and sometimes need to get lines from some other `InputStream`, for example, a web page or a web socket.

For this purpose, Commons IO provides a very helpful utility class `IOUtils`. Using it, reading the entire input stream into string or a list of strings is quite easy:

```
try (InputStream is = new FileInputStream("data/text.txt")) {
    String content = IOUtils.toString(is, StandardCharsets.UTF_8);
    System.out.println(content);
}

try (InputStream is = new FileInputStream("data/text.txt")) {
    List<String> lines = IOUtils.readLines(is, StandardCharsets.UTF_8);
    System.out.println(lines);
}
```

Although we use `FileInputStream` objects in this example, it can be any other stream. The first method, `IOUtils.toString`, is particularly useful, and we will use it later for crawling web pages and processing the responses from web services.

There are a lot more useful methods for I/O in this library, and to get a good overview, you can consult the documentation available at `https://commons.apache.org/io`.

Commons Collections

The Java Collections API is very powerful and it defines a good set of abstractions for data structures in Java. The Commons Collections use these abstractions and extend the standard Collections API with new implementations as well as new collections. To include the library, use this snippet:

```
<dependency>
  <groupId>org.apache.commons</groupId>
  <artifactId>commons-collections4</artifactId>
  <version>4.1</version>
</dependency>
```

Some useful collections from this library are:

- `Bag`: This is an interface for sets that can hold the same element multiple times
- `BidiMap`: This stands for Bi-directional map. It can map from keys to values and from values to keys

It has some overlap with collections from Google Guava, explained in the next session, but has some additional collections that aren't implemented there. For example,

- `LRUMap`: This is used for implementing caches
- `PatriciaTrie`: This is used for fast string prefix lookups

Other commons modules

Commons Lang, IO, and Collections are a few commons libraries out of many. There are other commons modules that are useful for data science:

- Commons compress is used for reading compressed files such as, `bzip2` (for reading Wikipedia dumps), `gzip`, `7z`, and others

- Commons CSV is used for reading and writing CSV files (we will use it later)
- Commons math is used for statistical calculation and linear algebra (we will also use it later)

You can refer to `https://commons.apache.org/` for the whole list.

Google Guava

Google Guava is very similar to Apache Commons; it is a set of utilities that extend the standard Java API and make life easier. But unlike Apache Commons, Google Guava is one library that covers many areas at once, including collections and I/O.

To include it in a project, use `dependency`:

```xml
<dependency>
  <groupId>com.google.guava</groupId>
  <artifactId>guava</artifactId>
  <version>19.0</version>
</dependency>
```

We will start with the Guava I/O module. To give an illustration, we will use some generated data. We already used the `word` class, which contains a token and its part-of-speech tag, and here we will generate more words. To do that, we can use a data generation tool such as `http://www.generatedata.com/`. Let's define the following schema as shown in the following screenshot:

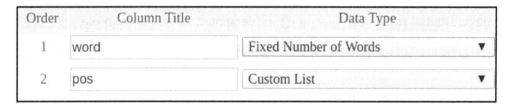

Order	Column Title	Data Type
1	word	Fixed Number of Words ▼
2	pos	Custom List ▼

After that it is possible to save the generated data to the CSV format, set the delimiter to tab (t), and save it to `words.txt`. We already generated a file for you; you can find it in the `chapter2` repository.

Guava defines a few abstractions for working with I/O. One of them is `CharSource`, an abstraction for any source of character-based data, which, in some sense, is quite similar to the standard `Reader` class. Additionally, similarly to Commons IO, there is a utility class for working with files. It is called `Files` (not to be confused with `java.nio.file.Files`), and contains helper functions that make file I/O easier. Using this class, it is possible to read all lines of a text file as follows:

```
File file = new File("data/words.txt");
CharSource wordsSource = Files.asCharSource(file, StandardCharsets.UTF_8);
List<String> lines = wordsSource.readLines();
```

Google Guava Collections follows the same idea as Commons Collections; it builds on the Standard Collections API and provides new implementations and abstractions. There are a few utility classes such as `Lists`, for working with lists, `Sets` for working with sets, and so on.

One of the methods from `Lists` is `transform`, it is like `map` on streams and it is applied to every element from the list. The elements of the resulting list are evaluated lazily; the computation of the function is triggered only when the element is needed. Let's use it for transforming the lines from the text file to a list of `Word` objects:

```
List<Word> words = Lists.transform(lines, line -> {
    String[] split = line.split("t");
    return new Word(split[0].toLowerCase(), split[1]);
});
```

The main difference between this and map from the Streams API is that transform immediately returns a list, so there is no need to first create a stream, call the `map` function, and finally collect the results to list.

Similarly to Commons Collections, there are new collections that are not available in the Java API. The most useful collections for data science are `Multiset`, `Multimap`, and `Table`.

Multisets are sets where the same element can be stored multiple times, and they are usually used for counting things. This class is especially useful for text processing, when we want to calculate how many times each term appears.

Let's take the words that we read and calculate how many times each `pos` tag appeared:

```
Multiset<String> pos = HashMultiset.create();
for (Word word : words) {
    pos.add(word.getPos());
}
```

If we want to output the results sorted by counts, there is a special utility function for that:

```
Multiset<String> sortedPos = Multisets.copyHighestCountFirst(pos);
System.out.println(sortedPos);
```

Multimap is a map that for each key can have multiple values. There are several types of multimaps. The two most common maps are as follows:

- `ListMultimap`: This associates a key with a list of values, similar to `Map<Key, List<Value>>`
- `SetMultimap`: This associates a key to a set of values, similar to `Map<Key, Set<Value>>`

This can be quite useful for implementing `group by` logic. Let's look at the average length per `POS` tag:

```
ArrayListMultimap<String, String> wordsByPos = ArrayListMultimap.create();
for (Word word : words) {
    wordsByPos.put(word.getPos(), word.getToken());
}
```

It is possible to view a multimap as a map of collections:

```
Map<String, Collection<String>> wordsByPosMap = wordsByPos.asMap();
wordsByPosMap.entrySet().forEach(System.out::println);
```

Finally, the `Table` collection can be seen as a two-dimensional extension of the `map` interface; now, instead of one key, each entry is indexed by two keys, `row` keys and `column` keys. In addition to that, it is also possible to get the entire column using the `column` key or a row using the `row` key.

For example, we can count how many times each (word, POS) pair appeared in the dataset:

```
Table<String, String, Integer> table = HashBasedTable.create();
for (Word word : words) {
    Integer cnt = table.get(word.getPos(), word.getToken());
    if (cnt == null) {
        cnt = 0;
    }
    table.put(word.getPos(), word.getToken(), cnt + 1);
}
```

Once the data is put to the table, we can access the rows and columns individually:

```
Map<String, Integer> nouns = table.row("NN");
System.out.println(nouns);
```

```
String word = "eu";
Map<String, Integer> posTags = table.column(word);
System.out.println(posTags);
```

Like in Commons Lang, Guava also contains utility classes for working with primitives such as `Ints` for `int` primitives, `Doubles` for `double` primitives, and so on. For example, it can be used to convert a collection of primitive wrappers to a primitive array:

```
Collection<Integer> values = nouns.values();
int[] nounCounts = Ints.toArray(values);
int totalNounCount = Arrays.stream(nounCounts).sum();
System.out.println(totalNounCount);
```

Finally, Guava provides a nice abstraction for sorting data--`Ordering`, which extends the standard `Comparator` interface. It provides a clean fluent interface for creating comparators:

```
Ordering<Word> byTokenLength =
        Ordering.natural().<Word> onResultOf(w ->
w.getToken().length()).reverse();
List<Word> sortedByLength = byTokenLength.immutableSortedCopy(words);
System.out.println(sortedByLength);
```

Since `Ordering` implements the `Comparator` interface, it can be used wherever a comparator is expected. For example, for `Collections.sort`:

```
List<Word> sortedCopy = new ArrayList<>(words);
Collections.sort(sortedCopy, byTokenLength);
```

In addition to that, it provides other methods such as extracting the top-k or bottom-k elements:

```
List<Word> first10 = byTokenLength.leastOf(words, 10);
System.out.println(first10);
List<Word> last10 = byTokenLength.greatestOf(words, 10);
System.out.println(last10);
```

It is the same as first sorting and then taking the first or last k elements, but more efficient.

There are other useful classes:

- Customizable hash implementations such as Murmur hash and others
- `Stopwatch` for measuring time

For more insights, you can refer to `https://github.com/google/guava` and `https://github.com/google/guava/wiki`.

You may have noticed that Guava and Apache Commons have a lot in common. Selecting which one to use is a matter of taste--both libraries are very well tested and actively used in many production systems. However, Guava is more actively developed and new features appear more often, so if you want to use only one of them, then Guava may be a better choice.

AOL Cyclops React

As we already learned, Java Streams API is a very powerful way of dealing with data in a functional way. The Cyclops React library extends this API by adding new operations on streams and allows for more control of the flow execution. To include the library, add this to the `pom.xml` file:

```
<dependency>
  <groupId>com.aol.simplereact</groupId>
  <artifactId>cyclops-react</artifactId>
  <version>1.0.0-RC4</version>
</dependency>
```

Some of the methods it adds are `zipWithIndex` and cast and convenience collectors such as `toList`, `toSet`, and `toMap`. What is more, it gives more control for parallel execution, for example, it is possible to provide a custom executor, which will be used for processing data or intercepting exceptions declaratively.

Also, with this library, it is easy to create a parallel stream from the iterator--it is hard to do it with the standard library.

For example, let's take `words.txt`, extract all POS tags from it, and then create a map that associates each tag with a unique index. For reading data, we will use `LineIterator` from Commons IO, which otherwise would be hard to parallelize using only standard Java APIs. Additionally, we create a custom executor, which will be used for executing the stream operations in parallel:

```
LineIterator it = FileUtils.lineIterator(new File("data/words.txt"),
"UTF-8");
ExecutorService executor = Executors.newCachedThreadPool();
LazyFutureStream<String> stream =
        LazyReact.parallelBuilder().withExecutor(executor).from(it);

Map<String, Integer> map = stream
        .map(line -> line.split("t"))
        .map(arr -> arr[1].toLowerCase())
        .distinct()
        .zipWithIndex()
```

```
       .toMap(Tuple2::v1, t -> t.v2.intValue());

System.out.println(map);
executor.shutdown();
it.close();
```

It is a very simple example and does not come close to describing all the functionality available in this library. For more information, refer to their documentation, which can be found at `https://github.com/aol/cyclops-react`. We will also use it in other examples in later chapters.

Accessing data

By now we already have spent a lot of time describing how to read and write data. But there is much more to that: data often comes in different formats such as CSV, HTML, or JSON or it can be stored in a database. Knowing how to access and process this data is important for Data Science and now we will describe in detail how to do it for the most common data formats and sources.

Text data and CSV

We already have spoken about reading text data in great detail, and it can be done, for example, using the `Files` helper class from the NIO API or `IOUtils` from Commons IO.

CSV (Comma Separated Values) is a common way to organize tabular data in plain text files. While it is possible to parse CSV files by hand, there are some corner cases, which make it a bit cumbersome. Luckily, there are nice libraries for that purpose, and one of them is Apache Commons CSV:

```xml
<dependency>
  <groupId>org.apache.commons</groupId>
  <artifactId>commons-csv</artifactId>
  <version>1.4</version>
</dependency>
```

To illustrate how to use this library, let's generate some random data once again. This time we can also use `http://www.generatedata.com/` and define the following schema:

Now we can create a special class for holding this data:

```
public static class Person {
    private final String name;
    private final String email;
    private final String country;
    private final int salary;
    private final int experience;
    // constructor and getters are omitted
}
```

Then, to read a CSV file you can do the following:

```
List<Person> result = new ArrayList<>();

Path csvFile = Paths.get("data/csv-example-generatedata_com.csv");
try (BufferedReader reader = Files.newBufferedReader(csvFile,
StandardCharsets.UTF_8)) {
    CSVFormat csv = CSVFormat.RFC4180.withHeader();
    try (CSVParser parser = csv.parse(reader)) {
        Iterator<CSVRecord> it = parser.iterator();
        it.forEachRemaining(rec -> {
            String name = rec.get("name");
            String email = rec.get("email");
            String country = rec.get("country");
            int salary = Integer.parseInt(rec.get("salary").substring(1));
            int experience = Integer.parseInt(rec.get("experience"));
            Person person = new Person(name, email, country, salary,
experience);
            result.add(person);
        });
    }
}
```

The preceding code creates an iterator of `CSVRecord` objects, and from each such object we extract the values and pass them to a data object. Creating an iterator is useful when the CSV file is very large and may not fit entirely into available memory.

If the file is not too large, it is also possible to read the entire CSV at once and put the results into a list:

```
List<CSVRecord> records = parse.getRecords();
```

Finally, tab-separated files can be seen as a special case of CSV and also can be read using this library. To do it, you just need to use the `TDF` format for parsing:

```
CSVFormat tsv = CSVFormat.TDF.withHeader();
```

Web and HTML

There is a lot of data on the Internet nowadays, and being able to access this data and transform it into something machine-readable is a very important skill for a Data Scientist.

There are multiple ways of accessing data from the Internet. Luckily for us, the standard Java API provides a special class for doing that, `URL`. With `URL`, it is possible to open an `InputStream`, which will contain the response body. For web pages it typically is its HTML content. With `IOUtils` from Commons IO, doing this is simple:

```
try (InputStream is = new URL(url).openStream()) {
    return IOUtils.toString(is, StandardCharsets.UTF_8);
}
```

This piece of code is quite useful, so putting it into some helper method, for example, `UrlUtils.request`, will be helpful.

 Here we assume that the content of a web page is always UTF-8. It may work for many cases, especially for pages in English, but it occasionally may fail. For more complex crawlers, you can use encoding detection from Apache Tika (https://tika.apache.org/).

The preceding method returns raw HTML data, which is not useful in itself; most of the time we are interested in the text content rather than markup. There are libraries for processing HTML and one of them is Jsoup:

```
<dependency>
  <groupId>org.jsoup</groupId>
  <artifactId>jsoup</artifactId>
  <version>1.9.2</version>
</dependency>
```

Let's consider an example. Kaggle.com is a website for hosting data science competitions, and for each competition there is a leader board that shows the performance of each participant. Suppose you are interested in extracting this information from `https://www.kaggle.com/c/avito-duplicate-ads-detection/leaderboard` as shown in the following screenshot:

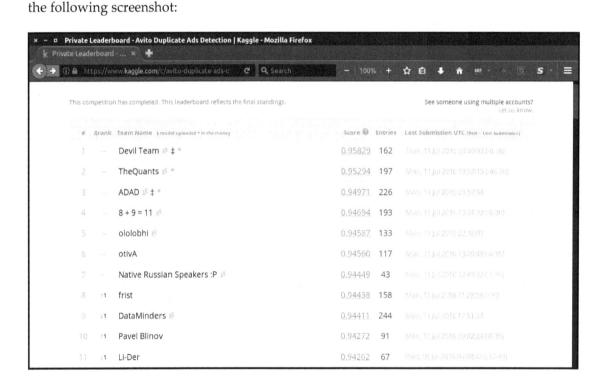

This information is contained in a table, and to extract the data from this table we need to find an anchor that uniquely points to this table. To do that, you can have a look at the page using an inspector (pressing *F12* in Mozilla Firefox or Google Chrome will open the **Inspector** window):

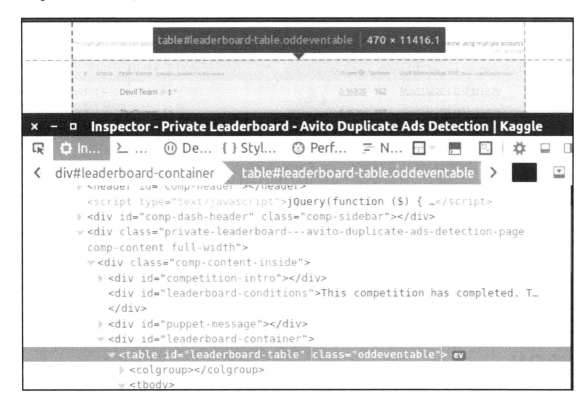

Using the **Inspector**, we can notice that the ID of the table is `leaderboard-table`, and to get this table in Jsoup, we can use the following CSS selector, `#leaderboard-table`. Since we are actually interested in the rows of the table, we will use `#leaderboard-table tr`.

The information about the team name is contained in the third column of the table in the list. Thus, to extract it, we need to get the third `<td>` tag and then look inside its `<a>` tag. Likewise, to extract the score, we get the content of the fourth `<td>` tag.

The code for doing this is as follows:

```
Map<String, Double> result = new HashMap<>();

String rawHtml =
UrlUtils.request("https://www.kaggle.com/c/avito-duplicate-ads-detection/le
```

```
aderboard");
Document document = Jsoup.parse(rawHtml);
Elements tableRows = document.select("#leaderboard-table tr");
for (Element tr : tableRows) {
    Elements columns = tr.select("td");
    if (columns.isEmpty()) {
        continue;
    }

    String team = columns.get(2).select("a.team-link").text();
    double score = Double.parseDouble(columns.get(3).text());
    result.put(team, score);
}

Comparator<Map.Entry<String, Double>> byValue =
Map.Entry.comparingByValue();
result.entrySet().stream()
        .sorted(byValue.reversed())
        .forEach(System.out::println);
```

Here we reuse the `UrlUtils.request` function to get the HTML that we defined previously, and then process it with Jsoup.

Jsoup makes use of CSS selectors for accessing items inside the parsed HTML document. To learn more about them, you can read the related documentation, which is accessible at `https://jsoup.org/cookbook/extracting-data/selector-syntax`.

JSON

JSON is becoming more and more popular as a way of communicating between web services, steadily displacing XML and other formats. Knowing how to process it lets you extract data from a huge variety of data sources available on the Internet.

There are quite a few JSON libraries available for Java. Jackson is one of them and there is its simplified version, called `jackson-jr`, which works for most simple cases when all we need is to quickly extract data from JSON. To add it, use the following:

```
<dependency>
  <groupId>com.fasterxml.jackson.jr</groupId>
  <artifactId>jackson-jr-all</artifactId>
  <version>2.8.1</version>
</dependency>
```

To illustrate it, let's consider a simple API that returns JSON. We can use `http://www.jsont` `est.com/`, which provides a number of dummy web services. One of them is an MD5 service at `http://md5.jsontest.com`; given a string it returns its MD5 hash.

Here is an example of its output:

```
{
   "original": "mastering java for data science",
   "md5": "f4c8637d7274f13b58940ff29f669e8a"
}
```

Let us use it:

```
String text = "mastering java for data science";
String json = UrlUtils.request("http://md5.jsontest.com/?text=" +
text.replace(' ', '+'));

Map<String, Object> map = JSON.std.mapFrom(json);
System.out.println(map.get("original"));
System.out.println(map.get("md5"));
```

In this example, the JSON response of a web service is quite simple. However, there are more complex cases with lists and nested objects. For example, `www.github.com` provides a number of APIs, one of which is `https://api.github.com/users/alexeygrigorev/repos`. For a given user it returns all their repositories. It has a list of objects and each object has a nested object.

In languages with dynamic typing, such as Python, it is quite simple--the language does not force you to have a specific type, which, for this particular case, is good. In Java, however, the static type system requires defining a type; every time you need to extract something, you need to do casting.

For example, if we want to get the element ID of the first object, we would need to do something like this:

```
String username = "alexeygrigorev";
String json = UrlUtils.request("https://api.github.com/users/" + username +
"/repos");

List<Map<String, ?>> list = (List<Map<String, ?>>) JSON.std.anyFrom(json);
String name = (String) list.get(0).get("name");
System.out.println(name);
```

As you can see, we need to do a lot of type casting and the code quickly becomes pretty cluttered. A solution to that may be using a query language similar to Xpath, called JsonPath. An implementation available for Java is accessible at `https://github.com/jayway/JsonPath`. To use it, add the following:

```
<dependency>
  <groupId>com.jayway.jsonpath</groupId>
  <artifactId>json-path</artifactId>
  <version>2.2.0</version>
</dependency>
```

If we want to retrieve all repositories, which are written in Java and have at least one start, then the following query will do it:

```
ReadContext ctx = JsonPath.parse(json);
String query = "$..[?(@.language=='Java' && @.stargazers_count >
0)]full_name";
List<String> javaProjects = ctx.read(query);
```

It definitely will save some time for simple data manipulations such as filtering, but, unfortunately, for more complex things, you may still need to do manual conversions with a lot of casting.

 For more complex queries (for example, sending a POST request), it is better to use a special library such as Apache HttpComponents (`https://hc.apache.org/`).

Databases

In organizations, data is usually kept in relational databases. Java defines **Java Database Connectivity (JDBC)** as an abstraction for accessing any database that supports SQL.

In our example, we will use MySQL, which can be downloaded from `https://www.mysql.com/`, but in principle it can be any other database, such as PostgreSQL, Oracle, MS SQL and many others. To connect to a MySQL server, we can use a JDBC MySQL driver:

```
<dependency>
  <groupId>mysql</groupId>
  <artifactId>mysql-connector-java</artifactId>
  <version>5.1.39</version>
</dependency>
```

If you would like to use a different database, then you can use your favorite search engine and find the suitable JDBC driver. The interaction code will remain the same, and if you use the standard SQL, the query code should not change as well.

For example, we will use the same data we generated for the CSV example. First, we will load it to the database, and then do a simple select.

Let's define the following schema:

```
CREATE SCHEMA `people` DEFAULT CHARACTER SET utf8 ;
CREATE TABLE `people`.`people` (
  `person_id` INT UNSIGNED NOT NULL AUTO_INCREMENT,
  `name` VARCHAR(45) NULL,
  `email` VARCHAR(100) NULL,
  `country` VARCHAR(45) NULL,
  `salary` INT NULL,
  `experience` INT NULL,
  PRIMARY KEY (`person_id`));
```

Now, to connect to the database, we typically use the `DataSource` abstraction. The MySQL driver provides an implementation: `MysqlDataSource`:

```
MysqlDataSource datasource = new MysqlDataSource();
datasource.setServerName("localhost");
datasource.setDatabaseName("people");
datasource.setUser("root");
datasource.setPassword("");
```

Now using the `DataSource` object, we can load the data. There are two ways of doing it; the simple way, when we insert each object individually, and batch mode, where we first prepare a batch, and then insert all the objects of a batch. The batch mode option typically works faster.

Let's first look at the usual mode:

```
try (Connection connection = datasource.getConnection()) {
    String sql = "INSERT INTO people (name, email, country, salary,
experience) VALUES (?, ?, ?, ?, ?);";
    try (PreparedStatement statement = connection.prepareStatement(sql)) {
        for (Person person : people) {
            statement.setString(1, person.getName());
            statement.setString(2, person.getEmail());
            statement.setString(3, person.getCountry());
            statement.setInt(4, person.getSalary());
            statement.setInt(5, person.getExperience());
            statement.execute();
        }
```

```
        }
    }
```

 Note that the enumeration of indexes starts from 1 in JDBC, not from 0.

Batch is very similar. To prepare the batches, we first use a `Lists.partition` function from Guava, and chuck all the data into batches of 50 objects. Then each object of a chunk is added to a batch with the `addBatch` function:

```
List<List<Person>> chunks = Lists.partition(people, 50);

try (Connection connection = datasource.getConnection()) {
    String sql = "INSERT INTO people (name, email, country, salary,
experience) VALUES (?, ?, ?, ?, ?);";
    try (PreparedStatement statement = connection.prepareStatement(sql)) {
        for (List<Person> chunk : chunks) {
            for (Person person : chunk) {
                statement.setString(1, person.getName());
                statement.setString(2, person.getEmail());
                statement.setString(3, person.getCountry());
                statement.setInt(4, person.getSalary());
                statement.setInt(5, person.getExperience());
                statement.addBatch();
            }
            statement.executeBatch();
        }
    }
}
```

Batch mode is faster than the usual way of processing the data, but requires more memory. If you need to process a lot of data and care about speed, then batch mode is a better choice, but it makes the code a bit more complex. For that reason, it may be better to use the simpler approach.

Now, when the data is loaded, we can query the database. For instance, let us select all the people from a country:

```
String country = "Greenland";
try (Connection connection = datasource.getConnection()) {
    String sql = "SELECT name, email, salary, experience FROM people WHERE
country = ?;";
    try (PreparedStatement statement = connection.prepareStatement(sql)) {
        List<Person> result = new ArrayList<>();
```

```
            statement.setString(1, country);
            try (ResultSet rs = statement.executeQuery()) {
                while (rs.next()) {
                    String name = rs.getString(1);
                    String email = rs.getString(2);
                    int salary = rs.getInt(3);
                    int experience = rs.getInt(4);
                    Person person = new Person(name, email, country, salary,
experience);
                    result.add(person);
                }
            }
        }
    }
}
```

This way we can execute any SQL query we want and put the results into Java objects for further processing.

 You may have noticed that there is a lot of boilerplate code in JDBC. The boilerplate can be reduced with the Spring JDBC Template library (see `http://www.springframework.org`).

DataFrames

DataFrames are a convenient way of representing tabular data in memory. Originally DataFrames came from the R programming language, but they are now common in other languages; for example, in Python the pandas library offers a DataFrame data structure similar to R's.

The usual way of storing data in Java is lists, maps, and other collections of objects. We can think of these collections as tables, but we can assess the data only by row. However, for data science manipulation columns are equally important, and this is where DataFrames are helpful.

For example, they allow you to apply the same function over all values of the same column or look at the distribution of the values.

In Java there are not so many mature implementations, but there are some that have all the needed functionality. In our examples we will use `joinery`:

```
<dependency>
  <groupId>joinery</groupId>
  <artifactId>joinery-dataframe</artifactId>
```

```
    <version>1.7</version>
</dependency>
```

Unfortunately, `joinery` is not available on Maven Central; thus, to include it to a Maven project, you need to point to `bintray`, another Maven repository. To do this, add this `repository` to the repositories section in the `pom` file:

```
<repository>
  <id>bintray</id>
  <url>http://jcenter.bintray.com</url>
</repository>
```

Joinery depends on `Apache POI`, so you need to add it as well:

```
<dependency>
  <groupId>org.apache.poi</groupId>
  <artifactId>poi</artifactId>
  <version>3.14</version>
</dependency>
```

With Joinery it is very easy to read the data:

```
DataFrame<Object> df = DataFrame.readCsv("data/csv-example-
generatedata_com.csv");
```

Once the data is read, we can access not only every row, but also every column of the DataFrame. Given a column name, Joinery returns a `List` of values that are stored in the column, and we can use it to apply various transformations to it.

For example, suppose we want to associate every country that we have with a unique index. We can do it like this:

```
List<Object> country = df.col("country");
Map<String, Long> map = LazyReact.sequentialBuilder()
        .from(country)
        .cast(String.class)
        .distinct()
        .zipWithIndex()
        .toMap(Tuple2::v1, Tuple2::v2);

List<Object> indexes =
country.stream().map(map::get).collect(Collectors.toList());
```

After that, we can drop the old column with `country` and include the new index column instead:

```
df = df.drop("country");
df.add("country_index", indexes);
System.out.println(df);
```

Joinery can do a lot more--group by, joins, pivoting, and creating design matrices for machine learning models. We will use it again in the future in almost all the chapters. Meanwhile, you can read more about joinery at `https://cardillo.github.io/joinery/`.

Search engine - preparing data

In the first chapter, we introduced the running example, building a search engine. A search engine is a program that, given a query from the user, returns results ordered by relevance with respect to the query. In this chapter, we will perform the first steps--obtaining and processing data.

Suppose we are working on a web portal where users generate a lot of content, but they have trouble finding what other people have created. To overcome this problem, we propose to build a search engine, and product management has identified the typical queries that the users will put in.

For example, "Chinese food", "homemade pizza", and "how to learn programming" are typical queries from this list.

Now we need to collect the data. Luckily for us, there are already search engines on the Internet that can take in a query and return a list of URLs they consider relevant. We can use them for obtaining the data. You probably already know such engines--Google or Bing, to name just two.

Thus, we can apply what we learned in this chapter and parse the data from Google, Bing, or any other search engine using JSoup. Alternatively, it is possible to use services such as `https://flow-app.com/` to do this extraction for you, but it requires registration.

In the end, what we need is a query and a list of the most relevant URLs. Extraction of the relevant URLs is left as an exercise, but we already prepared some results that you can use if you wish: for each query there are 30 most relevant pages from the first three pages of the search results. Additionally, you can find useful code for crawling in the code bundle.

Now, when we have the URLs, we are interested in retrieving them and saving their HTML code. For this purpose, we need a crawler that is a bit smarter than what we already have in our `UrlUtils.request`.

One particular thing that we must add is timeouts: some pages take a lot of time to load, because they are either big or the server is experiencing some troubles and takes a while to respond. In these cases, it makes sense to give up when a page cannot be downloaded in, for example, 30 seconds.

In Java, this can be done with `Executors`. First, let's create a `Crawler` class, and declare the `executor` field:

```
int numProc = Runtime.getRuntime().availableProcessors();
executor = Executors.newFixedThreadPool(numProc);
```

Then, we can use this executor as follows:

```
try {
    Future<String> future = executor.submit(() -> UrlUtils.request(url));
    String result = future.get(30, TimeUnit.SECONDS);
    return Optional.of(result);
} catch (TimeoutException e) {
    LOGGER.warn("timeout exception: could not crawl {} in {} sec", url,
timeout);
    return Optional.empty();
}
```

This code will drop pages that are taking too long to retrieve.

We need to store the crawled HTML pages somewhere. There are a few options: a bunch of HTML files on the filesystem, a relational store such as MySQL, or a key-value store. The key-value storage looks like the best choice because we have a key, the URL, and the value, the HTML. For that we can use MapDB, a pure Java key-value storage that implements the `Map` interface. In essence, it's a `Map` that is supported by a file on disk.

Since it is pure Java, all you need to do to use it is to include its dependency:

```
<dependency>
  <groupId>org.mapdb</groupId>
  <artifactId>mapdb</artifactId>
  <version>3.0.1</version>
</dependency>
```

And now we can use it:

```
DB db = DBMaker.fileDB("urls.db").closeOnJvmShutdown().make();
HTreeMap<?, ?> htreeMap = db.hashMap("urls").createOrOpen();
Map<String, String> urls = (Map<String, String>) htreeMap;
```

Since it implements the Map interface, it can be treated as a usual Map and we can put the HTML there. So, let's read the relevant URLs, download their HTML, and save it to the map:

```
Path path = Paths.get("data/search-results.txt");
List<String> lines = FileUtils.readLines(path.toFile(),
StandardCharsets.UTF_8);

lines.parallelStream()
    .map(line -> line.split("t"))
    .map(split -> "http://" + split[2])
    .distinct()
    .forEach(url -> {
        try {
            Optional<String> html = crawler.crawl(url);
            if (html.isPresent()) {
                LOGGER.debug("successfully crawled {}", url);
                urls.put(url, html.get());
            }
        } catch (Exception e) {
            LOGGER.error("got exception when processing url {}", url, e);
        }
    });
```

Here we do that in a parallelStream to make the execution faster. The timeouts will ensure that it finishes in a reasonable amount of time.

For starters, let's extract something very simple from the pages, as follows:

- Length of the URL
- Length of the title
- Whether or not the query is contained in the title
- Length of entire text in body
- Number of <h1>-<h6> tags
- Number of links

To hold this information, we can create a special class, `RankedPage`.

```
public class RankedPage {
    private String url;
    private int position;
    private int page;
    private int titleLength;
    private int bodyContentLength;
    private boolean queryInTitle;
    private int numberOfHeaders;
    private int numberOfLinks;
    // setters, getters are omitted
}
```

Now, let us crawl the for each page create an object of this class. We use `flatMap` for this because for some URLs there is no HTML data.

```
Stream<RankedPage> pages = lines.parallelStream().flatMap(line -> {
    String[] split = line.split("t");
    String query = split[0];
    int position = Integer.parseInt(split[1]);
    int searchPageNumber = 1 + (position - 1) / 10; // converts position to
a page number
    String url = "http://" + split[2];
    if (!urls.containsKey(url)) { // no crawl available
        return Stream.empty();
    }

    RankedPage page = new RankedPage(url, position, searchPageNumber);
    String html = urls.get(url);
    Document document = Jsoup.parse(html);
    String title = document.title();
    int titleLength = title.length();
    page.setTitleLength(titleLength);

    boolean queryInTitle =
title.toLowerCase().contains(query.toLowerCase());
    page.setQueryInTitle(queryInTitle);

    if (document.body() == null) { // no body for the document
        return Stream.empty();
    }
    int bodyContentLength = document.body().text().length();
    page.setBodyContentLength(bodyContentLength);

    int numberOfLinks = document.body().select("a").size();
    page.setNumberOfLinks(numberOfLinks);
```

```
    int numberOfHeaders =
document.body().select("h1,h2,h3,h4,h5,h6").size();
    page.setNumberOfHeaders(numberOfHeaders);

    return Stream.of(page);
});
```

In this piece of code, for each page we look up its HTML. If it is not crawled--we skip the page; then we parse the HTML and retrieve the preceding basic features.

This is only a small fraction of the possible page features that we can compute. Later on, we will build on this and add more features.

In this example, we get a stream of pages. We can do anything we want with this stream, for example, save it to JSON or convert it to a DataFrame. The code bundle that comes with this book has some examples and shows how to do these types of conversion. For example, conversion from a list of Java objects to a Joinery `DataFrame` is available in the `BeanToJoinery` utility class.

Summary

There are a few steps for approaching any data science problem, and the data preparation step is one of the first. The standard Java API has a tremendous number of tools that make this task possible, and there are a lot of libraries that make it a lot easier.

In this chapter, we discussed many of them, including extensions to the Java API such as Google Guava; we talked about ways to read the data from different sources such as text, HTML, and databases; and finally we covered the DataFrame, a useful structure for manipulating tabular data.

In the next chapter, we will take a closer look at the data that we extracted in this chapter and perform Exploratory Data Analysis.

3
Exploratory Data Analysis

In the previous chapter, we covered data processing, which is an important step for transforming data into a form usable for analysis. In this chapter, we take the next logical step after cleaning and look at data. This step is called **Exploratory Data Analysis** (**EDA**), and it consists of summarizing data and creating visualizations.

In this chapter, we will cover the following topics:

- Summary statistics with Apache Commons Math and Joinery
- Interactive shells for EDA in Java and JVM

By the end of this chapter, you will know how to calculate summary statistics and create simple graphs with Joinery.

Exploratory data analysis in Java

Exploratory Data Analysis is about taking a dataset and extracting the most important information from it, in such a way that it is possible to get an idea of what the data looks like. This includes two main parts: summarization and visualization.

The summarization step is very helpful for understanding data. For numerical variables, in this step we calculate the most important sample statistics:

- The extremes (the minimal and the maximal values)
- The mean value, or the sample average
- The standard deviation, which describes the spread of the data

Often we consider other statistics, such as the median and the quartiles (25% and 75%).

As we have already seen in the previous chapter, Java offers a great set of tools for data preparation. The same set of tools can be used for EDA, and especially for creating summaries.

Search engine datasets

In this chapter, we will use our running example--building a search engine. In `Chapter 2`, *Data Processing Toolbox*, we extracted some data from HTML pages returned by a search engine. This dataset included some numerical features, such as the length of the title and the length of the content.

For the purposes of storing these features, we created the following class:

```java
public class RankedPage {
    private String url;
    private int position;
    private int page;
    private int titleLength;
    private int bodyContentLength;
    private boolean queryInTitle;
    private int numberOfHeaders;
    private int numberOfLinks;
    // setters, getters are omitted
}
```

It is interesting to see if this information can be useful for the search engine. For example, given a URL, we may want to know whether it is likely to appear on the first page of the engine output or not. Looking at the data by means of EDA will help us know if it is possible.

Additionally, real-world data is rarely clean. We will use EDA to try to spot some strange or problematic observations.

Let's get started. We saved the data in the JSON format, and now we can read it back using streams and Jackson:

```java
Path path = Paths.get("./data/ranked-pages.json");
try (Stream<String> lines = Files.lines(path)) {
    return lines.map(line -> parseJson(line)).collect(Collectors.toList());
}
```

This is the body of a function that returns a list of `RankedPage` objects. We read them from the `ranked-page.json` file. And then we use the `parseJson` function to convert the JSON to the Java class:

```
JSON.std.beanFrom(RankedPage.class, line);
```

After reading the data, we can analyze it. Usually, the first step in the analysis is looking at the summary statistics, and we can use Apache Commons Math for that.

Apache Commons Math

Once we read the data, we can calculate the statistics. As we already mentioned earlier, we are typically interested in summaries such as min, max, mean, standard deviation, and so on. We can use the Apache Commons Math library for that. Let's include it in `pom.xml`:

```
<dependency>
  <groupId>org.apache.commons</groupId>
  <artifactId>commons-math3</artifactId>
  <version>3.6.1</version>
</dependency>
```

There is a `SummaryStatistics` class for calculating the summaries. Let's use it to calculate some statistics about the distribution of body content length of the pages we crawled:

```
SummaryStatistics statistics = new SummaryStatistics();
data.stream().mapToDouble(RankedPage::getBodyContentLength)
    .forEach(statistics::addValue);
System.out.println(statistics.getSummary());
```

Here, we create `SummaryStatistics` objects and add all body content lengths. After that, we can call a `getSummary` method to get all summary stats at once. This will print the following:

```
StatisticalSummaryValues:
n: 4067
min: 0.0
max: 8675779.0
mean: 14332.239242685007
std dev: 144877.54551111493
variance: 2.0989503193325176E10
sum: 5.8289217E7
```

The `DescriptiveStatistics` method is another useful class from this library. It allows getting more values, such as median and percentiles, and percentiles; give a better idea of what the data looks like:

```
double[] dataArray = data.stream()
        .mapToDouble(RankedPage::getBodyContentLength)
        .toArray();
DescriptiveStatistics desc = new DescriptiveStatistics(dataArray);
System.out.printf("min: %9.1f%n", desc.getMin());
System.out.printf("p05: %9.1f%n", desc.getPercentile(5));
System.out.printf("p25: %9.1f%n", desc.getPercentile(25));
System.out.printf("p50: %9.1f%n", desc.getPercentile(50));
System.out.printf("p75: %9.1f%n", desc.getPercentile(75));
System.out.printf("p95: %9.1f%n", desc.getPercentile(95));
System.out.printf("max: %9.1f%n", desc.getMax());
```

This will produce the following output:

```
min: 0.0
p05: 527.6
p25: 3381.0
p50: 6612.0
p75: 11996.0
p95: 31668.4
max: 8675779.0
```

From the output, we can note that the minimum length is zero, which is strange; most likely, there was a data processing issue. Also, the maximal value is very high, which suggests that there are outliers. Later on, it will make sense to exclude these values from our analysis.

Probably the pages with zero content length are crawling errors. Let's see the proportion of these pages:

```
double proportion = data.stream()
        .mapToInt(p -> p.getBodyContentLength() == 0 ? 1 : 0)
        .average().getAsDouble();
System.out.printf("proportion of zero content length: %.5f%n", proportion);
```

We see that not so many pages have zero length, so it is quite safe to just drop them.

Later on, in the next chapter, we will try to predict whether a URL comes from the first search page result or not. If some features have different values for each page, then a machine learning model will be able to see this difference and use it for more accurate predictions. Let's see whether the value for content length is similar across the different pages.

For this purpose, we can group the URLs by page and calculate the mean content length. As we already know, Java streams can be used to do this:

```
Map<Integer, List<RankedPage>> byPage = data.stream()
    .filter(p -> p.getBodyContentLength() != 0)
    .collect(Collectors.groupingBy(RankedPage::getPage));
```

Note that we added a filter for empty pages, so they do not appear in the groups. Now, we can use the groups to calculate the average:

```
List<DescriptiveStatistics> stats = byPage.entrySet().stream()
    .sorted(Map.Entry.comparingByKey())
    .map(e -> calculate(e.getValue(), RankedPage::getBodyContentLength))
    .collect(Collectors.toList());
```

Here, `calculate` is a function that takes in a collection, computes the provided function on every element (using `getBodyContentLength` in this case), and creates a `DescriptiveStatistics` object from it:

```
private static DescriptiveStatistics calculate(List<RankedPage> data,
            ToDoubleFunction<RankedPage> getter) {
    double[] dataArray = data.stream().mapToDouble(getter).toArray();
    return new DescriptiveStatistics(dataArray);
}
```

Now, in the list, you will have the descriptive statistics for each group (page, in this case). Then, we can display them in any way we want. Consider the following example:

```
Map<String, Function<DescriptiveStatistics, Double>> functions = new
LinkedHashMap<>();
functions.put("min", d -> d.getMin());
functions.put("p05", d -> d.getPercentile(5));
functions.put("p25", d -> d.getPercentile(25));
functions.put("p50", d -> d.getPercentile(50));
functions.put("p75", d -> d.getPercentile(75));
functions.put("p95", d -> d.getPercentile(95));
functions.put("max", d -> d.getMax());
System.out.print("page");

for (Integer page : byPage.keySet()) {
    System.out.printf("%9d ", page);
}
System.out.println();

for (Entry<String, Function<DescriptiveStatistics, Double>> pair :
functions.entrySet()) {
    System.out.print(pair.getKey());
    Function<DescriptiveStatistics, Double> function = pair.getValue();
```

```
        System.out.print(" ");
        for (DescriptiveStatistics ds : stats) {
            System.out.printf("%9.1f ", function.apply(ds));
        }
        System.out.println();
    }
```

This produces the following output:

```
page 0 1 2
min 5.0 1.0 5.0
p05 1046.8 900.6 713.8
p25 3706.0 3556.0 3363.0
p50 7457.0 6882.0 6383.0
p75 13117.0 12067.0 11309.8
p95 42420.6 30557.2 27397.0
max 390583.0 8675779.0 1998233.0
```

The output suggests that the distribution of content length is different across URLs coming from different pages of search engine results. Thus, this can potentially be useful when predicting the search page number for a given URL.

Joinery

You might notice that the code we just wrote is quite verbose. Of course, it is possible to put it inside a helper function and call it when needed, but there is another more concise way of computing these statistics--with joinery and its DataFrames.

In Joinery, the DataFrame object has a method called describe, which creates a new DataFrame with summary statistics:

```
List<RankedPage> pages = Data.readRankedPages();
DataFrame<Object> df = BeanToJoinery.convert(pages, RankedPage.class);
df = df.retain("bodyContentLength", "titleLength", "numberOfHeaders");
DataFrame<Object> describe = df.describe();
System.out.println(describe.toString());
```

In the preceding code, Data.readRankedPages is a helper method that reads JSON data and converts it to a list of Java objects, and BeanToJoinery.convert is a helper class that converts a list of Java objects to a DataFrame.

Then, we keep only three columns and drop everything else. The following is the output:

```
body     contentLength    numberOfHeaders  titleLength
count    4067.00000000    4067.00000000    4067.00000000
mean     14332.23924269   25.25325793      46.17334645
std      144877.5455111   32.13788062      27.72939822
var      20989503193.32   1032.84337047    768.91952552
max      8675779.000000   742.00000000     584.00000000
min      0.00000000       0.00000000       0.00000000
```

We can also look at the means across different groups, for example, across different pages. For that, we can use the `groupBy` method:

```java
DataFrame<Object> meanPerPage = df.groupBy("page").mean()
    .drop("position")
    .sortBy("page")
    .transpose();
System.out.println(meanPerPage);
```

Apart from applying mean after `groupBy`, we also remove one column position because we already know that position will be different for different pages. Additionally, we apply the transpose operation at the end; this is a trick to make the output fit into a screen when there are many columns. This produces the following output:

```
page 0 1 2
bodyContentLength 12577 18703 11286
numberOfHeaders 30 23 21
numberOfLinks 276 219 202
queryInTitle 0 0 0
titleLength 46 46 45
```

We can see that the averages are quite different for some variables. For other variables, such as `queryInTitle`, there does not seem to be any difference. However, remember that this is a Boolean variable, so the mean is between 0 and 1. For some reason, Joinery decided not to show the decimal part here.

Now, we know how to compute some simple summary statistics in Java, but to do that, we first need to write some code, compile it, and then run it. This is not the most convenient procedure, and there are better ways to do it interactively, that is, avoiding compilation and getting the results right away. Next, we will see how to do it in Java.

Interactive Exploratory Data Analysis in Java

Java is a statically typed programming language and code written in Java needs compiling. While Java is good for developing complex data science applications, it makes it harder to interactively explore the data; every time, we need to recompile the source code and re-run the analysis script to see the results. This means that, if we need to read some data, we will have to do it over and over again. If the dataset is large, the program takes more time to start.

So it is hard to interact with data and this makes EDA more difficult in Java than in other languages. In particular, **Read-Evaluate-Print Loop** (**REPL**), an interactive shell, is quite an important feature for doing EDA.

Unfortunately, Java 8 does not have REPL, but there are several alternatives:

- Other interactive JVM languages such as JavaScript, Groovy, or Scala
- Java 9 with jshell
- Completely alternative platforms such as Python or R

In this chapter, we will look at the first two options--JVM languages and Java 9's REPL.

JVM languages

As you probably know, the Java platform is not only the Java programming language, but also the **Java Virtual Machine** (JVM) can run code from other JVM languages. There are a number of languages that run on JVM and have REPL, for example, JavaScript, Scala, Groovy, JRuby, and Jython. There are many more. All these languages can access any code written in Java and they have interactive consoles.

For example, Groovy is very similar to Java, and prior to Java 8 almost any code written in Java could be run in Groovy. However, for Java 8, this is no longer the case. Groovy does not support the new Java syntax for lambda expressions and functional interfaces, so we will not be able to run most of the code from this book there.

Scala is another popular functional JVM language, but its syntax is very different from Java. It is a very powerful and expressive language for data processing, it has a nice interactive shell, and there are many libraries for doing data analysis and data science.

Additionally, there are a couple of JavaScript implementations available for JVM. One of them is Nashorn, which comes with Java 8 out-of-the-box; there is no need to include it as a separate dependency. Joinery also comes in with a built-in interactive console, which utilizes JavaScript, and later in this chapter, we will see how to use it.While all these languages are nice, they are beyond the scope of this book. You can learn more about them from these books:

- *Groovy in Action, Dierk Konig, Manning*
- *Scala Data Analysis Cookbook, Arun Manivannan, Packt Publishing*

Interactive Java

It would not be fair to say that Java is a 100% not-interactive language; there are some extensions that provide a REPL environment directly for Java.

One such environment is a scripting language (BeanShell) that looks exactly like Java. However, it is quite old and the new Java 8 syntax is not supported, so it is not very useful for doing interactive data analysis.

What is more interesting is Java 9, which comes with an integrated REPL called JShell and supports autocompletion on tab, Java Streams, and the Java 8 syntax for lambda expressions. At the time of writing, Java 9 is only available as an Early Access Release. You can download it from `https://jdk9.java.net/download/`.

Starting the shell is easy:

```
$ jshell
```

But typically you would like to access some libraries, and for that they need to be on the classpath. Usually, we use Maven for managing the dependencies, so we can run the following to copy all the `jar` libraries specified in the `pom` file to a directory of our choice:

```
mvn dependency:copy-dependencies -DoutputDirectory=lib
mvn compile
```

After doing it, we can run the shell like this:

```
jshell -cp lib/*:target/classes
```

If you are on Windows, replace the colon with a semicolon:

```
jshell -cp lib/*;target/classes
```

However, our experiments showed that JShell is unfortunately quite raw yet and sometimes crashes. At the time of writing, the plan is to release it at the end of March 2017. For now, we will not cover JShell in more detail, but all the code from the first half of the chapter should work in that console with no additional configuration. And what is more, we should be able to see the output immediately.

By now, we have used Joinery a couple of times already, and it has also some support for performing simple EDA. Next, we will look at how to do the analysis with the Joinery shell.

Joinery shell

Joinery has already proved useful multiple times for doing data processing and simple EDA. It has an interactive shell for doing EDA and you get an answer instantly.

If the data is already in the CSV format, then the Joinery shell can be called from the system console:

```
$ java joinery.DataFrame shell
```

You can see the examples at https://github.com/cardillo/joinery. So if your data is already in CSV, you are good to go, just follow the instructions from there.

Here, in this book, we will look at a more complex example when the DataFrame is not in CSV. In our case the data is in JSON, and the Joinery shell does not support that format, so we need to do some pre-processing first.

What we can do is to create a DataFrame object inside the Java code and then create the interactive shell and pass the DataFrame there. Let's see how it can be done.

But before we can do this, we need to add a few dependencies to make it possible. First, the Joinery shell uses JavaScript, but it does not use the Nashorn engin shipped along with the JVM; instead it uses the Mozilla's engine called **Rhino**. Thus, we need to include it to our pom:

```
<dependency>
  <groupId>rhino</groupId>
  <artifactId>js</artifactId>
  <version>1.7R2</version>
</dependency>
```

Second, it relies on a special library for autocompletion, `jline`. Let's add it as well:

```
<dependency>
  <groupId>jline</groupId>
  <artifactId>jline</artifactId>
  <version>2.14.2</version>
</dependency>
```

Using Maven gives you a lot of flexibility; it is simpler and does not require you to download all the libraries manually and build Joinery from the source code to be able to execute the shell. So, we let Maven take care of it.

Now we are ready to use it:

```
List<RankedPage> pages = Data.readRankedPages();
DataFrame<Object> dataFrame = BeanToJoinery.convert(pages,
'RankedPage.class);
Shell.repl(Arrays.asList(dataFrame));
```

Let's save this code to a `chapter03.JoineryShell` class. After that, we can run it with the following Maven command:

```
mvn exec:java -Dexec.mainClass="chapter03.JoineryShell"
```

This will bring us to the Joinery shell:

```
# DataFrames for Java -- null, 1.7-8e3c8cf
# Java HotSpot(TM) 64-Bit Server VM, Oracle Corporation, 1.8.0_91
# Rhino 1.7 release 2 2009 03 22
>
```

All the DataFrames that we pass to the Shell object in Java are available in the frames variable in the shell. So, to get `DataFrame`, we can do this:

```
> var df = frames[0]
```

To see the content of `DataFrame`, just write its name:

```
> df
```

And you will see a couple of first rows of `DataFrame`. Note that the autocompletion works as expected:

```
> df.<tab>
```

You will see a list of options.

We can use this shell to call the same methods on the DataFrames as we would use in the usual Java application. For example, you can compute the mean as follows:

```
> df.mean().transpose()
```

We will see the following output:

```
bodyContentLength 14332.23924269
numberOfHeaders 25.25325793
numberOfLinks 231.16867470
page 1.03221047
position 18.76518318
queryInTitle 0.59822965
titleLength 46.17334645
```

Alternatively. we can perform the same `groupBy` example:

```
> df.drop('position').groupBy('page').mean().sortBy('page').transpose()
```

This will produce the following output:

```
page 0 1 2
bodyContentLength 12577 18703 11286
numberOfHeaders 30 23 21
numberOfLinks 276 219 202
queryInTitle 0 0 0
titleLength 46 46 45
```

Finally, it is also possible to create some simple plots with Joinery. For that, we will need to use an additional library. For plotting, Joinery uses `xchart`. Let's include it:

```
<dependency>
  <groupId>com.xeiam.xchart</groupId>
  <artifactId>xchart</artifactId>
  <version>2.5.1</version>
</dependency>
```

And run the console again. Now we can use the `plot` function:

```
> df.retain('titleLength').plot(PlotType.SCATTER)
```

And we will see this:

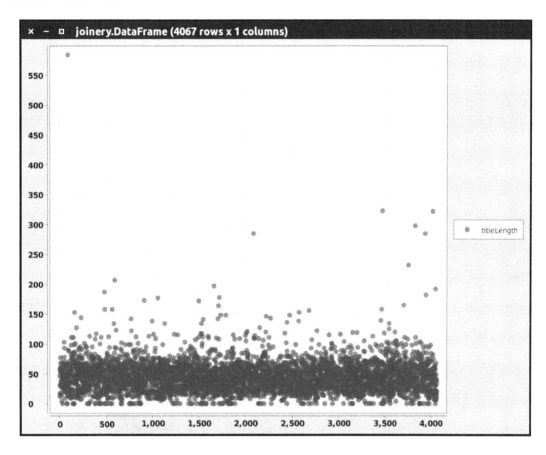

Here, we see an outlier whose title length is more than 550 characters. Let's remove everything that is above 200 and have a look at the picture again. Also, remember that there are some zero-length content pages, so we can filter them out as well.

To keep only those rows that satisfy some condition, we use the `select` method. It takes a function, which is applied to every row; if a function returns `true`, the row is kept.

We can use it like this:

```
> df.retain('titleLength')
    .select(function(list) { return list.get(0) <= 200; })
    .select(function(list) { return list.get(0) > 0;})
    .plot(PlotType.SCATTER)
```

The line-breaks in the preceding code are added for better readability, but they will not work in the console, so do not use them.

Now, we get a clearer picture:

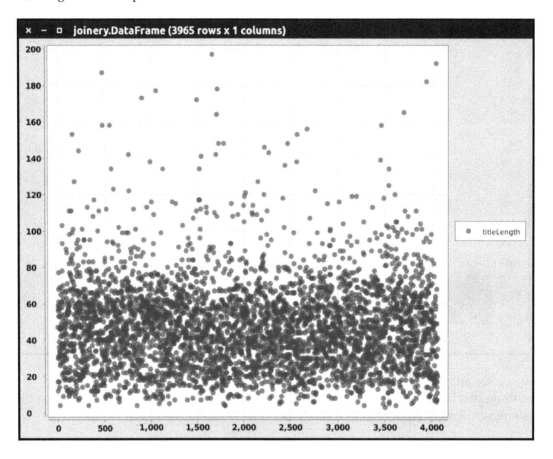

Unfortunately, the plotting capabilities of joinery are quite limited, and it takes a lot of effort to produce graphs using `xchart`.

As we already know, in Joinery, it is easy to calculate statistics across different groups; we just need to use the `groupBy` method. However, it is not possible to easily use this method for plotting data so that it is easy to compare the distributions for each group.

There are other tools that you can also use for EDA:

- Weka, which is written in Java, is a library used for performing data mining. It has a GUI interface for performing EDA.
- Smile, another Java library, has a Scala shell and a smile-plot library for creating visualizations.

Unfortunately, Java is typically not the ideal choice for performing EDA and there are other better suited dynamic languages for that. For example, R and Python are ideal for this task, but covering them is beyond the scope of this book. You can learn more about them from the following books:

- Mastering Data Analysis with R, Gergely Daroczi
- Python Machine Learning, Sebastian Raschka

Summary

In this chapter, we talked about Exploratory Data Analysis, or EDA for short. We discussed how to do EDA in Java, which included creating summaries and simple visualizations.

Throughout the chapter, we used our search engine example and analyzed the data we collected previously. Our analysis showed that the distribution of some variables looks different for URLs coming from different pages of the search engine results. This suggests that it is possible to use these differences to build a model that will predict whether a URL comes from the first page or not.

In the next chapter, we will look at how to do it and discuss of supervised machine learning algorithms, such as classification and regression.

4

Supervised Learning - Classification and Regression

In previous chapters, we looked at how to pre-process data in Java and how to do Exploratory Data Analysis. Now, as we covered the foundation, we are ready to start creating machine learning models.

First, we start with supervised learning. In the supervised settings, we have some information attached to each observation, called labels, and we want to learn from it, and predict it for observations without labels.

There are two types of labels: the first are discrete and finite, such as true/false or buy/sell, and the second are continuous, such as salary or temperature. These types correspond to two types of supervised learning: classification and regression. We will talk about them in this chapter.

This chapter covers the following points:

- Classification problems
- Regression problems
- Evaluation metrics for each type
- An overview of the available implementations in Java

By the end of this chapter, you will know how to use Smile, LIBLINEAR, and other Java libraries for building supervised machine learning models.

Classification

In machine learning, the classification problems deal with discrete targets with a finite set of possible values. What this means is that there is a set of possible outcomes, and given some features we want to predict the outcome.

The **binary classification** is the most common type of classification problem, as the `target` variable can have only two possible values, such as `True`/`False`, `Relevant`/`Not Relevant`, `Duplicate`/`Not Duplicate`, `Cat`/`Dog`, and so on.

Sometimes the target variable can have more than two outcomes, for example, colors, category of an item, model of a car, and so on, and we call this **multi-class classification**. Typically, each observation can only have one label, but in some settings an observation can be assigned several values. Multi-class classification can be converted to a set of binary classification problems, which is why we will mostly concentrate on binary classification.

Binary classification models

As we have already discussed, the binary classification model deals with the case when there are only two possible outcomes that we want to predict. Typically, in these settings, we have items of the positive class (the presence of some effect) and items of the negative class (the absence of some effect).

For example, the positive label can be relevant, duplicate, fail to pay the debts, and so on. The instances of the positive class are typically assigned the target value of 1. Also, we have negative instances, such as not relevant, not duplicate, pays the debts, and they are assigned the target value of 0.

This separation into positive and negative classes is somewhat artificial, and in some cases does not really make sense. For example, if we have images of cats and dogs, even though there are just two classes, it would be a stretch to say that `Cat` is a positive class and `Dog` is negative. But it is not important for the model, so we can still assign the labels in such a way that `Cat` is 1, and `Dog` is 0.

Once we have trained a model, we are not typically interested in a hard prediction such as *the positive effect is there*, or *this is a cat*. What is more interesting is the degree of the positive or negative effect, and this is typically achieved by predicting probabilities. For example, if we want to build a model to predict whether a client will fail to pay the debts, then saying *this client has 30% of defaulting* is more useful than *this client will not default*.

There are many models solve the binary classification problem and it is not possible to cover all of them. We will briefly cover the ones that are most often used in practice. They include the following:

- Logistic regression
- Support Vector Machines
- Decision trees
- Neural networks

We assume that you are already familiar with these methods, and at least have some idea as to how they work. Deep familiarity is not required, but for more information, you can check the following books:

- *An Introduction to Statistical Learning, G. James, D. Witten, T. Hastie, and R. Tibshirani, Springer*
- *Python Machine Learning, S. Raschka, Packt Publishing*

When it comes to libraries, we will cover Smile, JSAT, LIBSVM, LIBLINEAR, and Encog. Let's start with Smile.

Smile

Statistical Machine Intelligence and Learning Engine (**Smile**) is a library with a large set of classification and other machine learning algorithms. For us, the most interesting ones are logistic regression, SVM, and random forest, but you can see the full list of available algorithms on their official GitHub page at `https://github.com/haifengl/smile`.

The library is available on Maven Central and the latest version at the time of writing is 1.1.0. To include it to your project, add the following dependency:

```
<dependency>
  <groupId>com.github.haifengl</groupId>
  <artifactId>smile-core</artifactId>
  <version>1.1.0</version>
</dependency>
```

It is being actively developed; new features and bug fixes are added quite often, but not released as frequently. We recommend using the latest available version of Smile, and to get it, you will need to build it from the sources. To do this:

- Install `sbt`, which is a tool used for building scala projects. You can follow the instruction
  at `http://www.scala-sbt.org/release/docs/Manual-Installation.html`
- Use git to clone the project from `https://github.com/haifengl/smile`
- To build and publish the library to a local Maven repository, run the following command:

`sbt core/publishM2`

The Smile library consists of several submodules, such as `smile-core`, `smile-nlp`, `smile-plot`, and so on. For the purposes of this chapter, we only need the core package, and the preceding command will build only that. At the moment of writing, the current version available on GitHub is 1.2.0. So, after building it, add the following dependency to your pom:

```
<dependency>
  <groupId>com.github.haifengl</groupId>
  <artifactId>smile-core</artifactId>
  <version>1.2.0</version>
</dependency>
```

The models from Smile expect the data to be in a form of two-dimensional arrays of doubles, and the label information as a one dimensional array of integers. For binary models, the values should be 0 or 1. Some models in Smile can handle multi-class classification problems, so it is possible to have more labels, not just 0 and 1, but also 2, 3, and so on.

In Smile, the models are built using the `builder` pattern; you create a special class, set some parameters and at the end it returns the object it builds. This `builder` class is typically called `Trainer`, and all models should have a `Trainer` object for them.

For example, consider training a RandomForest model:

```
double[] X = ... // training data
int[] y = ... // 0 and 1 labels
RandomForest model = new RandomForest.Trainer()
    .setNumTrees(100)
    .setNodeSize(4)
    .setSamplingRates(0.7)
    .setSplitRule(SplitRule.ENTROPY)
```

```
.setNumRandomFeatures(3)
.train(X, y);
```

The `RandomForest.Trainer` class takes in a set of parameters and the training data, and in the end produces the trained `RandomForest` model. The implementation of RandomForest from Smile has the following parameters:

- `numTrees`: This is the number of trees to train in the model
- `nodeSize`: This is the minimum number of items in the leaf nodes
- `samplingRate`: This is the ratio of training data used to grow each tree
- `splitRule`: This is the impurity measure used for selecting the best split
- `numRandomFeatures`: This is the number of features the model randomly chooses for selecting the best split

Similarly, a logistic regression is trained as follows:

```
LogisticRegression lr = new LogisticRegression.Trainer()
        .setRegularizationFactor(lambda)
        .train(X, y);
```

Once we have a model, we can use it for predicting the label of previously unseen items. For that we use the `predict` method:

```
double[] row = // data
int prediction = model.predict(row);
```

This code outputs the most probable class for the given item. However, we are often more interested not in the label itself, but in the probability of having the label. If a model implements the `SoftClassifier` interface, then it is possible to get these probabilities like this:

```
double[] probs = new double[2];
model.predict(row, probs);
```

After running this code, the `probs` array will contain the probabilities.

JSAT

Java Statistical Analysis Tool (JSAT) is another Java library which contains a lot of implementations of commonly-used machine learning algorithms. You can check the full list of implemented models at `https://github.com/EdwardRaff/JSAT/wiki/Algorithms`.

To include JSAT to a Java project, add the following snippet to pom:

```
<dependency>
  <groupId>com.edwardraff</groupId>
  <artifactId>JSAT</artifactId>
  <version>0.0.5</version>
</dependency>
```

Unlike Smile models, which require just an array of doubles with the feature information, JSAT requires a special wrapper class for data. If we have an array, it is converted to the JSAT representation like this:

```
double[][] X = ... // data
int[] y = ... // labels

// change to more classes for more classes for multi-classification
CategoricalData binary = new CategoricalData(2);

List<DataPointPair<Integer>> data = new ArrayList<>(X.length);
for (int i = 0; i < X.length; i++) {
    int target = y[i];
    DataPoint row = new DataPoint(new DenseVector(X[i]));
    data.add(new DataPointPair<Integer>(row, target));
}

ClassificationDataSet dataset = new ClassificationDataSet(data, binary);
```

Once we have prepared the dataset, we can train a model. Let's consider the Random Forest classifier again:

```
RandomForest model = new RandomForest();
model.setFeatureSamples(4);
model.setMaxForestSize(150);
model.trainC(dataset);
```

First, we set some parameters for the model, and then, in the end, we call the trainC method (which means train a classifier).

In the JSAT implementation, Random Forest has fewer options for tuning than Smile, only the number of features to select and the number of trees to grow.

Also, JSAT contains several implementations of Logistic Regression. The usual Logistic Regression model does not have any parameters, and it is trained like this:

```
LogisticRegression model = new LogisticRegression();
model.trainC(dataset);
```

If we want to have a regularized model, then we need to use the `LogisticRegressionDCD` class. **Dual Coordinate Descent** (**DCD**) is the optimization method used to train the logistic regression). We train it like this:

```
LogisticRegressionDCD model = new LogisticRegressionDCD();
model.setMaxIterations(maxIterations);
model.setC(C);
model.trainC(fold.toJsatDataset());
```

In this code, `C` is the regularization parameter, and the smaller values of `C` correspond to stronger regularization effect.

Finally, for outputting probabilities, we can do the following:

```
double[] row = // data
DenseVector vector = new DenseVector(row);
DataPoint point = new DataPoint(vector);
CategoricalResults out = model.classify(point);
double probability = out.getProb(1);
```

The `CategoricalResults` class contains a lot of information, including probabilities for each class and the most likely label.

LIBSVM and LIBLINEAR

Next, we consider two similar libraries, LIBSVM and LIBLINEAR.

- LIBSVM (`https://www.csie.ntu.edu.tw/~cjlin/libsvm/`) is a library with implementation of Support Vector Machine models, which include support vector classifiers
- LIBLINEAR (`https://www.csie.ntu.edu.tw/~cjlin/liblinear/`) is a library for fast linear classification algorithms such as Liner SVM and Logistic Regression

Both these libraries come from the same research group and have very similar interfaces. We will start with LIBSVM.

LIBSVM is a library that implements a number of different SVM algorithms. It is implemented in C++ and has an officially supported Java version. It is available on Maven Central:

```
<dependency>
  <groupId>tw.edu.ntu.csie</groupId>
  <artifactId>libsvm</artifactId>
  <version>3.17</version>
</dependency>
```

Note that the Java version of LIBSVM is updated not as often as the C++ version. Nevertheless, the preceding version is stable and should not contain bugs, but it might be slower than its C++ version.

To use SVM models from LIBSVM, you first need to specify the parameters. For this, you create a `svm_parameter` class. Inside, you can specify many parameters, including:

- The kernel type (`RBF`, `POLY`, or `LINEAR`)
- The regularization parameter `C`
- `probability` which you can set to `1` to be able to get probabilities
- `svm_type` should be set to `C_SVC`; this tells that the model should be a classifier

Recall that SVM models can have different kernels, and depending on which kernel we use, we have different models with different parameters. Here, we will consider the most commonly used kernels; linear (or no kernel), polynomial and **Radial Basis Function** (**RBF**), also known as Gaussian kernel).

First, let's start with the linear kernel. First, we create an `svm_paramter` object, where we set the kernel type to `LINEAR` and also ask it to output probabilities:

```
svm_parameter param = new svm_parameter();
param.svm_type = svm_parameter.C_SVC;
param.kernel_type = svm_parameter.LINEAR;
param.probability = 1;
param.C = C;

// default parameters
param.cache_size = 100;
param.eps = 1e-3;
param.p = 0.1;
param.shrinking = 1;
```

Next, we have a polynomial kernel. Recall that the polynomial kernel is specified by the following formula:

$$(\text{gamma} \cdot u^T v + \text{coef0})^{\text{degree}}$$

It has three additional parameters, that is, `gamma`, `coef0`, and `degree`, which control the kernel, and also `C`--the regularization parameter. We can configure the `svm_parameter` class for `POLY` SVM like this:

```
svm_parameter param = new svm_parameter();
```

```
param.svm_type = svm_parameter.C_SVC;
param.kernel_type = svm_parameter.POLY;
param.C = C;
param.degree = degree;
param.gamma = 1;
param.coef0 = 1;
param.probability = 1;
// plus defaults from the above
```

Finally, the Gaussian kernel (or RBF) has the following formula:

$$\exp(-\mathbf{gamma} \cdot \| u\text{-}v \|^2)$$

So there is one parameter, gamma, which controls the width of the Gaussians. We can specify the model with the RBF kernel like this:

```
svm_parameter param = new svm_parameter();
param.svm_type = svm_parameter.C_SVC;
param.kernel_type = svm_parameter.RBF;
param.C = C;
param.gamma = gamma;
param.probability = 1;
// plus defaults from the above
```

Once we have created the configuration object, we need to convert the data in the right format. The library expects the data to be represented in the sparse format. For a single data row, the conversion to the required format is as follows:

```
double[] dataRow = // single row vector
svm_node[] svmRow = new svm_node[dataRow.length];

for (int j = 0; j < dataRow.length; j++) {
    svm_node node = new svm_node();
    node.index = j;
    node.value = dataRow[j];
    svmRow[j] = node;
}
```

Since we typically have a matrix, not just a single row, we apply the preceding code to each row of this matrix:

```
double[][] X = ... // data
int n = X.length;
svm_node[][] nodes = new svm_node[n][];

for (int i = 0; i < n; i++) {
```

```
        nodes[i] = wrapAsSvmNode(X[i]);
    }
```

Here, `wrapAsSvmNode` is a function, that wraps a vector into an array of `svm_node` objects.

Now, we can put the data and the labels together into the `svm_problem` object:

```
double[] y = ... // labels
svm_problem prob = new svm_problem();
prob.l = n;
prob.x = nodes;
prob.y = y;
```

Finally, we can use the parameters and the problem specification to train an SVM model:

```
svm_model model = svm.svm_train(prob, param);
```

Once the model is trained, we can use it to classify unseen data. Getting probabilities is done this way:

```
double[][] X = // test data
int n = X.length;
double[] results = new double[n];
double[] probs = new double[2];

for (int i = 0; i < n; i++) {
    svm_node[] row = wrapAsSvmNode(X[i]);
    svm.svm_predict_probability(model, row, probs);
    results[i] = probs[1];
}
```

Since we used `param.probability = 1`, we can use the `svm.svm_predict_probability` method to predict probabilities. Like in Smile, the method takes an array of doubles and writes the output there. After this operation, it will contain the probabilities in this array.

Finally, while training, LIBSVM outputs a lot of things on the console. If we are not interested in this output, we can disable it with the following code snippet:

```
svm.svm_set_print_string_function(s -> {});
```

Just add this in the beginning of your code and you will not see the debugging information anymore.

The next library is LIBLINEAR, which provides very fast and high-performing linear classifiers, such as SVM with linear kernel and logistic regression. It can easily scale to tens and hundreds of millions of data points. Its interface is quite similar to LIBSVM, where we need to specify the parameters and the data, and then train a model.

Unlike LIBSVM, there is no official Java version of LIBLINEAR, but there is an unofficial Java port available at `http://liblinear.bwaldvogel.de/`. To use it, include the following:

```
<dependency>
 <groupId>de.bwaldvogel</groupId>
 <artifactId>liblinear</artifactId>
 <version>1.95</version>
</dependency>
```

The interface is very similar to LIBSVM. First, we define the parameters:

```
SolverType solverType = SolverType.L1R_LR;
double C = 0.001;
double eps = 0.0001;
Parameter param = new Parameter(solverType, C, eps);
```

In this example, we specify three parameters:

- `solverType`: This defines the model that will be used
- `C`: This is the amount of regularization, the smaller the C, the stronger the regularization
- `epsilon`: This is the level of tolerance for stopping the training process; a reasonable default is `0.0001`

For the classification problem, the following are the solvers that we can use:

- **Logistic regression**: L1R_LR or L2R_LR
- **SVM**: L1R_L2LOSS_SVC or L2R_L2LOSS_SVC

Here, we have two models; logistic regression and SVM, and two regularization types, L1 and L2. How can we decide which model to choose and which regularization to use? According to the official FAQ (which can be found here: `https://www.csie.ntu.edu.tw/~cjlin/liblinear/FAQ.html`), we should:

- Prefer SVM to logistic regression as it trains faster and usually gives higher accuracy
- Try L2 regularization first unless you need a sparse solution, in this case use L1

Next, we need to prepare our data. As previously, we need to wrap it to some special format. First, let's see how to wrap a single data row:

```
double[] row = // data
int m = row.length;
Feature[] result = new Feature[m];

for (int i = 0; i < m; i++) {
    result[i] = new FeatureNode(i + 1, row[i]);
}
```

 Note that we add 1 to the index. The 0 is the bias term, so the actual features should start from 1.

We can put this code into a `wrapRow` function and then wrap the entire dataset as follows:

```
double[][] X = // data
int n = X.length;
Feature[][] matrix = new Feature[n][];
for (int i = 0; i < n; i++) {
    matrix[i] = wrapRow(X[i]);
}
```

Now, we can create the `Problem` class with the data and labels:

```
double[] y = // labels

Problem problem = new Problem();
problem.x = wrapMatrix(X);
problem.y = y;
problem.n = X[0].length + 1;
problem.l = X.length;
```

Note that here we also need to provide the dimensionality of the data, and it's the number of features plus one. We need to add one because it includes the bias term.

Now we are ready to train the model:

```
Model model = LibLinear.train(fold, param);
```

When the model is trained, we can use it to classify unseen data. In the following example, we will output probabilities:

```
double[] dataRow = // data
Feature[] row = wrapRow(dataRow);
Linear.predictProbability(model, row, probs);
```

```
double result = probs[1];
```

The preceding code works fine for the logistic regression model, but it will not work for SVM, SVM cannot output probabilities, so the preceding code will throw an error for solvers such as L1R_L2LOSS_SVC. What we can do instead is to get the raw output:

```
double[] values = new double[1];
Feature[] row = wrapRow(dataRow);
Linear.predictValues(model, row, values);
double result = values[0];
```

In this case, the results will not contain probability, but some real value. When this value is greater than zero, the model predicts that the class is positive.

If we would like to map this value to the [0, 1] range, we can use the sigmoid function for that:

```
public static double[] sigmoid(double[] scores) {
    double[] result = new double[scores.length];

    for (int i = 0; i < result.length; i++) {
        result[i] = 1 / (1 + Math.exp(-scores[i]));
    }

    return result;
}
```

Finally, like LIBSVM, LIBLINEAR also outputs a lot of things to standard output. If you do not wish to see it, you can mute it with the following code:

```
PrintStream devNull = new PrintStream(new NullOutputStream());
Linear.setDebugOutput(devNull);
```

Here, we use NullOutputStream from Apache IO, which does nothing, so the screen stays clean.

Want to know when to use LIBSVM and when to use LIBLINEAR? For large datasets, it is not often possible to use any kernel methods. In this case, you should prefer LIBLINEAR. Additionally, LIBLINEAR is especially good for text processing purposes such as document classification. We will cover these cases in more detail in Chapter 6, *Working with Texts - Natural Language Processing and Information Retrieval*.

Encog

So far, we have covered many models, that is, logistic regression, SVM, and RandomForest, and we have looked at multiple libraries that implement them. But we have not yet covered neural networks. In Java, there is a special library that deals exclusively with neural networks--Encog. It is available on Maven Central and can be added with the following snippet:

```
<dependency>
  <groupId>org.encog</groupId>
  <artifactId>encog-core</artifactId>
  <version>3.3.0</version>
</dependency>
```

After including the library, the first step is to specify the architecture of a neural network. We can do it like this:

```
BasicNetwork network = new BasicNetwork();
network.addLayer(new BasicLayer(new ActivationSigmoid(), true,
noInputNeurons));
network.addLayer(new BasicLayer(new ActivationSigmoid(), true, 30));
network.addLayer(new BasicLayer(new ActivationSigmoid(), true, 1));
network.getStructure().finalizeStructure();
network.reset();
```

Here, we create a network with one input layer, one inner layer with 30 neurons, and one output layer with 1 neuron. In each layer we use sigmoid as the activation function and add the bias input (the `true` parameter). Finally, the `reset` method randomly initializes the weights in the network.

For both input and output, Encog expects two-dimensional double arrays. In the case of binary classification, we typically have a one dimensional array, so we need to convert it:

```
double[][] X = // data
double[] y = // labels
double[][] y2d = new double[y.length][];

for (int i = 0; i < y.length; i++) {
    y2d[i] = new double[] { y[i] };
}
```

Once the data is converted, we wrap it into a special wrapper class:

```
MLDataSet dataset = new BasicMLDataSet(X, y2d);
```

Then, this dataset can be used for training:

```
MLTrain trainer = new ResilientPropagation(network, dataset);
double lambda = 0.01;
trainer.addStrategy(new RegularizationStrategy(lambda));

int noEpochs = 101;
for (int i = 0; i < noEpochs; i++) {
    trainer.iteration();
}
```

We won't cover Encog in much detail here, but we will come back to neural networks in Chapter 8, *Deep Learning with DeepLearning4j*, where we will look at a different library-- DeepLearning4J.

There are a lot of other machine learning libraries available in Java. For example Weka, H2O, JavaML, and others. It is not possible to cover all of them, but you can also try them and see if you like them more than the ones we have covered.

Next, we will see how we can evaluate the classification models.

Evaluation

We have covered many machine learning libraries, and many of them implement the same algorithms such as random forest or logistic regression. Also, each individual model can have many different parameters, a logistic regression has the regularization coefficient, an SVM is configured by setting the kernel and its parameters.

How do we select the best single model out of so many possible variants?

For that, we first define some evaluation metric and then select the model which achieves the best possible performance with respect to this metric. For binary classification, there are many metrics that we can use for comparison, and the most commonly used ones are as follows:

- Accuracy and error
- Precision, recall, and F1
- AUC (AU ROC)

We use these metrics to see how well the model will be able to generalize to new unseen data. Therefore, it is important to model this situation when the data is new to the model. This is typically done by splitting the data into several parts. So, we will also cover the following:

- Result evaluation
- K-fold cross-validation
- Training, validation, and testing

Let us start with the most intuitive evaluation metric, accuracy.

Accuracy

Accuracy is the most straightforward way of evaluating a classifier: we make a prediction, look at the predicted label and then compare it with the actual value. If the values agree, then the model got it right. Then, we can do it for all the data that we have and see the ratio of the correctly predicted examples; and this is exactly what accuracy describes. So, accuracy tells us for how many examples the model predicted the correct label. Calculating it is trivial:

```
int n = actual.length;
double[] proba = // predictions;

double[] prediction = Arrays.stream(proba).map(p -> p > threshold ? 1.0 :
0.0).toArray();
int correct = 0;

for (int i = 0; i < n; i++) {
    if (actual[i] == prediction[i]) {
        correct++;
    }
}

double accuracy = 1.0 * correct / n;
```

Accuracy is the simplest evaluation metric, and it is easy to explain it to anybody, even to nontechnical people.

However sometimes, accuracy is not the best measure of model performance. Next we will see what are its problems and what to use instead.

Precision, recall, and F1

In some cases, accuracy values are deceiving: they suggest that the classifier is good, although it is not. For example, suppose we have an unbalanced dataset: there are only 1% of examples that are positive, and the rest (99%) are negative. Then, a model that always predicts negative is right in 99% of the cases, and hence will have an accuracy of 0.99. But this model is not useful.

There are alternatives to accuracy that can overcome this problem. Precision and recall are among these metrics, as they both look at the fraction of positive items that the model correctly recognized. So, if we have a large number of negative examples, we can still perform some meaningful evaluation of the model.

Precision and recall can be calculated using the confusion matrix, a table which summarizes the performance of a binary classifier:

		Actual Class y	
		Positive	Negative
$h_\theta(x)$ **Predicted outcome**	Predicted positive outcome	**True positive** (TP)	**False positive** (FP)
	Predicted negative outcome	**False negative** (FN)	**True negative** (TN)

When we use a binary classification model to predict the actual value of some data item, there are four possible outcomes:

- **True positive** (**TP**): The actual class is positive, and we predict positive
- **True negative** (**TN**): The actual class is negative, and we predict negative
- **False positive** (**FP**): The actual class is negative, but we say it is positive
- **False negative** (**FN**): The actual class is positive, but we say it is negative

The first two cases (TP and TN) are correct predictions the actual and the predicted values are the same. The last two cases (FP and FN) are incorrect classification, as we fail to predict the correct label.

Now, suppose that we have a dataset with known labels, and run our model against it. Then, let TP be the number of true positive examples, TN the true negative examples, and so on.

Then we can calculate precision and recall using these values:

- Precision is the fraction of correctly--predicted positive items among all items the model predicted positive. In terms of the confusion matrix, precision is TP / (TP + FP).
- Recall is the fraction of correctly-- predicted positive items among items that are actually positive. With values from the confusion matrix, recall is TP / (TP + FN).
- It is often hard to decide whether one should optimize precision or recall. But there is another metric which combines both precision and recall into one number, and it is called **F1 score**.

For calculating precision and recall, we first need to calculate the values for the cells of the confusion matrix:

```
int tp = 0, tn = 0, fp = 0, fn = 0;

for (int i = 0; i < actual.length; i++) {
    if (actual[i] == 1.0 && proba[i] > threshold) {
        tp++;
    } else if (actual[i] == 0.0 && proba[i] <= threshold) {
        tn++;
    } else if (actual[i] == 0.0 && proba[i] > threshold) {
        fp++;
    } else if (actual[i] == 1.0 && proba[i] <= threshold) {
        fn++;
    }
}
```

Then, we can use the values to calculate precision and recall:

```
double precision = 1.0 * tp / (tp + fp);
double recall = 1.0 * tp / (tp + fn);
```

Finally, f1 can be calculated using the following formula:

```
double f1 = 2 * precision * recall / (precision + recall);
```

These metrics are quite useful when the dataset is imbalanced.

ROC and AU ROC (AUC)

The preceding metrics are good for binary classifiers which produce a hard output; they only tell whether the class should be assigned a positive label or negative. If, instead, our model outputs some score such that the higher the values of the score the more likely the item is to be positive, then the binary classifier is called a **ranking classifier**.

Most of the models can output probabilities of belonging to a certain class, and we can use it to rank examples such that the positives are likely to come first.

The ROC curve visually tells us how good a ranking classifier separates positive examples from negative ones. The way a ROC curve is built is as follows:

- Sort the observations by their score and then start from the origin
- Go up if the observation is positive and right if it is negative.

This way, in the ideal case, we first always go up, and then always go right and this will result in the best possible ROC curve. In this case, we can say that the separation between positive and negative examples is perfect. If the separation is not perfect, but still **OK**, the curve will go up for positive examples, but sometimes will turn right when a misclassification occurs. Finally, a bad classifier will not be able to tell positive and negative examples apart and the curve would alternate between going up and right.

Let's look at some examples:

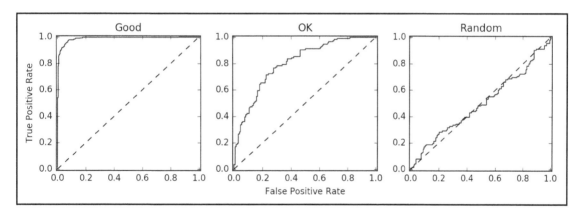

The diagonal line on the plot represents the baseline--the performance that a random classifier would achieve. The further away the curve is from the baseline, the better.

Unfortunately, there is no available easy-to-use implementation of ROC curves in Java. It is not hard to implement the code ourselves. Here, we will outline how to do it, and you will find the implementation in the chapter code repository.

So the algorithm for drawing a ROC curve is as follows:

- Let POS be the number of positive labels, and NEG be the number of negative labels
- Order data by the score, decreasing
- Start from (0, 0)
- For each example in the sorted order,
    - o if the example is positive, move 1 / POS up in the graph,
    - o otherwise, move 1 / NEG right in the graph.

This is a simplified algorithm and assumes that the scores are distinct. If the scores aren't distinct, and there are different actual labels for the same score, some adjustment needs to be made.

It is implemented in the `RocCurve` class, which you will find in the source code. You can use it as follows:

```
RocCurve.plot(actual, prediction);
```

Calling it will create a plot similar to this one:

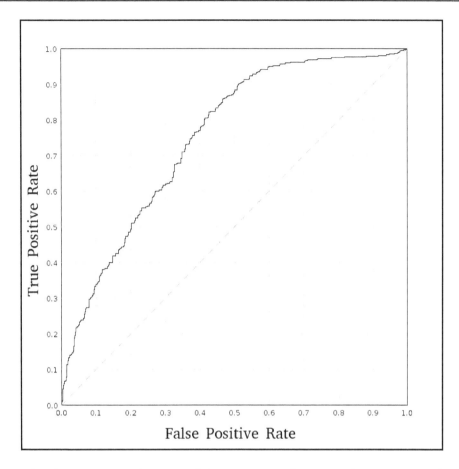

The area under the curve says how good the separation between the positive and negative examples is. If the separation is very good, then the area will be close to one. But if the classifier cannot distinguish between positive and negative examples, the curve will go around the random baseline curve, and the area will be close to **0.5**.

The area under the curve is often abbreviated as AUC, or, sometimes, AU ROC to emphasize that the curve is a ROC curve.

AUC has a very nice interpretation--the value of AUC corresponds to probability that a randomly selected positive example is scored higher than a randomly selected negative example. Naturally, if this probability is high, our classifier does a good job separating positive and negative examples.

This makes AUC a to-go evaluation metric for many cases, especially when the dataset is unbalanced in the sense that there are a lot more examples of one class than another.

Luckily, there are implementations of AUC in Java. For example, it is implemented in Smile. You can use it like this:

```
double[] predicted = ...  //
int[] truth = ... //
double auc = AUC.measure(truth, predicted);
```

Now, when we discussed the possible evaluation metrics, we need to apply them to test our models. We need to handle it with care. If we perform the evaluation on the same data which we used for training, then the evaluation results will be overly optimistic. Next, we will see what is the correct way of doing it.

Result validation

When learning from data, there is always the danger of overfitting. Overfitting occurs when the model starts learning the noise in the data instead of detecting useful patterns. It is always important to check if a model overfits, otherwise it will not be useful when applied to unseen data.

The typical and most practical way of checking whether a model overfits or not is to emulate unseen data, that is, take a part of the available labeled data and do not use it for training.

This technique is called **hold out**, where we hold out a part of the data and use it only for evaluation.

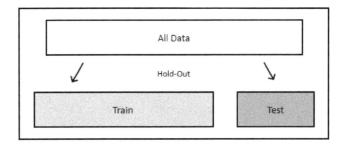

We also shuffle the original dataset before splitting. In many cases, we make a simplifying assumption that the order of data is not important, that is, one observation has no influence on another. In this case, shuffling the data prior to splitting will remove effects that the order of items might have. On the other hand, if the data is a time series data, then shuffling it is not a good idea, because there is some dependency between observations.

So, let's implement the hold out split. We assume that the data that we have is already represented by X--a two-dimensional array of doubles with features and y--a one-dimensional array of labels.

First, we create a helper class for holding the data:

```
public class Dataset {
    private final double[][] X;
    private final double[] y;
    // constructor and getters are omitted
}
```

Splitting our dataset should produce two datasets, so let's create a class for that as well:

```
public class Split {
    private final Dataset train;
    private final Dataset test;
    // constructor and getters are omitted
}
```

Now, suppose we want to split the data into two parts: train and test. We also want to specify the size of the train set, and we will do it using a testRatio parameter: the percentage of items that should go to the test set.

The first thing we do is to generate an array with indexes and then split it according to testRatio:

```
int[] indexes = IntStream.range(0, dataset.length()).toArray();
int trainSize = (int) (indexes.length * (1 - testRatio));
int[] trainIndex = Arrays.copyOfRange(indexes, 0, trainSize);
int[] testIndex = Arrays.copyOfRange(indexes, trainSize, indexes.length);
```

We can also shuffle the indexes if we want:

```
Random rnd = new Random(seed);

for (int i = indexes.length - 1; i > 0; i--) {
    int index = rnd.nextInt(i + 1);
    int tmp = indexes[index];
    indexes[index] = indexes[i];
    indexes[i] = tmp;
}
```

Then we can select instances for the training set as follows:

```
int trainSize = trainIndex.length;
double[][] trainX = new double[trainSize][];
double[] trainY = new double[trainSize];
for (int i = 0; i < trainSize; i++) {
    int idx = trainIndex[i];
    trainX[i] = X[idx];
    trainY[i] = y[idx];
}
```

And then, finally, wrap it into our `Dataset` class:

```
Dataset train = new Dataset(trainX, trainY);
```

If we repeat the same for the test set, we can put both train and test sets into a `Split` object:

```
Split split = new Split(train, test);
```

Now we can use train fold for training and test fold for testing the models.

If we put all the previous code into a function of the `Dataset` class, for example, `trainTestSplit`, we can use it as follows:

```
Split split = dataset.trainTestSplit(0.2);

Dataset train = split.getTrain();
// train the model using train.getX() and train.getY()

Dataset test = split.getTest();
// test the model using test.getX(); test.getY();
```

Here, we train a model on the `train` dataset, and then calculate the evaluation metric on the `test` set.

K-fold cross-validation

Holding out only one part of the data may not always be the best option. What we can do instead is splitting it into *K* parts and then testing the models only on *1/K*th of the data.

This is called **k-fold cross-validation**; it not only gives the performance estimation, but also the possible spread of the error. Typically, we are interested in models that give good and consistent performance. K-fold cross-validation helps us to select such models.

Next we prepare the data for k-fold cross-validation as follows:

- First, split the data into *K* parts
- Then, for each of these parts:
    - Take one part as the validation set
    - Take the remaining *K-1* parts as the training set

If we translate this into Java, the first step will look like this:

```
int[] indexes = IntStream.range(0, dataset.length()).toArray();
int[][] foldIndexes = new int[k][];

int step = indexes.length / k;
int beginIndex = 0;

for (int i = 0; i < k - 1; i++) {
    foldIndexes[i] = Arrays.copyOfRange(indexes, beginIndex, beginIndex +
step);
    beginIndex = beginIndex + step;
}

foldIndexes[k - 1] = Arrays.copyOfRange(indexes, beginIndex,
indexes.length);
```

This creates an array of indexes for each of the *K* folds. We can also shuffle the indexes array as previously.

Now we can create splits from each fold:

```
List<Split> result = new ArrayList<>();

for (int i = 0; i < k; i++) {
    int[] testIdx = folds[i];
    int[] trainIdx = combineTrainFolds(folds, indexes.length, i);
    result.add(Split.fromIndexes(dataset, trainIdx, testIdx));
}
```

In the preceding code we have two additional methods:

- `combineTrainFolds`: This takes in *K-1* arrays with indexes and combines them into one
- `Split.fromIndexes`: This creates a split that trains and tests indexes.

We have already covered the second function when we created a simple hold-out test set.

The first function, `combineTrainFolds`, is implemented like this:

```
private static int[] combineTrainFolds(int[][] folds, int totalSize, int
excludeIndex) {
    int size = totalSize - folds[excludeIndex].length;
    int result[] = new int[size];

    int start = 0;
    for (int i = 0; i < folds.length; i++) {
        if (i == excludeIndex) {
            continue;
        }
        int[] fold = folds[i];
        System.arraycopy(fold, 0, result, start, fold.length);
        start = start + fold.length;
    }

    return result;
}
```

Again, we can put the preceding code into a function of the `Dataset` class and call it like follows:

```
List<Split> folds = train.kfold(3);
```

Now, when we have a list of `Split` objects, we can create a special function for performing cross-validation:

```
public static DescriptiveStatistics crossValidate(List<Split> folds,
        Function<Dataset, Model> trainer) {
    double[] aucs = folds.parallelStream().mapToDouble(fold -> {
        Dataset foldTrain = fold.getTrain();
        Dataset foldValidation = fold.getTest();
        Model model = trainer.apply(foldTrain);
        return auc(model, foldValidation);
    }).toArray();

    return new DescriptiveStatistics(aucs);
}
```

What this function does is, it takes a list of folds and a callback that is inside and creates a model. After the model is trained, we calculate AUC for it.

Additionally, we take advantage of Java's ability to parallelize loops and train models on each fold at the same time.

Finally, we put the AUCs calculated on each fold into a `DescriptiveStatistics` object, which can later on be used to return the mean and standard deviation of the AUCs. As you probably remember, the `DescriptiveStatistics` class comes from the Apache Commons Math library.

Let's consider an example. Suppose we want to use logistic regression from `LIBLINEAR` and select the best value for the regularization parameter, `C`. We can use the preceding function this way:

```
double[] Cs = { 0.01, 0.05, 0.1, 0.5, 1.0, 5.0, 10.0 };

for (double C : Cs) {
    DescriptiveStatistics summary = crossValidate(folds, fold -> {
        Parameter param = new Parameter(SolverType.L1R_LR, C, 0.0001);
        return LibLinear.train(fold, param);
    });

    double mean = summary.getMean();
    double std = summary.getStandardDeviation();
    System.out.printf("L1 logreg C=%7.3f, auc=%.4f &pm; %.4f%n", C, mean,
std);
}
```

Here, `LibLinear.train` is a helper method that takes a `Dataset` object and a `Parameter` object and then trains a LIBLINEAR model. This will print AUC for all the provided values of `C`, so you can see which one is the best, and pick the one with the highest mean AUC.

Training, validation, and testing

When doing cross-validation, there's still a danger of overfitting. Since we try a lot of different experiments on the same validation set, we might accidentally pick the model which just happened to do well on the validation set--but it may later on fail to generalize to unseen data.

The solution to this problem is to hold out a test set at the very beginning and do not touch it at all until we select what we think is the best model. And we use it only for evaluating the final model on it.

So how do we select the best model? What we can do is to do cross-validation on the remaining train data. It can be hold out or k-fold cross-validation. In general, you should prefer doing k-fold cross-validation because it also gives you the spread of performance, and you may use it in for model selection as well.

The following diagram illustrates the process:

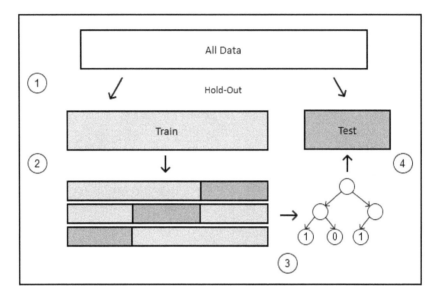

According to the diagram, a typical data science workflow should be the following:

- **0**: Select some metric for validation, for example, accuracy or AUC
- **1**: Split all the data into train and test sets
- **2**: Split the training data further and hold out a validation dataset or split it into k folds
- **3**: Use the validation data for model selection and parameter optimization
- **4**: Select the best model according to the validation set and evaluate it against the hold out test set

It is important to avoid looking at the test set too often, it should be used very rarely, and only for final evaluation to make sure the selected model does not overfit. If the validation scheme is set up properly, the validation score should correspond to the final test score. If this happens, we can be sure that the model does not overfit and is able to generalize to unseen data.

Using the classes and the code we created previously, it translates to the following Java code:

```
Dataset data = new Dataset(X, y);
Dataset train = split.getTrain();
List<Split> folds = train.kfold(3);
// now use crossValidate(folds, ...) to select the best model

Dataset test = split.getTest();
// do final evaluation of the best model on test
```

With this information, we are ready to do a project on binary classification.

Case study - page prediction

Now we will continue with our running example, the search engine. What we want to do here is to try to predict whether a URL comes from the first page of the search engine results or not. So, it is time to use the material we have covered so far in this chapter.

In `Chapter 2`, *Data Processing Toolbox*, we created the following object to store the information about pages:

```
public class RankedPage {
    private String url;
    private int position;
    private int page;
    private int titleLength;
    private int bodyContentLength;
    private boolean queryInTitle;
    private int numberOfHeaders;
    private int numberOfLinks;
}
```

First, we can start by adding a few methods to this object, as follows:

- `isHttps`: This should tell us if the URL is HTTPS and can be implemented with `url.startsWith("https://")`
- `isComDomain`: This should tells us if the URL belongs to the COM domain and whether we can implement it with `url.contains(".com")`
- `isOrgDomain`, `isNetDomain`: This is the same as the previous one, but for ORG and NET, respectively

- `numberOfSlashes`: This is the number of slash characters in the URL and can be implemented with Guava's `CharMatcher`:
  `CharMatcher.is('/').countIn(url)`

These models describe each URL that we get, so we call them feature methods, and we can use the results of these methods in our machine learning models.

As previously, we have a method which reads the JSON data and creates a Joinery DataFrame from it:

```
List<RankedPage> pages = RankedPageData.readRankedPages();
DataFrame<Object> dataframe = BeanToJoinery.convert(pages,
RankedPage.class);
```

When we have the data, the first step is to extract the values of the target variable:

```
List<Object> page = dataframe.col("page");
double[] target = page.stream()
                    .mapToInt(o -> (int) o)
                    .mapToDouble(p -> (p == 0) ? 1.0 : 0.0)
                    .toArray();
```

To get the feature matrix X, we can use Joinery to create a two-dimensional array for us. First, we need to drop some of the variables, namely, the target variable, the URL, and also the position, because the position clearly correlates with the page. We can do it like this:

```
dataframe = dataframe.drop("page", "url", "position");
double[][] X = dataframe.toModelMatrix(0.0);
```

Next, we can use the `Dataset` class we have created in this chapter and split it into train and test parts:

```
Dataset dataset = new Dataset(X, target);
Split split = dataset.trainTestSplit(0.2);
Dataset train = split.getTrain();
Dataset test = split.getTest();
```

Additionally, for some algorithms, it is helpful to standardize the features such that they have zero mean and unit standard deviation. The reason for doing this is to help the optimization algorithms converge faster.

To do it, we calculate mean and standard deviation for each column of the matrix, and then subtract the mean from each value and divide it by the standard deviation. We omit the code of this function here for brevity, but you can find it in the chapter code repository.

The following code does this:

```
preprocessor = StandardizationPreprocessor.train(train);
train = preprocessor.transform(train);
test = preprocessor.transform(test);
```

Now we are ready to start training different models. Let's try logistic regression implementation from Smile first. We will use k-fold cross-validation to select the best value of lambda, its regularization parameter.

```
List<Fold> folds = train.kfold(3);
double[] lambdas = { 0, 0.5, 1.0, 5.0, 10.0, 100.0, 1000.0 };
for (double lambda : lambdas) {
    DescriptiveStatistics summary = Smile.crossValidate(folds, fold -> {
        return new LogisticRegression.Trainer()
                .setRegularizationFactor(lambda)
                .train(fold.getX(), fold.getYAsInt());
    });

    double mean = summary.getMean();
    double std = summary.getStandardDeviation();
    System.out.printf("logreg, λ=%8.3f, auc=%.4f &pm; %.4f%n", lambda,
mean, std);
}
```

Note that the `Dataset` class here has a new method, `getYAsInt`, which simply returns the target variable represented as an array of integers. When we run this, it produces the following output:

```
logreg, λ=   0.000, auc=0.5823 &pm; 0.0041
logreg, λ=   0.500, auc=0.5822 &pm; 0.0040
logreg, λ=   1.000, auc=0.5820 &pm; 0.0037
logreg, λ=   5.000, auc=0.5820 &pm; 0.0030
logreg, λ=  10.000, auc=0.5823 &pm; 0.0027
logreg, λ= 100.000, auc=0.5839 &pm; 0.0009
logreg, λ=1000.000, auc=0.5859 &pm; 0.0036
```

It shows the value of lambda, the AUC we got for this value, and the standard deviation of AUCs across different folds.

We see that the AUCs that we get are quite low. This should not be a surprise: using only the information that we have now is clearly not enough to fully reverse-engineer the ranking algorithm of the search engine. In the following chapters, we will learn how to extract more information from the pages and these techniques will help to increase AUC greatly.

Another thing we can notice is that the AUCs are quite similar across different values of lambda, but one of them has the lowest standard deviation. In situations like this, we always should prefer models with smallest variance.

We can also try a more complex classifier such as RandomForest:

```
DescriptiveStatistics rf = Smile.crossValidate(folds, fold -> {
    return new RandomForest.Trainer()
            .setNumTrees(100)
            .setNodeSize(4)
            .setSamplingRates(0.7)
            .setSplitRule(SplitRule.ENTROPY)
            .setNumRandomFeatures(3)
            .train(fold.getX(), fold.getYAsInt());
});

System.out.printf("random forest auc=%.4f &pm; %.4f%n", rf.getMean(),
rf.getStandardDeviation());
```

This creates the following output:

```
random forest auc=0.6093 &pm; 0.0209
```

This classifier is, on average, 2% better than the logistic regression one, but we can also notice that the standard deviation is quite high. Because it is a lot higher, we can suspect that on the test data this model may perform significantly worse than the logistic regression model.

Next, we can try training other models as well. But, let's assume we did that and at the end we came to the conclusion that the logistic regression with `lambda=100` gives the best performance. We can then take it and retrain on the entire train dataset, and then use the test set for the final evaluation:

```
LogisticRegression logregFinal = new LogisticRegression.Trainer()
        .setRegularizationFactor(100.0)
        .train(train.getX(), train.getYAsInt());

double auc = Smile.auc(logregFinal, test);
System.out.printf("final logreg auc=%.4f%n", auc);
```

This code produces the following output:

```
final logreg auc=0.5807
```

So, indeed, we can see that the AUC produced by the selected model is the same as in our cross-validation. This is a good sign that the model can generalize well and does not overfill.

For curiosity, we can also check how the RandomForest model would perform on the training set. Since it has high variance, it may perform worse than logistic regression, but also can perform way better. Let's retrain it on the entire train set:

```
RandomForest rfFinal = new RandomForest.Trainer()
        .setNumTrees(100)
        .setNodeSize(4)
        .setSamplingRates(0.7)
        .setSplitRule(SplitRule.ENTROPY)
        .setNumRandomFeatures(3)
        .train(train.getX(), train.getYAsInt());

double auc = Smile.auc(rfFinal, test);
System.out.printf("final rf auc=%.4f%n", finalAuc);
```

It prints the following:

```
final rf auc=0.5778
```

So, indeed, high variance of the model resulted in a test score lower than the cross-validation score. This is not a good sign, and such models should not be preferred.

Thus, for such a dataset, the best performing model is logistic regression.

If you wonder how to use other machine learning libraries to solve this problem, you can check the chapter's code repository. There we created some examples for JSAT, JavaML, LIBSVM, LIBLINEAR, and Encog.

With this, we conclude the part of this chapter on classification and next we will look into another supervised learning problem called **regression**.

Regression

In machine learning, regression problems deal with situations when the label information is continuous. This can be predicting the temperature for tomorrow, the stock price, the salary of a person or the rating of an item on an e-commerce website.

There are many models which can solve the regression problem:

- **Ordinary Least Squares** (**OLS**) is the usual linear regression
- Ridge regression and LASSO are the regularized variants of OLS
- Tree-based models such as RandomForest
- Neural networks

Approaching a regression problem is very similar to approaching a classification problem, and the general framework stays the same:

- First, you select an evaluation metric
- Then, you split the data into training and testing
- You train the model on training, tune parameters using cross-validation, and do the final verification using the held out testing set.

Machine learning libraries for regression

We have already discussed many machine learning libraries that can deal with classification problems. Typically, these libraries also have regression models. Let's briefly go over them.

Smile

Smile is a general purpose machine learning library, so it has regression models as well. You can have a look at the list of models, here: `https://github.com/haifengl/smile`.

For example, this is how you can create a simple linear regression:

```
OLS ols = new OLS(data.getX(), data.getY());
```

For regularized regression, you can use ridge or LASSO:

```
double lambda = 0.01;
RidgeRegression ridge = new RidgeRegression(data.getX(), data.getY(),
lambda);
LASSO lasso = new LASSO(data.getX(), data.getY(), lambda);
```

Using a RandomForest is very similar to the classification case:

```
int nbtrees = 100;
RandomForest rf = new RandomForest.Trainer(nbtrees)
        .setNumRandomFeatures(15)
        .setMaxNodes(128)
```

```
.setNodeSize(10)
.setSamplingRates(0.6)
.train(data.getX(), data.getY());
```

Predicting is identical to the classification case as well. What we need to do is just use the `predict` method:

```
double result = model.predict(row);
```

JSAT

JSAT is also a general purpose library and contains a lot of implementations for solving regression problems.

As with classification, it needs a wrapper class for data and a special wrapper for regression:

```
double[][] X = ... //
double[] y = ... //
List<DataPointPair<Double>> data = new ArrayList<>(X.length);

for (int i = 0; i < X.length; i++) {
    DataPoint row = new DataPoint(new DenseVector(X[i]));
    data.add(new DataPointPair<Double>(row, y[i]));
}

RegressionDataSet dataset = new RegressionDataSet(data);
```

Once the dataset is wrapped in the right class, we can train models like this:

```
MultipleLinearRegression linreg = new MultipleLinearRegression();
linreg.train(dataset);;
```

The preceding code trains the usual OLS linear regression.

 Unlike Smile, OLS does not produce a stable solution when the matrix is ill-conditioned, that is, it has some linearly dependent solutions. Use a regularized model in this case.

Training a regularized linear regression can be done with the following code:

```
RidgeRegression ridge = new RidgeRegression();
ridge.setLambda(lambda);
ridge.train(dataset);
```

Then, for predicting, we also need to do some conversion:

```
double[] row = .. . //
DenseVector vector = new DenseVector(row);
DataPoint point = new DataPoint(vector);
double result = model.regress(point);
```

Other libraries

Other libraries that we previously covered also have models for solving the regression problem.

For example, in LIBSVM, it is possible to do regression by setting the `svm_type` parameter to `EPSILON_SVR` or `NU_SVR`, and the rest of the code stays almost the same as in the classification case. Likewise, in LIBLINEAR, the regression problem is solved by choosing `L2R_L2LOSS_SVR` or `L2R_L2LOSS_SVR_DUAL` models.

It is also possible to solve the regression problem with neural networks, for example, in Encog. The only thing you need to change is the loss function: instead of minimizing a classification loss function (such as `logloss`) you should use a regression loss function, such as mean-squared error.

Since most of the code is pretty similar, there is no need to cover it in detail. As always, we have prepared some code examples in the chapter code repository, so feel free to have a look at them.

Evaluation

As with classification, we also need to evaluate the results of our models. There are some metrics that help to do that and select the best model. Let's go over the two most popular ones: **Mean Squared Error** (**MSE**) and **Mean Absolute Error** (**MAE**).

MSE

Mean Squared Error (**MSE**) is the sum of squared differences between the actual and predicted values. It is quite easy to compute it in Java:

```
double[] actual, predicted;

int n = actual.length;
double sum = 0.0;
for (int i = 0; i < n; i++) {
```

```
    diff = actual[i] - predicted[i];
    sum = sum + diff * diff;
}

double mse = sum / n;
```

Typically, the value of MSE is hard to interpret, which is why we often take a square root of MSE; this is called **Root Mean Squared Error** (**RMSE**). It is easier to interpret because it is in the same units as the target variable.

```
double rmse = Math.sqrt(mse);
```

MAE

Mean Absolute Error (**MAE**), is an alternative metric for evaluating performance. Instead of taking the squared error, it only takes the absolute value of the difference between the actual and predicted value. This is how we can compute it:

```
double sum = 0.0;
for (int i = 0; i < n; i++) {
    sum = sum + Math.abs(actual[i] - predicted[i]);
}

double mae = sum / n;
```

Sometimes we have outliers in the data--the values with quite irregular values. If we have a lot of outliers, we should prefer MAE to RMSE, since it is more robust to them. If we do not have many outliers, then RMSE should be the preferred choice.

There are also other metrics such as MAPE or RMSE, but they are used less often, so we won't cover them.

While we went over the libraries for solving the regression problem only briefly, with the foundation we got from the overview for solving the classification problem, it is enough to do a project on regression.

Case study - hardware performance

In this project, we will try to predict how much time it will take to multiply two matrices on different computers.

The dataset for this project originally comes from the paper *Automatic selection of the fastest algorithm implementation* by Sidnev and Gergel (2014), and it was made available at a machine learning competition organized by Mail.RU. You can check the details at `http://m lbootcamp.ru/championship/7/`.

 The content is in Russian, so if you do not speak it, it is better to use a browser with translation support.

You will find a copy of the dataset along with the code for this chapter.

This dataset has the following data:

- m, k, and n represent the dimensionality of the matrices, with m*k being the dimensionality of matrix A and k*n being the dimensionality of matrix B
- Hardware characteristics such as CPU speed, number of cores, whether hyper-threading is enabled or not, and the type of CPU
- The operation system

The solution for this problem can be quite useful for research, when selecting hardware to buy for running the experiment. In that case. you can can use the model for selecting a build which should result in the best performance.

So, the goal is to predict how many seconds it will take to multiply two matrices given their size and the characteristics of the environment. Although the paper uses MAPE as the evaluation metric, we will use RMSE as it is easier to implement and interpret.

First, we need to read the data. There are two files, one with features and one with labels. Let's read the target first:

```
DataFrame<Object> targetDf =
DataFrame.readCsv("data/performance/y_train.csv");
List<Double> targetList = targetDf.cast(Double.class).col("time");
double[] target = Doubles.toArray(targetList);
```

Next, we read the features:

```
DataFrame<Object> dataframe =
DataFrame.readCsv("data/performance/x_train.csv");
```

If we look at the data, we can notice that sometimes the missing values are encoded as a string `None`. We need to convert it to a real Java `null`. To do this, we can define a special function:

```
private static List<Object> noneToNull(List<Object> memfreq) {
    return memfreq.stream()
                .map(s -> isNone(s) ? null : Double.parseDouble(s.toString()))
                .collect(Collectors.toList());
}
```

Now, use it to process the original columns, then remove them, and add the transformed ones:

```
List<Object> memfreq = noneToNull(dataframe.col("memFreq"));
List<Object> memtRFC = noneToNull(dataframe.col("memtRFC"));
dataframe = dataframe.drop("memFreq", "memtRFC");
dataframe.add("memFreq", memfreq);
dataframe.add("memtRFC", memtRFC);
```

There are some categorical variables in the dataset. We can look at them. First, let's create a data frame, which contains the types of original frames:

```
List<Object> types = dataframe.types().stream()
                .map(c -> c.getSimpleName())
                .collect(Collectors.toList());
List<Object> columns = new ArrayList<>(dataframe.columns());
DataFrame<Object> typesDf = new DataFrame<>();
typesDf.add("column", columns);
typesDf.add("type", types);
```

Since we are interested only in categorical values, we need to select the features that are of type `String`:

```
DataFrame<Object> stringTypes = typesDf.select(p ->
p.get(1).equals("String"));
```

The way categorical variables are often used in the machine learning problem is called dummy-coding, or one hot encoding. In this coding scheme:

- We create as many columns as there are possible values
- For each observation, we put the number 1 for the column, which corresponds to the value of the categorical variable, and the remaining columns get 0

Joinery can do this conversion automatically for us:

```
double[][] X = dataframe.toModelMatrix(0.0);
```

The preceding code will apply one hot encoding scheme to all categorical variables.

However, for the data that we have, some values of the categorical variables occur only once or just a few times. Typically, we are not interested in such infrequently occurring values, so we can replace them with some artificial value such as OTHER.

This is how we do this in Joinery:

- Remove all categorical columns from DataFrame
- For each column, we calculate how many times the values occur and replace infrequent with OTHER

Let's translate it into Java code. This way we get the categorical variables:

```
Object[] columns = stringTypes.col("column").toArray();
DataFrame<Object> categorical = dataframe.retain(columns);
dataframe = dataframe.drop(stringTypes.col("column").toArray());
```

For counting, we can use a Multiset collection from Guava. Then, we replace the infrequent ones with OTHER and put the result back to the DataFrame:

```
for (Object column : categorical.columns()) {
    List<Object> data = categorical.col(column);
    Multiset<Object> counts = HashMultiset.create(data);

    List<Object> cleaned = data.stream()
            .map(o -> counts.count(o) >= 50 ? o : "OTHER")
            .collect(Collectors.toList());

    dataframe.add(column, cleaned);
}
```

After this processing, we can convert the DataFrame into the matrix and put it into our Dataset object:

```
double[][] X = dataframe.toModelMatrix(0.0);
Dataset dataset = new Dataset(X, target);
```

Now we are ready to start training models. Again, we will use Smile for the implementation of machine learning algorithms, and the code for other libraries is available in the chapter code repository.

We already decided that we will use RMSE as the evaluation metrics. Now we need to set up the cross-validation scheme and hold out the data for final evaluation:

```
Split trainTestSplit = dataset.shuffleSplit(0.3);
Dataset train = trainTestSplit.getTrain();
Dataset test = trainTestSplit.getTest();
List<Split> folds = train.shuffleKFold(3);
```

We can reuse the function we wrote for the classification case and slightly adapt it to the regression case:

```
public static DescriptiveStatistics crossValidate(List<Split> folds,
        Function<Dataset, Regression<double[]>> trainer) {
    double[] aucs = folds.parallelStream().mapToDouble(fold -> {
        Dataset train = fold.getTrain();
        Dataset validation = fold.getTest();
        Regression<double[]> model = trainer.apply(train);
        return rmse(model, validation);
    }).toArray();

    return new DescriptiveStatistics(aucs);
}
```

In the preceding code, we first train a regression model and then evaluate its RMSE on the validation dataset.

Before going into modeling, let's first come with a simple baseline solution. In case of Regression, always predicting the mean can be such a baseline:

```
private static Regression<double[]> mean(Dataset data) {
    double meanTarget = Arrays.stream(data.getY()).average().getAsDouble();
    return x -> meanTarget;
}
```

Let's use it as the function for cross-validation for the baseline calculation:

```
DescriptiveStatistics baseline = crossValidate(folds, data -> mean(data));
System.out.printf("baseline: rmse=%.4f &pm; %.4f%n", baseline.getMean(),
baseline.getStandardDeviation());
```

It prints the following to the console:

```
baseline: rmse=25.1487 &pm; 4.3445
```

Our baseline solution is wrong by 25 seconds on average and the spread is 4.3 seconds.

Now we can try to train a simple OLS regression:

```
DescriptiveStatistics ols = crossValidate(folds, data -> {
    return new OLS(data.getX(), data.getY());
});

System.out.printf("ols: rmse=%.4f &pm; %.4f%n", ols.getMean(),
ols.getStandardDeviation());
```

We should note that Smile gives us a warning that the matrix is not full rank and it will use **Singular Value Decomposition (SVD)** to solve the OLS problem. We can either ignore it or explicitly tell it to use SVD:

```
new OLS(data.getX(), data.getY(), true);
```

In either case, it prints the following to the console:

```
ols: rmse=15.8679 &pm; 3.4587
```

When we use a regularized model, we do not typically worry about correlated columns. Let's try LASSO with different values of `lambda`:

```
double[] lambdas = { 0.1, 1, 10, 100, 1000, 5000, 10000, 20000 };
for (double lambda : lambdas) {
    DescriptiveStatistics summary = crossValidate(folds, data -> {
        return new LASSO(data.getX(), data.getY(), lambda);
    });

    double mean = summary.getMean();
    double std = summary.getStandardDeviation();
    System.out.printf("lasso λ=%9.1f, rmse=%.4f &pm; %.4f%n", lambda, mean,
std);
}
```

It produces the following output:

```
lasso λ=       0.1, rmse=15.8679 &pm; 3.4587
lasso λ=       1.0, rmse=15.8678 &pm; 3.4588
lasso λ=      10.0, rmse=15.8650 &pm; 3.4615
lasso λ=     100.0, rmse=15.8533 &pm; 3.4794
lasso λ=    1000.0, rmse=15.8650 &pm; 3.5905
lasso λ=    5000.0, rmse=16.1321 &pm; 3.9813
lasso λ=   10000.0, rmse=16.6793 &pm; 4.3830
lasso λ=   20000.0, rmse=18.6088 &pm; 4.9315
```

Note that the LASSO implementation from Smile version 1.1.0 will have a problem with this dataset because there are linearly dependent columns. To avoid this, you should use the 1.2.0 version, which, at the moment of writing, is not available from Maven Central, and you need to build it yourself if you want to use it. We have already discussed how to do this.

We can also try RidgeRegression, but its performance is very similar to OLS and LASSO, so we will omit it here.

It seems that the results of OLS is not so different from LASSO, so we select it as the final model and use it since it's the simplest model:

```
OLS ols = new OLS(train.getX(), train.getY(), true);
double testRmse = rmse(lasso, test);
System.out.printf("final rmse=%.4f%n", testRmse);
```

This gives us the following output:

```
final rmse=15.0722
```

So the performance of the selected model is consistent with our cross-validation, which means that the model is able to generalize to the unseen data well.

Summary

In this chapter, we spoke about supervised machine learning and about two common supervised problems: classification and regression. We also covered the libraries, which are commonly-used algorithms, implemented them, and learned how to evaluate the performance of these algorithms.

There is another family of machine learning algorithms that do not require the label information; these methods are called unsupervised learning--in the next chapter, we will talk about them.

5
Unsupervised Learning - Clustering and Dimensionality Reduction

In the previous chapter, covered with with machine learning in Java and discussed how to approach the supervised learning problem when the label information is provided.

Often, however, there is no label information, and all we have is just some data. In this case, it is still possible to use machine learning, and this class of problems is called **unsupervised learning**; there are no labels, hence no **supervision**. Cluster analysis belongs to one of these algorithms. Given some dataset, the goal is to group the items from there such that similar items are put into the same group.

Additionally, some unsupervised learning techniques can be useful when there is label information.

For example, the dimensionality reduction algorithm tries to *compress* the dataset such that most of the information is preserved and the dataset can be represented with fewer features. What is more, dimensionality reduction is also useful for performing cluster analysis, and cluster analysis can be used for performing dimensionality reduction.

We will see how to do it all of this in this chapter. Specifically, we will cover the following topics:

- Unsupervised dimensionality reduction methods, such as PCA and SVD
- Cluster analysis algorithms, such as k-means
- Available implementations in Java

By the end of this chapter, you will know how to cluster the data you have and how to perform dimensionality reduction in Java using Smile and other Java libraries.

Dimensionality reduction

Dimensionality reduction, as the name suggests, reduces the dimensionality of your dataset. That is, these techniques try to compress the dataset such that only the most useful information is retained, and the rest is discarded.

By dimensionality of a dataset, we mean the number of features of this dataset. When the dimensionality is high, that is, there are too many features, it can be bad due to the following reasons:

- If there are more features than the items of the dataset, the problem becomes ill-defined and some linear models, such as **ordinary least squares** (**OLS**) regression cannot handle this case
- Some features may be correlated and cause problems with training and interpreting the models
- Some of the features can turn out to be noisy or irrelevant and confuse the model
- Distances start to make less sense in high dimensions -- this problem is commonly referred to as the curse of dimensionality
- Processing a large set of features may be computationally expensive

In the case of high dimensionality, we are interested in reducing the dimensionality such that it becomes manageable. There are several ways of doing so:

- **Supervised dimensionality reduction methods such as feature selection**: We use the information we have about the labels to help us decide which features are useful and which are not
- **Unsupervised dimensionality reduction such as feature extraction**: We do not use the information about labels (either because we do not have it or would not like to do it) and try to compress the large set of features into smaller ones

In this chapter, we will speak about the second type, that is, unsupervised dimensionality reduction, and in particular, about feature extraction.

Unsupervised dimensionality reduction

The main idea behind feature extraction algorithms is that they take in some dataset with high dimensionality, process it, and return a dataset with much smaller set of new features.

Note that the returned features are new, they are **extracted** or **learned** from the data. But this extraction is performed in such a way that the new representation of data retains as much information from the original features as possible. In other words, it takes the data represented with old features, transforms it, and returns a new dataset with entirely new features.

There are many feature extraction algorithms for dimensionality reduction, including:

- **Principal Component Analysis** (**PCA**) and **Singular Value Decomposition** (**SVD**)
- **Non-Negative Matrix Factorization** (**NNMF**)
- Random projections
- **Locally Linear Embedding** (**LLE**)
- t-SNE

In this chapter we will cover PCA, SVD, and random projections. The other techniques are less popular and less often used in practice, so we will not discuss them in this book.

Principal Component Analysis

Principal Component Analysis (**PCA**) is the most famous algorithm for feature extraction. The new feature representation learned by PCA is a linear combination of the original features such that the variance within the original data is preserved as much as possible.

Let's look at this algorithm in action. First, we will consider the dataset we already used the performance prediction. For this problem, the number of features is relatively large; after encoding categorical variables with one-hot-encoding there are more than 1,000 features, and only 5,000 observations. Clearly, 1,000 features is quite a lot for such a small sample size, and this may cause problems when building a machine learning model.

Let's see if we can reduce the dimensionality of this dataset without harming the performance of our model.

But first, let's recall how PCA works. There are usually the following steps to complete:

1. First, you perform mean-normalization of the datasets -- transform the dataset such that the mean value of each column becomes zero.
2. Then, compute the covariance or correlation matrix.
3. After that, perform **Eigenvalue Decomposition** (**EVD**) or **Singular Value Decomposition** (**SVD**) of the covariance/correlation matrix.
4. The result is a set of principal components, each of which explains a part of the variance. The principal components are typically ordered such that the first components explain most of the variance, and last components explain very little of it.
5. In the last step, we throw away components that do not carry any variance on them, and keep only first principal components with large variance. To select the number of components to keep, we typically use the cumulated ratio of explained variance to the total variance.
6. We use these components to compress the original dataset by performing the projection of the original data on the basis formed by these components.
7. After doing these steps, we have a dataset with smaller number of features, but most of the information of the original dataset is preserved.

There are a number of ways we can implement PCA in Java, but we can take one of the libraries such as Smile, which offers off-the-shelf implementations. In Smile, PCA already performs mean-normalization, then computes the covariance matrix and automatically decides whether to use EVD or SVD. All we need to do is to give it a data matrix, and it will do the rest.

Typically, PCA is performed on the covariance matrix, but sometimes, when some of the original features are on a different scale, the ratio of the explained variance can become misleading.

For example, if one of the features we have is distance in kilometers, and the other one is time is milliseconds, then the second feature will have larger variance simply because the numbers are a lot higher in the second feature. Thus, this feature will have the dominant presence in the resulting components.

To overcome this problem, we can use the correlation matrix instead of the covariance one, and since the correlation coefficient is unitless, the PCA results will not be affected by different scales. Alternatively, we can perform standardization of the features in our dataset, and, in effect, computing covariance will be the same as computing correlation.

So, first we will standardize the data using the `StandardizationPreprocessor` we wrote previously:

```
StandardizationPreprocessor preprocessor =
StandardizationPreprocessor.train(dataset);
dataset = preprocessor.transform(dataset)
```

Then we can run PCA on the transformed dataset and have a look at the cumulative variance:

```
PCA pca = new PCA(dataset.getX(), false);
double[] variance = pca.getCumulativeVarianceProportion();
System.out.println(Arrays.toString(variance));
```

If we take the output and plot the first one hundred components, we will see the following picture:

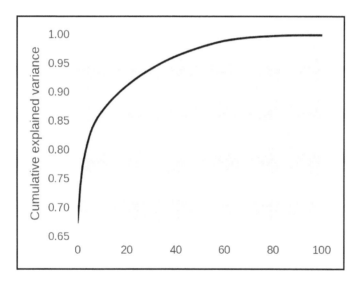

As we can see, the principal component explains about 67% of variance, and the cumulative explained ratio quite quickly reaches 95% at less than **40** components, 99% at 61, and it is almost 100% at **80** components. This means that if we take only the first **80** components, it will be enough to capture almost all variance present in the dataset. This means that we should be able to safely compress our 1,000 plus dimensional datasets into only 80 dimensions.

Let's test it. First, let's try to do OLS without PCA. We will take the code from the previous chapter:

```
Dataset train = trainTestSplit.getTrain();

List<Split> folds = train.shuffleKFold(3);
DescriptiveStatistics ols = crossValidate(folds, data -> {
    return new OLS(data.getX(), data.getY());
});
```

This prints the following output:

```
ols: rmse=15.8679 &pm; 3.4587
```

Now let's try to cap the number of principal components at the 95%, 99%, and 99.9% levels and see what happens with the error:

```
double[] ratios = { 0.95, 0.99, 0.999 };

for (double ratio : ratios) {
    pca = pca.setProjection(ratio);
    double[][] projectedX = pca.project(train.getX());
    Dataset projected = new Dataset(projectedX, train.getY());

    folds = projected.shuffleKFold(3);
    ols = crossValidate(folds, data -> {
        return new OLS(data.getX(), data.getY());
    });

    double mean = ols.getMean();
    double std = ols.getStandardDeviation();
    System.out.printf("ols (%.3f): rmse=%.4f &pm; %.4f%n", ratio, mean,
std);
}
```

This produces the following output:

```
ols (0.950): rmse=18.3331 &pm; 3.6308
ols (0.990): rmse=16.0702 &pm; 3.5046
ols (0.999): rmse=15.8656 &pm; 3.4625
```

As we see, keeping 99.9% of variance with PCA gives the same performance as the OLS regression fit on the original dataset. For this dataset, 99.9% of variance is explained by only 84 principal components, and there are 1070 features in the original dataset. Thus, we managed to reduce the dimensionality of the data by keeping only 7.8% of the original data size without loosing any performance.

Sometimes, however, the implementation of PCA from Smile and other similar packages is not the best in terms of performance. Next, we will see why and how to deal with it.

Truncated SVD

The previous code (in this case, using Smile) performs full PCA via full SVD or EVD. Here, **full** means that it computes all eigenvalues and eigenvectors, which may be computationally expensive, especially when we only need the first 7.8% of the principal components. However, we do not necessarily have to always compute the full PCA, and instead we can use truncated SVD. Truncated SVD computes only the specified number of principal components, and it is usually a lot faster than the full version.

Smile also provides an implementation of truncated SVD. But before using it, let's quickly revise SVD.

SVD of a matrix X computes the bases for the rows and the columns of X such that:

$$XV = US$$

Here, the equation is explained as follows:

- The columns of V form the basis for the rows of X
- The columns of U form the basis for the rows of X
- S is a diagonal matrix with the singular values of X

Often, SVD is written in this form:

$$X = USV^T$$

So, SVD decomposes the matrix X into three matrices U, S, and V.

When SVD is truncated to dimensionality K, the matrices U and V have only K columns, and we compute only K singular values. If we then multiply the original matrix X by the truncated V, or, alternatively, multiply S by U, we will obtain the reduced projection of the rows of X to this new SVD basis.

This will bring the original matrix to the new reduced space, and we can use the results as features instead of the original one.

Now, we are ready to apply it. In Smile it will look like this:

```
double[][] X = ... // X is mean-centered
Matrix matrix = new Matrix(X);
SingularValueDecomposition svd =
SingularValueDecomposition.decompose(matrix, 100);
```

Here, `Matrix` is a class from Smile for storing dense matrices. The matrices U, S, and V are returned inside the `SingularValueDecomposition` object, U and V as two-dimensional double arrays and S as a one-dimensional array of doubles.

Now, we need to get the reduced representation of our data matrix X. As we discussed earlier, there are two ways of doing it:

- By computing $X \cdot V$
- By computing $U \cdot S$

First, let's have a look at computing $U \cdot S$.

In Smile, the `decompose` method from `SingularValueDecomposition` returns S as a one-dimensional array of doubles, so we need to convert it to the matrix form. We can take advantage of the fact that S is diagonal and use it for speeding up the multiplication.

Let's use the Commons Math library for that. There is a special implementation for diagonal matrices, so we will use it, and usual array-backed matrix for U.

```
DiagonalMatrix S = new DiagonalMatrix(svd.getSingularValues());
Array2DRowRealMatrix U = new Array2DRowRealMatrix(svd.getU(), false);
```

Now we can multiply these two matrices:

```
RealMatrix result = S.multiply(U.transpose()).transpose();
double[][] data = result.getData();
```

Note that instead of multiplying U by S, we do it in the opposite direction and then transpose: this takes advantage of S being diagonal, and makes the matrix multiplications a lot faster. In the end, we extract the array of doubles to be used in Smile.

If we use this code for the problem of predicting performance, it takes less than 4 seconds, and that's including the matrix multiplication part. This is a great speed improvement over the full PCA version, which, on our laptop, takes more than 1 minute.

Another way to compute the projection is to calculate $X \cdot V$. Let's once again use Commons Math for that:

```
Array2DRowRealMatrix X = new Array2DRowRealMatrix(dataX, false);
Array2DRowRealMatrix V = new Array2DRowRealMatrix(svd.getV(), false);
double[][] data = X.multiply(V).getData();
```

This takes slightly more time than computing $U \cdot S$, since neither of the matrices are diagonal. However, the difference in speed is only marginal: computing SVD and reducing the dimensionality this way takes less than 5 seconds for the performance prediction problem.

When you use SVD to reduce the dimensionality of *training* data, there is no difference between these two methods. However, we cannot apply the $U \cdot S$ approach to new unseen data, because both *U* and *S* are produced for the matrix X, for which we trained the SVD. Instead we use the $X \cdot V$ approach. Note that X in this case will be the new matrix containing the test data, not the same X we used for training the SVD.

In code it will look like this:

```
double[] trainX = ...;
double[] testX = ...;

Matrix matrix = new Matrix(trainX);
SingularValueDecomposition svd =
SingularValueDecomposition.decompose(matrix, 100);

double[][] trainProjected = mmult(trainX, svd.getV());
double[][] testProjected = mmult(testX, svd.getV());
```

Here, `mmult` is a method that multiplies the matrix X by the matrix V.

There is another implementation detail: in Smile's PCA implementation, we determine the number of needed dimensionality using the ratio of explained variance. Recall that we do this by invoking `getCumulativeVarianceProportion` on the PCA object, and usually keep the number of components high enough to get at least 95% or 99% of variance.

However, since we use SVD directly, we do not know this ratio now. It means that to be able to choose the right dimensionality, we need to implement this ourselves. Luckily, it is not very complex to do; first, we need to calculate the overall variance of the dataset, and then the variances of all the principal components. The latter can be obtained from the singular values (the matrix *S*). The singular values correspond to standard deviations, so to get the variance, we just need to square them. Finally, finding the ratio is simple, and we just need to divide one by another.

Let's see how it looks in code. First, we use Commons Math to compute the total variance:

```
Array2DRowRealMatrix matrix = new Array2DRowRealMatrix(dataset.getX(),
false);
int ncols = matrix.getColumnDimension();

double totalVariance = 0.0;
for (int col = 0; col < ncols; col++) {
    double[] column = matrix.getColumn(col);
    DescriptiveStatistics stats = new DescriptiveStatistics(column);
    totalVariance = totalVariance + stats.getVariance();
}
```

Now we can compute the cumulated ratios from singular values:

```
int nrows = X.length;
double[] singularValues = svd.getSingularValues();
double[] cumulatedRatio = new double[singularValues.length];

double acc = 0.0;
for (int i = 0; i < singularValues.length; i++) {
    double s = singularValues[i];
    double ratio = (s * s / nrows) / totalVariance;
    acc = acc + ratio;
    cumulatedRatio[i] = acc;
}
```

After running this code, the `cumulatedRatio` array will contain the desired ratios. The result should be exactly the same as from Smile's PCA implementation from `pca.getCumulativeVarianceProportion()`.

Truncated SVD for categorical and sparse data

Dimensionality reduction can be very useful for datasets with many categorical variables, especially when each of these variables have a lot of possible values.

When we have sparse matrices of very high dimensionality, computing full SVD is typically very expensive. Thus, truncated SVD is especially for this case, and here we will see how we can use it. Later on in the next chapter, we will see that this is also pretty useful for text data, and we will cover this case in the next chapter. For now, we will have a look at how to use it for categorical variables.

For this, we will use a dataset about customer complaints from Kaggle. You can download it from here: `https://www.kaggle.com/cfpb/us-consumer-finance-complaints`.

This dataset contains complaints that customers of banks and other financial institutions have filed, and also contains additional information about these complaints, as follows:

- The product for which the complaint is filed can be *Mortgage Loan, Student Loan, Debt Collection,* and so on. There are 11 types of products.
- The reported issue about the product, such as *incorrect information, false statements,* and so on. There are 95 types of issues.
- The company for which the complaint is filed, more than 3,000 companies.
- `submitted_via` is how the complaint was sent, 6 possible options such as, *web and e-mail.*
- The state and zipcode is 63 and 27,000 possible values respectively.
- `consumer_complaint_narrative` is a free text description of the problem.

We see that there is a large number of categorical variables in this dataset. As we have already discussed in previous chapters, the typical way of encoding categorical variables is one-hot-encoding (also called **dummy-coding**). The idea is that for each possible value of a variable, we create a separate feature, and put the value 1 there if an item has this particular value. Txhe columns for all other possible values will have 0 there.

The easiest way to implement this is to use feature hashing, which sometimes is referred as the hashing trick.

It can be done quite easily by following these steps:

- We specify the dimensionality of our sparse matrix beforehand, and for that we take some reasonably large number
- Then, for each value, we compute the hash of this value
- Using the hash, we compute the number of the column in the sparse matrix and set the value of this column to 1

So, let's try to implement it. First, we load the dataset and keep only the categorical variables:

```
DataFrame<Object> categorical = dataframe.retain("product", "sub_product",
    "issue",
        "sub_issue", "company_public_response", "company",
        "state", "zipcode", "consumer_consent_provided",
        "submitted_via");
```

Now, let's implement feature hashing for encoding them:

```
int dim = 50_000;
SparseDataset result = new SparseDataset(dim);
```

```
int ncolOriginal = categorical.size();
ListIterator<List<Object>> rows = categorical.iterrows();

while (rows.hasNext()) {
    int rowIdx = rows.nextIndex();
    List<Object> row = rows.next();
    for (int colIdx = 0; colIdx < ncolOriginal; colIdx++) {
        Object val = row.get(colIdx);
        String stringValue = colIdx + "_" + Objects.toString(val);
        int targetColIdx = Math.abs(stringValue.hashCode()) % dim;

        result.set(rowIdx, targetColIdx, 1.0);
    }
}
```

What happens here is that we first create a `SparseDataset`-- a class from Smile for keeping row-based sparse matrices. Next, we say that the matrix should have the dimensionality specified by the variable `dim`. The value of `dim` should be high enough so that the chance of collision is not very high. Typically, however, it is not a big deal if there are collisions.

 If you set the value of dim to a very large number, there could be some performance problems when we later decompose the matrix.

Feature hashing is a very simple approach and often works really well in practice. There is another approach, which is more complex to implement, but it ensures that there are no hash collisions. For that, we build a map from all the possible values to column indexes, and then build the sparse matrix.

Building the map will look like this:

```
Map<String, Integer> valueToIndex = new HashMap<>();
List<Object> columns = new ArrayList<>(categorical.columns());

int ncol = 0;

for (Object name : columns) {
    List<Object> column = categorical.col(name);
    Set<Object> distinct = new HashSet<>(column);
    for (Object val : distinct) {
        String stringValue = Objects.toString(name) + "_" +
Objects.toString(val);
        valueToIndex.put(stringValue, ncol);
        ncol++;
    }
}
```

The `ncol` variable contains the number of columns, which is the dimensionality of our future sparse matrix. Now we can construct the actual matrix. It is very similar to what we had before, but, instead of hashing, we now look the indexes up in the map:

```
SparseDataset result = new SparseDataset(ncol);

ListIterator<List<Object>> rows = categorical.iterrows();
while (rows.hasNext()) {
    int rowIdx = rows.nextIndex();
    List<Object> row = rows.next();
    for (int colIdx = 0; colIdx < columns.size(); colIdx++) {
        Object name = columns.get(colIdx);
        Object val = row.get(colIdx);
        String stringValue = Objects.toString(name) + "_" +
Objects.toString(val);
        int targetColIdx = valueToIndex.get(stringValue);

        result.set(rowIdx, targetColIdx, 1.0);
    }
}
```

After doing this, we have a `SparseDataset` object, which contains the data in a row-based format. Next, we need to be able to put it to the SVD solver, and for that we need to convert it to a different column-based format. This is implemented in the `SparseMatrix` class. Luckily, there is a special method in the `SparseDataset` class which does the conversion, so we use it:

```
SparseMatrix matrix = dataset.toSparseMatrix();
SingularValueDecomposition svd =
SingularValueDecomposition.decompose(matrix, 100);
```

The decomposition is quite fast; computing SVD of the feature hashing matrix took about 28 seconds and the usual one-hot-encoding took about 24 seconds. Remember that there are 0.5 million rows in this dataset, so the speed is pretty good. To our knowledge, other Java implementations of SVD are not able to provide the same performance.

Now, when SVD is computed, we need to project the original matrix to the reduced space, like we did in the case of dense matrices previously.

The $U \cdot S$ projection can be done exactly as before, because both U and S are dense. However, X is sparse, so we need to find a way to multiply sparse X and dense X efficiently.

Unfortunately, neither Smile nor Commons Math has a suitable implementation for this. Therefore, we need to use another library, and this problem can be solved with **Matrix Java Toolkit (MTJ)**. This library is based on netlib-java, which is a wrapper for low-level high-performance libraries such as BLAS, LAPACK, and ARPACK. You can read more on its GitHub page: `https://github.com/fommil/matrix-toolkits-java`.

Since we use Maven, it will take care of downloading the binary dependencies and linking them to the project. All we need need to do is to specify the following dependency:

```
<dependency>
  <groupId>com.googlecode.matrix-toolkits-java</groupId>
  <artifactId>mtj</artifactId>
  <version>1.0.2</version>
</dependency>
```

We need to multiply two matrices, *X* and *V*, with the condition that *X* is sparse while *V* is dense. Since *X* is on the left side of the multiplication operator, the most efficient way to store the values of *X* is a row-based sparse matrix representation. For *V* the most efficient representation is a column-based dense matrix.

But before we can do it, we first need to convert Smile's `SparseDataset` into MTJ's sparse matrix. For that we use a special builder: `FlexCompRowMatrix` class, which is good for populating a matrix with values, but not so good for multiplication. Once we constructed the matrix, we convert it to `CompRowMatrix`, which has a more efficient internal representation and is better suited for multiplication purposes.

Here's how we do it:

```
SparseDataset dataset = ... //
int ncols = dataset.ncols();
int nrows = dataset.size();
FlexCompRowMatrix builder = new FlexCompRowMatrix(nrows, ncols);

SparseArray[] array = dataset.toArray(new SparseArray[0]);
for (int rowIdx = 0; rowIdx < array.length; rowIdx++) {
    Iterator<Entry> row = array[rowIdx].iterator();
    while (row.hasNext()) {
        Entry entry = row.next();
        builder.set(rowIdx, entry.i, entry.x);
    }
}

CompRowMatrix X = new CompRowMatrix(builder);
```

The second step is to create a dense matrix. This step is simpler:

```
DenseMatrix V = new DenseMatrix(svd.getV());
```

Internally, MTJ stores dense matrices column-wise, and it is ideal for our purposes.

Next, we need to create a matrix object, which will contain the results, and then we multiply *X* by *V*:

```
DenseMatrix XV = new DenseMatrix(X.numRows(), V.numColumns());
X.mult(V, XV);
```

Finally, we need to extract the double array data from the result matrix. For performance purposes, MTJ stores the data as a one-dimensional double array, so we need to convert it to the conventional representation. We do it like this:

```
double[] data = XV.getData();
int nrows = XV.numRows();
int ncols = XV.numColumns();
double[][] result = new double[nrows][ncols];

for (int col = 0; col < ncols; col++) {
    for (int row = 0; row < nrows; row++) {
        result[row][col] = data[row + col * nrows];
    }
}
```

In the end, we have the result array, which captures most of the variability of the original dataset, and we can use it for cases where a small dense matrix is expected.

This transformation is especially useful for the second topic of this chapter: clustering. Typically, we use distances for clustering data points, but when it comes to high-dimensional spaces, the distances are no longer meaningful, and this phenomenon is known as the **curve of dimensionality**. However, in the reduced SVD space, the distances still make sense and when we apply cluster analysis, the results are typically better.

This is also a very useful method for processing natural language texts, as typically texts are represented as extremely high dimensional and very sparse matrices. We will come back to this in Chapter 6, *Working with Texts - Natural Language Processing and Information Retrieval*.

Note that unlike in the usual PCA case, we do not perform mean-centering here. There are a few reasons for this:

- If we do this, the matrix will become dense and will occupy too much memory, so it will not be possible to process it in a reasonable amount of time
- In sparse matrices, the mean is already very close to zero, so there is no need to perform mean normalization

Next, we will look at a different dimensionality reduction technique, which is extremely simple, requires no learning, and is pretty fast.

Random projection

PCA tries to find some structure in data and use it for reducing the dimensionality; it finds such a basis in which most of the original variance is preserved. However, there is an alternative approach instead of trying to learn the basis, just generate it randomly and then project the original data on it.

Surprisingly, this simple idea works quite well in practice. The reason for that is, this transformation preserves distances. What this means is that if we have two objects that are close to each other in the original space, then, when we apply the projection, they still remain close. Likewise, if the objects are far away from each other, then they will remain far in the new reduced space.

Smile already has implementation for random projection, which takes the input dimensionality and the desired output dimensionality:

```
double[][] X = ... // data
int inputDimension = X[0].length;
int outputDimension = 100;
smile.math.Math.setSeed(1);
RandomProjection rp = new RandomProjection(inputDimension,
outputDimension);
```

Note that we explicitly set the seed for random number generator; since the basis for random projections is generated randomly, we want to ensure reproducibility.

 Setting seed is only possible in version 1.2.1, which was not available on Maven Central at the moment of writing.

It is implemented in Smile in the following way:

- First, a set of random vectors are sampled from a Gaussian distribution
- Then, the vectors are made orthonormal via the Gram-Schmidt algorithm, that is, they are first made orthogonal and then the length is normalized to 1
- The projection is made on this orthonormal basis

Let's use it for performance prediction and then fit the usual OLS:

```
double[][] X = dataset.getX();
int inputDimension = X[0].length;
int outputDimension = 100;
smile.math.Math.setSeed(1);
RandomProjection rp = new RandomProjection(inputDimension,
outputDimension);

double[][] projected = rp.project(X);
dataset = new Dataset(projected, dataset.getY());

Split trainTestSplit = dataset.shuffleSplit(0.3);
Dataset train = trainTestSplit.getTrain();

List<Split> folds = train.shuffleKFold(3);
DescriptiveStatistics ols = crossValidate(folds, data -> {
    return new OLS(data.getX(), data.getY());
});

System.out.printf("ols: rmse=%.4f &pm; %.4f%n", ols.getMean(),
ols.getStandardDeviation());
```

It is very fast (it takes less than a second on our laptop) and this code produces the following result:

```
ols: rmse=15.8455 &pm; 3.3843
```

The result is pretty much the same as in plain OLS or OLS on PCA with 99.9% variance.

However, the implementation from Smile only works with dense matrices, and at the moment of writing there is no support for sparse matrices. Since the method is pretty straightforward, it is not difficult to implement it ourselves. Let's implement a simplified version of generating the random basis.

To generate the basis, we sample from the Gaussian distribution with zero mean and a standard deviation equal to `1 / new_dimensionality`, where `new_dimensionality` is the desired dimensionality of the new reduced space.

Let's use Commons Math for it:

```
NormalDistribution normal = new NormalDistribution(0.0, 1.0 /
outputDimension);
normal.reseedRandomGenerator(seed);
double[][] result = new double[inputDimension][];

for (int i = 0; i < inputDimension; i++) {
    result[i] = normal.sample(outputDimension);
}
```

Here, we have the following parameters:

- inputDimension: This is the dimensionality of the matrix we want to project, that is, the number of columns of this matrix
- outputDimension: This is the desired dimensionality of the projection
- seed: This is the random number generator seed for reproducibility

First, let's sanity-check the implementation and apply it to the same performance problem. Even though it is dense, it is enough for testing purposes:

```
double[][] X = dataset.getX();
int inputDimension = X[0].length;
int outputDimension = 100;
int seed = 1;
double[][] basis = Projections.randomProjection(inputDimension,
outputDimension, seed);
double[][] projected = Projections.project(X, basis);
dataset = new Dataset(projected, dataset.getY());

Split trainTestSplit = dataset.shuffleSplit(0.3);
Dataset train = trainTestSplit.getTrain();

List<Split> folds = train.shuffleKFold(3);
DescriptiveStatistics ols = crossValidate(folds, data -> {
    return new OLS(data.getX(), data.getY());
});

System.out.printf("ols: rmse=%.4f &pm; %.4f%n", ols.getMean(),
ols.getStandardDeviation());
```

Here we have two methods:

- Projections.randomProjection: This generates the random basis, which we implemented previously.

- `Projections.project`: This projects the matrix *X* onto the basis, and it is implemented by multiplying the matrix *X* onto the matrix of the basis.

After running the code, we see the following output:

```
ols: rmse=15.8771 &pm; 3.4332
```

This indicates that our implementation has passed the sanity check, the results make sense, and the method is implemented correctly.

Now we need to change the projection method such that it can be applied to sparse matrices. We have already done that, but let's once again take a look at the outline:

- Put the sparse matrix into `RompRowMatrix`, **compressed row storage** (**CRS**) matrix
- Put the basis into `DenseMatrix`
- Multiply the matrices and write the results into `DenseMatrix`
- Unwrap the underlying data from `DenseMatrix` into a two-dimensional double array

For the categorical example from the complaints dataset, it will look like the following:

```
DataFrame<Object> categorical = ... // data
SparseDataset sparse = OHE.hashingEncoding(categorical, 50_000);
double[][] basis = Projections.randomProjection(50_000, 100, 0);
double[][] proj = Projections.project(sparse, basis);
```

Here, we created some helper methods:

- `OHE.hashingEncoding` : This does one-hot-encoding of categorical data from the categorical `DataFrame`
- `Projections.randomProjection` : This generates a random basis
- `Projections.project` : This projects our sparse matrix on this generated basis

We wrote the code for these methods previously, and here we have placed them in helper methods for convenience. Of course, as usual, you can see the entire code in the code bundle provided for the chapter. So far, we have covered only one set of techniques from unsupervised learning dimensionality reduction. There is also cluster analysis, which we will cover next. Interestingly, clustering can also be used for reducing the dimensionality of the dataset, and soon we will see how.

Cluster analysis

Clustering, or cluster analysis, is another family of unsupervised learning algorithms. The goal of clustering is to organize data into clusters such that the similar items end up in the same cluster, and dissimilar items in different ones.

There are many different algorithm families for performing clustering, and they differ in how they group elements.

The most common families are as follows:

- **Hierarchical**: This organizes the dataset into a hierarchy, for example, agglomerative and divisive clustering. The result is typically a dendrogram.
- **Partitioning**: This splits the dataset into K disjoint classes--K is often specified in advance--for example, K-means.
- **Density-based**: This organizes the items based on density regions; if there are many items in some dense regions, they form a cluster, for example, DBSCAN.
- **Graph-based**: This represents the relations between items as a graph and applies grouping algorithms from the graph theory, for example, connected components and minimal spanning trees.

Hierarchical methods

Hierarchical methods are considered the simplest clustering algorithms; they are easy to understand and interpret. There are two families of clustering method, which belong to the hierarchical family:

- Divisive clustering algorithms
- Agglomerative clustering algorithms

In the divisive approach, we put all the data items into one cluster, and at each step we pick up a cluster and then split it into halves until every element is its own cluster. For this reason, this approach is sometimes called **top-down clustering**.

The agglomerative clustering approach is the opposite; at the beginning, each data point belongs to its own cluster, and then at each step, we select two closest clusters and merge them, until there is only one big cluster left. This is also called **bottom-up** approach.

Even though there are two types of hierarchical clustering algorithms, when people say hierarchical clustering, they typically mean agglomerative clustering, these algorithms are more common. So let's have a closer look at them.

In agglomerative clustering, at each step, we merge two closest clusters, but depending on how we define closest, the result can be quite different.

The process of merging two clusters is often called **linking**, and **linkage** describes how the distance between two clusters is calculated.

There are many types of linkages, and the most common ones are as follows:

- **Single linkage**: The distance between two clusters is the distance between two closest elements.
- **Complete linkage**: The distance between two clusters is the distance between two most distant elements.
- **Average linkage (also sometimes called UPGMA linkage)**: The distance between clusters is the distance between the centroids, where a centroid is the average across all items of the cluster.

These methods are usually suitable for a dataset of smaller sizes, and they work quite well for them. But for larger datasets, they are usually less useful and take a lot of time to finish. Still, it is possible to use it even with larger datasets, but we need to take a sample of some manageable size.

Let's look at the example. We can use the dataset of complaints we used previously, with categorical variables encoded via One-Hot-Encoding. If you remember, we then translated the sparse matrix with categorical variables into a dense matrix of smaller dimensionality by using SVD. The dataset is quite large to process, so let's first sample 10,000 records from there:

```
double[] data = ... // our data in the reduced SVD space
int size = 10000; // sample size
long seed = 0; // seed number for reproducibility
Random rnd = new Random(seed);

int[] idx = rnd.ints(0, data.length).distinct().limit(size).toArray();
double[][] sample = new double[size][];
for (int i = 0; i < size; i++) {
    sample[i] = data[idx[i]];
}

data = sample;
```

What we do here is take a stream of distinct integers from the random number generator and then limit it to 10,000. Then we use these integers as indexes for the sample.

After preparing the data and taking a sample, we can try to apply agglomerative cluster analysis to this dataset. Most of the Machine Learning libraries that we previously discussed have implementations of clustering algorithms, so we can use any of them. Since we have already used Smile quite extensively, and, in this chapter, we will also use the implementation from Smile.

When we use it, the first thing we need to specify is the **linkage**. To specify the linkage and create a `Linkage` object, we first need to compute a **proximity matrix**--a matrix that contains distances between each pair of object from the dataset.

We can use any distance measure there, but we will take the most commonly used one, the Euclidean distance. Recall that the Euclidean distance is a norm of the difference between two vectors. To efficiently compute it, we can use the following decomposition:

$$||a - b||^2 = (a-b)^T (a-b) = a^Ta - 2a^Tb + b^Tb$$

We represent the square of the distance as an inner product, and then decompose it. Next, we recognize that this is a sum of the norms of the individual vectors minus their product:

$$a^Ta - 2a^Tb + b^Tb = ||a||^2 - 2a^Tb + b^Tb$$

And this is the formula we can use for efficient calculation of the proximity matrix - the matrix of distances between each pair of items. In this formula, we have the inner product of the pair, which can be efficiently computed by using the matrix multiplication.

Let's see how to translate this formula into the code. The first two components are the individual norms, so let's compute them:

```
int nrow = data.length;

double[] squared = new double[nrow];
for (int i = 0; i < nrow; i++) {
    double[] row = data[i];

    double res = 0.0;
    for (int j = 0; j < row.length; j++) {
        res = res + row[j] * row[j];
    }

    squared[i] = res;
}
```

When it comes to the inner product, it is just a matrix multiplication of the data matrix with its transpose. We can compute it with any mathematical package in Java. For example, with Commons Math:

```
Array2DRowRealMatrix m = new Array2DRowRealMatrix(data, false);
double[][] product = m.multiply(m.transpose()).getData();
```

Finally, we put these components together to calculate the proximity matrix:

```
double[][] dist = new double[nrow][nrow];

for (int i = 0; i < nrow; i++) {
    for (int j = i + 1; j < nrow; j++) {
        double d = squared[i] - 2 * product[i][j] + squared[j];
        dist[i][j] = dist[j][i] = d;
    }
}
```

Because the distance matrix is symmetric, we can save time and loop only over the half of the indexes. There is no need to cover the case when `i == j`.

There are other distance measures we can use: it does not matter for the `Linkage` class. For example, instead of using Euclidean distance, we can take another one, for example, the cosine distance.

The cosine distance is another measure of dissimilarity between two vectors, and it is based on the cosine similarity. The cosine similarity geometrically corresponds to the angle between two vectors, and it is computed using the inner product:

$$cosine(a, b) = \frac{a^T b}{\| a \| \cdot \| b \|}$$

The inner product here is divided by the norms of each individual vector. But if the vectors are already normalized, that is, they have a norm, which is equal to 1, then the cosine is just the inner product. If the cosine similarity is equal to one, then the vectors are exactly the same.

The cosine distance is the opposite of the cosine similarity: it should be equal to zero when the vectors are the same, so we can compute it by just subtracting it from one:

$$cosine\text{-}dist(a, b) = 1 - \frac{a^T b}{\|a\| \cdot \|b\|}$$

Since we have the inner product here, it is easy to calculate this distance using the matrix multiplication.

Let's implement it. First, we do unit-normalization of each row vector of our data matrix:

```
int nrow = data.length;
double[][] normalized = new double[nrow][];

for (int i = 0; i < nrow; i++) {
    double[] row = data[i].clone();
    normalized[i] = row;
    double norm = new ArrayRealVector(row, false).getNorm();
    for (int j = 0; j < row.length; j++) {
        row[j] = row[j] / norm;
    }
}
```

Now we can multiply the normalized matrices to get the cosine similarity:

```
Array2DRowRealMatrix m = new Array2DRowRealMatrix(normalized, false);
double[][] cosine = m.multiply(m.transpose()).getData();
```

Finally, we get the cosine distance by subtracting the cosine similarity from 1:

```
for (int i = 0; i < nrow; i++) {
    double[] row = cosine[i];
    for (int j = 0; j < row.length; j++) {
        row[j] = 1 - row[j];
    }
}
```

Now, it is possible to pass the computed matrix to the `Linkage` instance. As we mentioned, any distance measure can be used with hierarchical clustering, and this is a nice property, which other clustering methods often lack.

Let's now use the computed distance matrix for clustering:

```
double[][] proximity = calcualateSquaredEuclidean(data);
Linkage linkage = new UPGMALinkage(proximity);
HierarchicalClustering hc = new HierarchicalClustering(linkage);
```

In agglomerative clustering, we take two most similar clusters and merge them, and we repeat that process until there is only one cluster left. This merging process can be visualized with a dendrogram. For drawing it in Java, we can use the plotting library that comes with Smile.

To illustrate how to do it, let's first sample only a few items and apply the clustering. Then we can get something similar to the following picture:

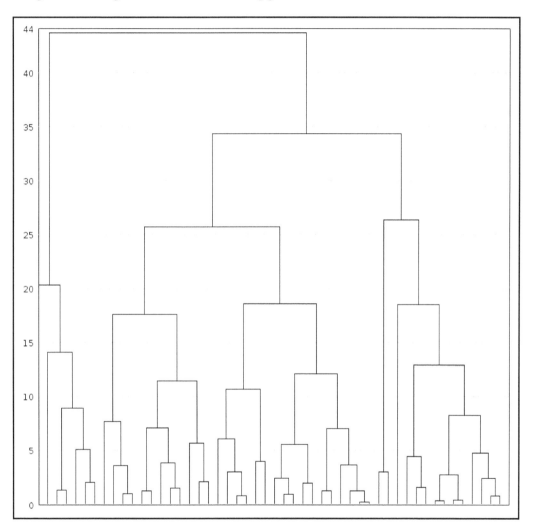

At the bottom on the *x* axis, we have the items that are merged into clusters. On the *y* axis, we have the distance at which the clusters are merged.

To create the plot, we use the following code:

```
Frame frame = new JFrame("Dendrogram");
frame.setDefaultCloseOperation(WindowConstants.DISPOSE_ON_CLOSE);
```

```
PlotCanvas dendrogram = Dendrogram.plot(hc.getTree(), hc.getHeight());
frame.add(dendrogram);

frame.setSize(new Dimension(1000, 1000));
frame.setLocationRelativeTo(null);
frame.setVisible(true);
```

This visualization is quite helpful when we need to analyze the resulting clusters. Since we know the distance at which the merge was done (on the y axis), we can get some idea how many clusters it may make sense to extract from the data. For example, after around 21, the mergers become quite distant from each other, which may suggest that there are 5 clusters.

To get these clusters, we can cut the dendrogram at some distance threshold. If some element was merged at a distance below the threshold, then they stay within the same cluster. Otherwise, if they are merged at the distance above the threshold, they are treated as separate clusters.

For the preceding dendrogram, if we cut at the height of 23, we should get 5 separate clusters. This is how we can do it:

```
double height = 23.0;
int[] labels = hc.partition(height);
```

Alternatively, we can ask for a specific number of clusters:

```
int k = 5;
int[] labels = hc.partition(k);
```

There are several advantages of hierarchical clusters:

- It can work with any distance function, all it needs is a distance matrix, so any function can be used to create the matrix
- It is easy to come up with the number of clusters with this clustering

However, there are some disadvantages:

- It does not work well with a large number of items in the dataset--the distance matrix is hard to fit into memory.
- It is usually slower than other method, especially when some linkage is used.

There is another very popular method, which works quite well for larger datasets, and next we will talk about it.

K-means

As we mentioned previously, Agglomerative clustering methods work quite well with small datasets, but they have some problems with bigger ones. *K*-means is another popular clusterization technique, which does not suffer from this problem.

K-means is a clustering method, which belongs to the partitioning family of clustering algorithm: given the number of clusters *K*, *K*-Means splits the data into *K* disjoint groups. Grouping items into clusters is done using centroids. A centroid represents the "center" of a cluster, and for each item, we assign it to the group of its closest centroid. The quality of clustering is measured by **distortion** - the sum of distances between each item and its centroid.

As with agglomerative clustering, there are multiple implementations of *K*-Means available in Java, and, like previously, we will use the one from Smile. Unfortunately, it does not support sparse matrices, and can work only with dense ones. If we want to use it for sparse data, we either need to convert it to dense matrix, or reduce its dimensionality with SVD or random projection.

Let's again use the categorical dataset of complaints, and project it to 30 components with SVD:

```
SingularValueDecomposition svd =
SingularValueDecomposition.decompose(sparse.toSparseMatrix(), 30);
double[][] proj = Projections.project(sparse, svd.getV());
```

As we see here, the *K*-means implementation in Smile takes in four arguments:

- The matrix that we want to cluster
- The number of clusters we want to find
- The number of iterations to run
- The number of trials before selecting the best one

K-means optimizes the distortion of the dataset, and this objective function has many local optima. This means, depending on the initial configuration, you may end up with entirely different results, and some may be better than others. The problem can be mitigated by running K-means multiple times, each time with different starting position, and then choosing the clustering with the best optimum. This is why we need the last parameters, the number of trials.

Now, let's run *K*-means in Smile:

```
int k = 10;
int maxIter = 100;
```

```
int runs = 3;
KMeans km = new KMeans(proj, k, maxIter, runs);
```

Although the implementation from Smile can only work with dense matrices, the implementation from JSAT does not have this limitation, it can work with any matrix, be it dense or sparse.

The way we do it in JSAT is as follows:

```
SimpleDataSet ohe = JsatOHE.oneHotEncoding(categorical);
EuclideanDistance distance = new EuclideanDistance();
Random rand = new Random(1);
SeedSelection seedSelection = SeedSelection.RANDOM;
KMeans km = new ElkanKMeans(distance, rand, seedSelection);

List<List<DataPoint>> clustering = km.cluster(ohe);
```

In this code, we use another implementation of One-Hot-Encoding, which produces sparse JSAT datasets. It very closely follows the implementation we have for Smile. For details, you can take a look at the code in the chapter's code repository.

There are multiple implementations of *K*-Means in JSAT. One of these implementations is `ElkanKMeans`, which we used earlier. The `ElkanKMeans` parameter from JSAT is quite different from the Smile version:

- First, it takes the distance function, typically Euclidean
- It creates an instance of the random class to ensure reproducibility
- It creates the algorithm for selecting the initial seeds for clusters, with random being fastest and KPP (which is *K*-means++) being most optimal in terms of the cost function

For sparse matrices, the JSAT implementation is too slow, so it is not suitable for the problem we have. For dense matrices, the results that JSAT implementations produce are comparable to Smile, but it also takes considerably more time.

K-means has a parameter *K*, which is the number of clusters we want to have. Often, it is challenging to come up with a good value of *K*, and next we will look at how to select it.

Choosing K in K-Means

K-means has a drawback: we need to specify the number of clusters *K*. Sometimes *K* can be known from the domain problem we are trying to solve. For example, if we know that there are 10 types of clients, we probably want to look for 10 clusters.

However, often we do not have this kind of domain knowledge. In situations like this, we can use a method often referred as the **elbow method**:

- Try different values of *K*, record the distortion for each
- Plot the distortion for each *K*
- Try to spot the **elbow**, the part of the graph where the error stops dropping rapidly and starts decreasing slowly

You can do it in the following way:

```
PrintWriter out = new PrintWriter("distortion.txt");

for (int k = 3; k < 50; k++) {
    int maxIter = 100;
    int runs = 3;
    KMeans km = new KMeans(proj, k, maxIter, runs);
    out.println(k + "/t" + km.distortion());
}

out.close();
```

Then, you can plot the content of the `distortion.txt` file with your favorite plotting library, and this is the result:

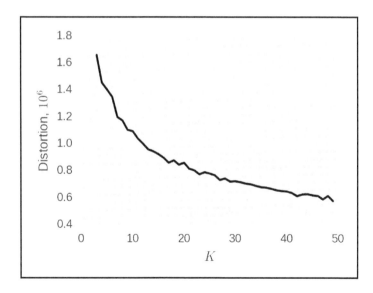

Here, we can see that it drops quickly initially, but then around 15-20 it starts to decrease slower. So we can select *K* from this region, for example, take *K* = 17.

Another solution would be to sample a small amount of data, and then build a dendrogram with hierarchical clustering. By looking at the dendrogram, it may become clear what is the best number of clusters K.

Both of these methods require human judgement and is hard to formalize. But there is another option--ask Machine Learning to choose the best K for us. To do it, we can use X-Means, which is an extension to the K-Means algorithm. X-Means tries to select the best K automatically using the **Bayesian Information Criterion** (**BIC**) score.

Smile already contains an implementation of X-Means, called `XMeans`, and running it is easy as follows:

```
int kmax = 300;
XMeans km = new XMeans(data, kmax);
System.out.println("selected number of clusters: " + km.getNumClusters());
```

This will output the optimal number of clusters according to BIC. JSAT also has an implementation of `XMeans`, and it works similarly.

It is never clear which approach is better, so you may need to try each of them and select the best one for a particular problem.

Apart from Agglomerative Clustering and K-Means, there are other clustering methods, which are also sometimes useful in practice. Next, we now look into one of them - DBSCAN.

DBSCAN

DBSCAN is another clustering quite popular technique. DBSCAN belongs to the density-based family of algorithms, and, unlike K-Means, it does not need to know the number of clusters, K, in advance.

In a few words, DBSCAN works as follows: at each step it takes an item to grow a cluster around it.

When we take an item from a high-density region, then there are many other data points close to the current item, and all these items are added to the cluster. Then the process is repeated for each newly added element of the cluster. If, however, the region is not dense enough, and there are not so many points nearby, then we do not form a cluster and say that this item is an outlier.

So, for DBSCAN to work, we need to provide the following parameters:

- The distance metric for calculating how close two items are
- The minimal number of neighbors within the radius to continue growing the cluster
- The radius around each point

As we can see, we do not need to specify *K* in advance for DBSCAN. Additionally, it naturally handles outliers, which may cause significant problems for methods like *K*-Means. There is an implementation of DBSCAN in Smile and here is how we use it:

```
double[] X = ... // data
EuclideanDistance distance = new EuclideanDistance();
int minPts = 5;
double radius = 1.0;
DBScan<double[]> dbscan = new DBScan<>(X, distance, minPts, radius);

System.out.println(dbscan.getNumClusters());
int[] assignment = dbscan.getClusterLabel();
```

In this code, we specify the following three parameters: distance, the minimum number of points around an item to be considered a cluster, and the radius.

After it is finished, we can get the cluster labels assignment using the `getClusterLabel` method. Since DBSCAN handles outliers, there is a special cluster ID for them, `Integer.MAX_VALUE`.

Agglomerative clustering, *K*-Means, and DBSCAN are one of the most commonly used clustering approaches, and they are useful when we need to group items that share some pattern. However, we can also use clustering for dimensionality reduction, and next we will see how.

Clustering for supervised learning

Like dimensionality reduction, clustering can also be useful for supervised learning.

We will talk about the following cases:

- Clustering as a feature engineering technique for creating extra features
- Clustering as a dimensionality reduction technique
- Clustering as a simple classification or regression method

Clusters as features

Clustering can be seen as a method for feature engineering, and the results of clustering can be added to a supervised model as a set of additional features.

The simplest way of doing it to use one-hot-encoding of clustering results is as follows:

- First, you run a clustering algorithm and as a result, you group the dataset into K clusters
- Then, you represent each datapoint as a cluster to which it belongs using the cluster ID
- Finally, you treat the IDs as a categorical feature and apply One-Hot-Encoding to it.

It looks very simple in code:

```
KMeans km = new KMeans(X, k, maxIter, runs);
int[] labels = km.getClusterLabel();

SparseDataset sparse = new SparseDataset(k);

for (int i = 0; i < labels.length; i++) {
    sparse.set(i, labels[i], 1.0);
}
```

After running it, the sparse object will contain one-hot-encoding of cluster IDs. Next, we can just append it to the existing features and run the usual supervised learning techniques on it.

Clustering as dimensionality reduction

Clustering can be seen as a special kind of dimensionality reduction. For example, if you group your data into K clusters, then you can compress it into K centroids. Once we have done it, each data point can be represented as a vector of distances to each of those centroids. If K is smaller than the dimensionality of your data, it can be seen as a way of reducing the dimensionality.

Let's implement this. First, let's run a K-means on some data. We can use the performance dataset we used previously.

We will use Smile again, and we already know how to run *K*-means. Here is the code:

```
double[][] X = ...; // data
int k = 60;
int maxIter = 10;
int runs = 1;
KMeans km = new KMeans(X, k, maxIter, runs);
```

Once it finishes, it is possible to extract the centroids for each cluster. They are stored in a two dimensional array row-wise:

```
double[][] centroids = km.centroids();
```

This should return a dataset of *K* rows (in our case, *K* = 60) with the number of columns equal to the number of features that we have in the dataset.

Next, for each observation, we can compute how far it is from each centroid. We already discussed how to implement the Euclidean distance efficiently via matrix multiplication, but previously we needed to compute the pair-wise distance between each element of the same set. Now, however, we need to compute the distance between each item from our dataset and each centroid, so we have two sets of data points. We will adapt the code slightly such that it can handle this case.

Recall the formula:

$$\|a - b\|^2 = \|a\|^2 - 2a^T b + \|b\|^2$$

We need to compute the squared norms for each vector individually and then an inner product between all items.

So, if we put all items of each set as rows of two matrices *A* and *B*, then we can use this formula to compute pair-wise distances between the two matrices via matrix multiplication.

First, we compute the norms and the product:

```
double[] squaredA = squareRows(A);
double[] squaredB = squareRows(B);

Array2DRowRealMatrix mA = new Array2DRowRealMatrix(A, false);
Array2DRowRealMatrix mB = new Array2DRowRealMatrix(B, false);
double[][] product = mA.multiply(mB.transpose()).getData();
```

Here, the `squareRows` function computes the squared norm of each row vector of the matrix:

```
public static double[] squareRows(double[][] data) {
    int nrow = data.length;

    double[] squared = new double[nrow];
    for (int i = 0; i < nrow; i++) {
        double[] row = data[i];

        double res = 0.0;
        for (int j = 0; j < row.length; j++) {
            res = res + row[j] * row[j];
        }

        squared[i] = res;
    }

    return squared;
}
```

Now we can use the formula from the preceding code to compute the distances:

```
int nrow = product.length;
int ncol = product[0].length;
double[][] distances = new double[nrow][ncol];
for (int i = 0; i < nrow; i++) {
    for (int j = 0; j < ncol; j++) {
        double dist = squaredA[i] - 2 * product[i][j] + squaredB[j];
        distances[i][j] = Math.sqrt(dist);
    }
}
```

If we wrap this into a function, for example, `distance`, we can use it like this:

```
double[][] centroids = km.centroids();
double[][] distances = distance(X, centroids);
```

Now we can use the distances array instead of the original dataset `X`, for example, like this:

```
OLS model = new OLS(distances, y);
```

Note that it does not necessarily have to be used as a dimensionality reduction technique. Instead, we can use it for engineering extra features, and just add these new features to the existing ones.

Supervised learning via clustering

Unsupervised learning can be used as a model for supervised learning, and depending on the supervised problem we have, it can be either *classification via clustering* or *regression via clustering*.

This approach is relatively straightforward. First, you associate each item with some cluster ID, and then:

- For the binary classification problem, you output the probability of seeing the positive class in the cluster
- For regression, you output the mean value across the cluster

Let's look at how we can do this for regression. At the beginning, we run *K*-means on the original data as usual:

```
int k = 250;
int maxIter = 10;
int runs = 1;

KMeans km = new KMeans(X, k, maxIter, runs);
```

 Often it makes sense to pick a relative large *K*, and the optimal value, as we do usually, should be determined by cross-validation.

Next, we calculate the mean target value for each cluster from the training data. For doing this, we first group by the cluster ID, and then calculate the mean of each group:

```
double[] y = ... // target variable
int[] labels = km.getClusterLabel();

Multimap<Integer, Double> groups = ArrayListMultimap.create();
for (int i = 0; i < labels.length; i++) {
    groups.put(labels[i], y[i]);
}

Map<Integer, Double> meanValue = new HashMap<>();
for (int i = 0; i < k; i++) {
    double mean = groups.get(i).stream()
                        .mapToDouble(d -> d)
                        .average().getAsDouble();
    meanValue.put(i, mean);
}
```

Now, if we want to apply this model to test data, we can do it the following way. First, for each unseen data item, we find the closest cluster ID, and then, using this ID, we look up the mean target value.

In code it looks like this:

```
double[][] testX = ... // test data
double[] testY = ... // test target
int[] testLabels = Arrays.stream(testX).mapToInt(km::predict).toArray();

double[] testPredict = Arrays.stream(testLabels)
                             .mapToDouble(meanValue::get)
                             .toArray();
```

Now, the `testPredict` array contains the prediction for each observation from the test data.

What is more, if instead of regression, you have a binary classification problem, and you keep the labels in array of doubles, the preceding code will output probabilities of belonging to a class based on clustering, without any changes! And the `testPredict` array will contain the predicted probabilities.

Evaluation

The most complex part of unsupervised learning is evaluating the quality of models. It is very hard to objectively tell if a clustering is good or whether one result is better than another.

There are a few ways to approach this:

- Manual evaluation
- Using label information, if present
- Unsupervised metrics

Manual evaluation

Manual evaluation means looking at the results manually and using the domain expertise to assess the quality of clusters and if they make any sense.

The manual check is usually done in the following way:

- For each cluster, we sample the same data points
- Then, we look at them to see if they should belong together or not

When looking at the data, we want to ask ourselves the following questions:

- Do these items look similar?
- Does it make sense to put these items into the same group?

If the answer to both the question is yes, then the clustering results are good. Additionally, the way we sample data is also important. For example, in case of *K*-means, we should sample some items that are close to the centroid, and some items that are far away from it. Then, we can compare the ones that are close with the ones that are far. If we look at them and still can spot some similarities between them, then the clustering is good.

This sort of evaluation always makes sense even if we use other sort of cluster validation techniques, and, if possible, it should be always done to sanity-check the models. For example, if we apply it for customer segregation, we always should manually see if two customers are indeed similar within clusters, otherwise the model results will not be useful.

However, it is clear that this approach is very subjective, not reproducible, and does not scale. Unfortunately, sometimes this is the only good option, and for many problems there is no proper way to evaluate the model quality. Still, for some problems other more automatic methods can provide good results, and next we will look at some such methods.

Supervised evaluation

Manual inspection of the output is always good, but it can be quite cumbersome. Often there is some extra data, which we can use for evaluating the result of our clustering in a more automatic fashion.

For example, if we use clustering for supervised learning, then we have labels. For example, if we solve the classification problem, then we can use the class information to measure how pure (or homogeneous) the discovered clusters are. That is, we can see what is the ratio of the majority class to the rest of the classes within the cluster.

If we take the complaints dataset, there are some variables, which we did not use for clustering, for example:

- **Timely response**: This is a binary variable indicating whether the company responded to the complaint in time or not.

- **Company response to consumer**: This states what kind of response the company gave to the complaint.
- **Consumer disputed**: This states whether the customer agreed with the response or not.

Potentially, we could be interested in predicting any of these variables, so we could use them as an indication of the quality of the clustering.

For example, suppose we are interested in predicting the response of the company. So we perform the clustering:

```
int maxIter = 100;
int runs = 3;
int k = 15;
KMeans km = new KMeans(proj, k, maxIter, runs);
```

And now want to see how useful it is for predicting the response. Let's calculate the ratio of the outcomes within each cluster.

For that we first group by the cluster ID, and then calculate the ratios:

```
int[] assignment = km.getClusterLabel();
List<Object> resp = data.col("company_response_to_consumer");
Multimap<Integer, String> respMap = ArrayListMultimap.create();

for (int i = 0; i < assignment.length; i++) {
    int cluster = assignment[i];
    respMap.put(cluster, resp.get(i).toString());
}
```

Now we can print it, sorting the values within the cluster by the most frequent one:

```
List<Integer> keys = Ordering.natural().sortedCopy(map.keySet());

for (Integer c : keys) {
    System.out.print(c + ": ");

    Collection<String> values = map.get(c);
    Multiset<String> counts = HashMultiset.create(values);
    counts = Multisets.copyHighestCountFirst(counts);

    int totalSize = values.size();
    for (Entry<String> e : counts.entrySet()) {
        double ratio = 1.0 * e.getCount() / totalSize;
        String element = e.getElement();
        System.out.printf("%s=%.3f (%d), ", element, ratio, e.getCount());
    }
}
```

```
    System.out.println();
}
```

This is the output for the first couple of clusters:

```
0: Closed with explanation=0.782 (12383), Closed with non-monetary
relief=0.094 (1495)...
1: Closed with explanation=0.743 (19705), Closed with non-monetary
relief=0.251 (6664)...
2: Closed with explanation=0.673 (18838), Closed with non-monetary
relief=0.305 (8536)...
```

We can see that the clustering is not really *pure:* there's one dominant class and the purity is more or less the same across the clusters. On the other hand, we see that the distribution of classes is different across clusters. For example, in cluster 2, 30% if items are *closed with non-monetary relief*, and in cluster 1, there is only 9% of them.

 Even though the majority class might not be useful by itself, the distribution within each cluster can be useful for a classification model, if we use it as a feature.

This brings us to a different evaluation method; if we use the clustering as a feature engineering technique, we can evaluate the quality of the clustering by how much performance gain it gives, and select the best clustering by picking up the one with the most gain.

This brings us to the next evaluation method. If we use the results of clustering in some supervised settings (say, by using it in as a feature engineering technique), then we can evaluate the quality of the clustering by looking at how much performance it gives.

For example, we have a model that has 85% accuracy without any clustering features. Then we use two different clustering algorithms and extract the features from them, and include them to the model. The features from the first algorithm improve the score by 2%, and the second algorithm gives a 3% improvement. Then, the second algorithm is better.

Finally, there are some special metrics that we can use to assess how good the clustering is with respect to a provided label. One such metric is Rand Index and Mutual Information. These metrics are implemented in JSAT, and you will find them in the `jsat.clustering.evaluation` package.

Unsupervised Evaluation

Lastly, there are unsupervised evaluation scores for assessing the quality of clustering when no labels are known.

We already mentioned one such metric: distortion, which is the sum of distances between each item and its closest centroid. There are other metrics such as:

- Maximal pairwise distance within clusters
- Mean pairwise distance
- Sum of squared pairwise distances

These and some other metrics are also implemented in JSAT and you will find them in the `jsat.clustering.evaluation.intra` package.

Summary

In this chapter, we talked about unsupervised machine learning and about two common unsupervised learning problems, dimensionality reduction and cluster analysis. We covered the most common algorithms from each type, including PCA and K-means. We also covered the existing implementations of these algorithms in Java, and implemented some of them ourselves. Additionally, we touched some important techniques such as SVD, which are very useful in general.

The previous chapter and this chapter have given us quite a lot of information already. With these chapters, we prepared a good foundation to look at how to process textual data with machine learning and data science algorithm--and this is what we will cover in the next chapter.

6
Working with Text - Natural Language Processing and Information Retrieval

In the previous two chapters, we covered the basics of machine learning: we spoke about supervised and unsupervised problems.

In this chapter, we will take a look at how to use these methods for processing textual information, and we will illustrate most of our ideas with our running example: building a search engine. Here, we will finally use the text information from the HTML and include it into the machine learning models.

First, we will start with the basics of natural language processing, and implement some of the basic ideas ourselves, and then look into efficient implementations available in NLP libraries.

This chapter covers the following topics:

- Basics of information retrieval
- Indexing and searching with Apache Lucene
- Basics of natural language processing
- Unsupervised models for texts - dimensionality reduction, clustering, and word embeddings
- Supervised models for texts - text classification and learning to rank

By the end of this chapter you will learn how to do simple text pre-processing for machine learning, how to use Apache Lucene for indexing, how to transform words into vectors, and finally, how to cluster and classify texts.

Natural Language Processing and information retrieval

Natural Language Processing (**NLP**) is a part of computer science and computational linguistics that deals with textual data. To a computer, texts are unstructured, and NLP helps find the structure and extract useful information from them.

Information retrieval (**IR**) is a discipline that studies searching in large unstructured datasets. Typically, these datasets are texts, and the IR systems help users find what they want. Search engines such as Google or Bing are examples of such IR systems: they take in a query and provide a collection of documents ranked according to relevance with respect to the query.

Usually, IR systems use NLP for understanding what the documents are about - so later, when the user needs, these documents can be retrieved. In this chapter, we will go over the basics of text processing for information retrieval.

Vector Space Model - Bag of Words and TF-IDF

For a computer, a text is just a string of characters with no particular structure imposed on it. Hence, we call texts **unstructured data**. However, to humans, texts certainly has a structure, which we use to understand the content. What IR and NLP models try to do is similar: they find the structure in texts, use it to extract the information there, and understand what the text is about.

The simplest possible way of achieving it is called **Bag of Words**: we take a text, split it into individual words (which we call **tokens**), and then represent the text as an unordered collection of tokens along with some weights associated with each token.

Let us consider an example. If we take a document, that consists of one sentence (*we use Java for Data Science because we like Java*), it can be represented as follows:

```
(because, 1), (data, 1), (for, 1), (java, 2), (science, 1), (use, 1), (we, 2)
```

Here, each word from the sentence is weighted by the number of times the word occurs there.

Now, when we are able to represent documents in such a way, we can use it for comparing one document to another.

For example, if we take another sentence such as *Java is good enterprise development*, we can represent it as follows:

```
(development, 1), (enterprise, 1), (for, 1), (good, 1), (java, 1)
```

We can see that there is some intersection between these two documents, which may mean that these two documents are similar, and the higher the intersection, the more similar the documents are.

Now, if we think of words as dimensions in some vector space, and weights as the values for these dimensions, then we can represent documents as vectors:

	because	data	development	enterprise	for	good	is	java	science	use	we
doc1	1	1			1			1	1	1	2
doc2			1	1	1	1	1	1			

If we take this vectorial representation, we can use the inner product between two vectors as a measure of similarity. Indeed, if two documents have a lot of common words, the inner product between them will be high, and if they share no documents, the inner product is zero.

This idea is called **Vector Space Model**, and this is what is used in many information retrieval systems: all documents as well as the user queries are represented as vectors. Once the query and the documents are in the same space, we can think of similarity between a query and a document as the relevance between them. So, we sort the documents by their similarity to the user query.

Going from raw text to a vector involves a few steps. Usually, they are as follows:

- First, we tokenize the text, that is, convert it into a collection of individual tokens.
- Then, we remove function words such as is, will, to, and others. They are often used for linking purposes only and do not carry any significant meaning. These words are called stop words.
- Sometimes we also convert tokens to some normal form. For example, we may want to map cat and cats to cat because the concept is the same behind these two different words. This is achieved through stemming or lemmatization.
- Finally, we compute the weight of each token and put them into the vector space.

Previously, we used the number of occurrences for weighting terms; this is called Term Frequency weighting. However, some words are more important than others and Term Frequency does not always capture that.

For example, *hammer* can be more important than *tool* because it is more specific. Inverse Document Frequency is a different weighting scheme that penalizes general words and favors specific ones. Inside, it is based on the number of documents that contain the term, and the idea is that more specific terms occur in fewer documents than general ones.

Finally, there is a combination of both Term Frequency and Inverse Document Frequency, which is abbreviated as TF-IDF. As the name suggests, the weight for the token t consists of two parts: TF and IDF:

```
weight(t) = tf(t) * idf(t)
```

Here is an explanation of the terms mentioned in the preceding equation:

- `tf(t)`: This is a function on the number of times the token t occurs in the text
- `idf(t)`: This is a function on the number of documents that contain the token

There are multiple ways to define these functions, but, most commonly, the following definitions are used:

- `tf(t)`: This is the number of times t occurs in the document
- `idf(t) = log(N / df(t))`: Here, `df(t)` is the number of documents, which contain t, and N - the total number of documents

Previously, we suggested that we can use the inner product for measuring the similarity between documents. There is a problem with this approach: it is unbounded, which means that it can take any positive value, and this makes it harder to interpret. Additionally, longer documents will tend to have higher similarity with everything else just because they contain more words.

The solution to this problem is to normalize the weights inside a vector such that its norm becomes 1. Then, computing the inner product will always result in a bounded value between 0 and 1, and longer documents will have less influence. The inner product between normalized vectors is usually called *cosine similarity* because it corresponds to the cosine of the angle that these two vectors form in the vector space.

Vector space model implementation

Now we have enough background information and are ready to proceed to the code.

First, suppose that we have a text file where each line is a document, and we want to index the content of this file and be able to query it. For example, we can take some text from `http s://ocw.mit.edu/ans7870/6/6.006/s08/lecturenotes/files/t8.shakespeare.txt` and save it to `simple-text.txt`.

Then we can read it this way:

```
Path path = Paths.get("data/simple-text.txt");
List<List<String>> documents = Files.lines(path, StandardCharsets.UTF_8)
    .map(line -> TextUtils.tokenize(line))
    .map(line -> TextUtils.removeStopwords(line))
    .collect(Collectors.toList());
```

We use the `Files` class from the standard library, and then use two functions:

- The first one, `TextUtils.tokenize`, takes a String and produces a list of tokens
- The second one, `TextUtils.removeStopwords`, removes the functional words such as a, the, and so on

A simple and naive way to implement tokenization is to split a string based on a regular expression:

```
public static List<String> tokenize(String line) {
    Pattern pattern = Pattern.compile("\W+");
    String[] split = pattern.split(line.toLowerCase());
    return Arrays.stream(split)
            .map(String::trim)
            .filter(s -> s.length() > 2)
            .collect(Collectors.toList());
}
```

The expression `\W+` means split the String on everything that is not a Latin character. Of course, it will fail to handle languages with non-Latin characters, but it is a fast way to implement tokenization. Also, it works quite well for English, and can be adapted to handle other European languages.

Another thing here is throwing away short tokens smaller than two characters - these tokens are often stopwords, so it is safe to discard them. The second function takes a list of tokens and removes all stopwords from it. Here is its implementation:

```
Set<String> EN_STOPWORDS = ImmutableSet.of("a", "an", "and", "are", "as",
"at", "be", ...
```

```
public static List<String> removeStopwords(List<String> line) {
    return line.stream()
            .filter(token -> !EN_STOPWORDS.contains(token))
            .collect(Collectors.toList());
}
```

It is pretty straightforward: we keep a set of English stopwords and then for each token we just check if it is in this set or not. You can get a good list of English stopwords from `http ://www.ranks.nl/stopwords`.

It is also quite easy to add token normalization to this pipeline. For now, we will skip it, but we will come back to it later in this chapter.

Now we have tokenized the texts, so the next step is to represent the tokens in the vector space. Let's create a special class for it. We will call it `CountVectorizer`.

 The name `CountVectorizer` is inspired by a class with similar functionality from scikit-learn - an excellent package for doing machine learning in Python. If you are familiar with the library, you may notice that we sometimes borrow the names from there (such as names `fit()` and `transform()` for methods).

Since we cannot directly create a vector space whose dimensions are indexed by words, we will first map all distinct tokens from all the texts to some column number.

Also, it makes sense to calculate the document frequency at this step, and use it to discard tokens that appear only in a few documents. Often, such terms are misspellings, non-existing words, or too infrequent to have any impact on the results.

In code it looks like this:

```
Multiset<String> df = HashMultiset.create();
documents.forEach(list -> df.addAll(Sets.newHashSet(list)));
Multiset<String> docFrequency = Multisets.filter(df, p -> df.count(p) >=
minDf);

List<String> vocabulary =
Ordering.natural().sortedCopy(docFrequency.elementSet());
Map<String, Integer> tokenToIndex = new HashMap<>(vocabulary.size());

for (int i = 0; i < vocabulary.size(); i++) {
    tokenToIndex.put(vocabulary.get(i), i);
}
```

We use a `Multiset` from Guava to count document frequency, then we apply the filtering, with `minDf` being a parameter, which specifies the minimal document frequency. After discarding infrequent tokens, we associate a column number with each remaining one, and put this to a `Map`.

Now we can use the document frequencies to calculate IDF:

```
int numDocuments = documents.size();
double numDocumentsLog = Math.log(numDocuments + 1);
double[] idfs = new double[vocabulary.size()];

for (Entry<String> e : docFrequency.entrySet()) {
    String token = e.getElement();
    double idfValue = numDocumentsLog - Math.log(e.getCount() + 1);
    idfs[tokenToIndex.get(token)] = idfValue;
}
```

After executing it, the `idfs` array will contain the IDF part of the weight for all the tokens in our vocabulary.

Now we are ready to put the tokenized documents into a vector space:

```
int ncol = vocabulary.size();
SparseDataset tfidf = new SparseDataset(ncol);

for (int rowNo = 0; rowNo < documents.size(); rowNo++) {
    List<String> doc = documents.get(rowNo);
    Multiset<String> row = HashMultiset.create(doc);
    for (Entry<String> e : row.entrySet()) {
        String token = e.getElement();
        double tf = e.getCount();
        int colNo = tokenToIndex.get(token);
        double idf = idfs[colNo];
        tfidf.set(rowNo, colNo, tf * idf);
    }
}

tfidf.unitize();
```

Since the resulting vectors are very sparse, we use `SparseDataset` from Smile to store them. Then, for each token in a document, we compute its TF and multiply it by IDF to get the TF-IDF weights.

The last line in the code applies the length normalization to the document vectors. With this, computing the inner product between vectors will result in the Cosine Similarity score, which is a bounded value between 0 and 1.

Now, let's put the code into a class, so we can reuse it afterwards:

```
public class CountVectorizer {
    void fit(List<List<String>> documents);
    SparseDataset tranform(List<List<String>> documents);
}
```

The functions we define does the following:

- `fit` creates the mapping from tokens to column numbers and calculates the IDF
- `transform` converts a collection of documents into a sparse matrix
- The constructor should take `minDf`, which specifies the minimal document frequency for a token.

Now we can use it for vectorizing our dataset:

```
List<List<String>> documents = Files.lines(path, StandardCharsets.UTF_8)
        .map(line -> TextUtils.tokenize(line))
        .map(line -> TextUtils.removeStopwords(line))
        .collect(Collectors.toList());

int minDf = 5;
CountVectorizer cv = new CountVectorizer(minDf);
cv.fit(documents);
SparseDataset docVectors = cv.transform(documents);
```

Now imagine that we, as users, want to query this collection of documents. To be able to do it, we need to implement the following:

1. First, represent a query in the same vector space: that is, apply the exact same procedure (tokenization, stopwords removal, and so on) to the documents.
2. Then, compute the similarity between the query and each document.
3. Finally, rank the documents using the similarity score, from largest to lowest.

Suppose our query is `the probabilistic interpretation of tf-idf`. Then, map it into the vector space in a similar way:

```
List<String> query = TextUtils.tokenize("the probabilistic interpretation
of tf-idf");
query = TextUtils.removeStopwords(query);
SparseDataset queryMatrix =
vectorizer.transfrom(Collections.singletonList(query));
SparseArray queryVector = queryMatrix.get(0).x;
```

The method we created previously accepts a collection of documents, rather than a single document, so first we wrap it into a list, and then get the first row of the matrix with results.

What we have now is `docVector`, which is a sparse matrix containing our collection of documents, and `queryVector`, a sparse vector containing the query. With this, getting similarities is easy: we just need to multiply the matrix with the vector and the result will contain the similarity scores.

As in the previous chapter, we will make use of **Matrix Java Toolkit** (**MTJ**) for that. Since we are doing matrix-vector multiplication, with the matrix being on the left side, the best way of storing the values is the row-based representation. We already wrote a utility method for converting `SparseDataset` from Smile into `CompRowMatrix` from MTJ.

Here it is again:

```
public static CompRowMatrix asRowMatrix(SparseDataset dataset) {
    int ncols = dataset.ncols();
    int nrows = dataset.size();

    FlexCompRowMatrix X = new FlexCompRowMatrix(nrows, ncols);
    SparseArray[] array = dataset.toArray(new SparseArray[0]);

    for (int rowIdx = 0; rowIdx < array.length; rowIdx++) {
        Iterator<Entry> row = array[rowIdx].iterator();
        while (row.hasNext()) {
            Entry entry = row.next();
            X.set(rowIdx, entry.i, entry.x);
        }
    }

    return new CompRowMatrix(X);
}
```

Now we also need to convert a `SparseArray` object into a `SparseVector` object from MTJ.

Let's also create a method for that:

```
public static SparseVector asSparseVector(int dim, SparseArray vector) {
    int size = vector.size();
    int[] indexes = new int[size];
    double[] values = new double[size];

    Iterator<Entry> iterator = vector.iterator();
    int idx = 0;

    while (iterator.hasNext()) {
        Entry entry = iterator.next();
```

```
        indexes[idx] = entry.i;
        values[idx] = entry.x;
        idx++;
    }

    return new SparseVector(dim, indexes, values, false);
}
```

Note that we also have to pass the dimensionality of the resulting vector to this method. This is due to a limitation of `SparseArray`, which does not store information about it.

Now we can use these methods for computing the similarities:

```
CompRowMatrix X = asRowMatrix(docVectors);
SparseVector v = asSparseVector(docVectors.ncols(), queryVector);
DenseVector result = new DenseVector(X.numRows());
X.mult(v, result);
double[] scores = result.getData();
```

The scores array now contains the cosine similarity scores of the query to each of the documents. The index of this array corresponds to the index of the original document collection. That is, to see the similarity between the query and the 10th document, we look at the 10th element of the array. So, we need to sort the array by the score, while keeping the original indexes.

Let's first create a class for it:

```
public class ScoredIndex implements Comparable<ScoredIndex> {
    private final int index;
    private final double score;

    // constructor and getters omitted

    @Override
    public int compareTo(ScoredIndex that) {
        return -Double.compare(this.score, that.score);
    }
}
```

This class implements the `Comparable` interface, so now we can put all objects of this class into a collection, and then sort it. At the end, the first elements in the collection will have the highest score. Let's do that:

```
double minScore = 0.2;
List<ScoredIndex> scored = new ArrayList<>(scores.length);

for (int idx = 0; idx < scores.length; idx++) {
```

```
    double score = scores[idx];
    if (score >= minScore) {
        scored.add(new ScoredIndex(idx, score));
    }
}

Collections.sort(scored);
```

We also add a similarity threshold of 0.2 to sort fewer elements: we assume that the elements below this score are not relevant, so we just ignore them.

Finally, we can just iterate over the results and see the most relevant documents:

```
for (ScoredIndex doc : scored) {
    System.out.printf("> %.4f ", doc.getScore());
    List<String> document = documents.get(doc.getIndex());
    System.out.println(String.join(" ", document));
}
```

With this, we implemented a simple IR system ourselves, entirely from scratch. However, the implementation is quite naive. In reality, there are a quite a lot of document candidates, so it is not feasible to compute the cosine similarity of a query with every one of them. There is a special data structure called inverted index, which can be used for solving the problem, and now we will look into one of its implementations: Apache Lucene.

Indexing and Apache Lucene

Previously, we looked at how to implement a simple search engine, but it will not scale well with the number of documents.

First of all, it requires a comparison of the query with each and every document in our collection, and it becomes very time-consuming as it grows. Most of the documents, however, are not relevant to the query, and only a small fraction are. We can safely assume that, if a document is relevant to a query, it should contain at least one word from it. This is the idea behind the Inverted Index data structure: for each word it keeps track of the documents that contain it. When a query is given, it can quickly find the documents that have at least one term from it.

There also is a memory problem: at some point, the documents will no longer fit into memory, and we need to be able to store them on disk and retrieve, when needed.

Apache Lucene solves these problems: it implements a persistent Inverted Index, which is very efficient in terms of both speed and storage, and it is highly optimized and time-proven. In `Chapter 2`, *Data Processing Toolbox* we collected some raw HTML data, so let's use Lucene to build an index for it.

First, we need to include the library to our pom:

```
<dependency>
    <groupId>org.apache.lucene</groupId>
    <artifactId>lucene-core</artifactId>
    <version>6.2.1</version>
</dependency>
<dependency>
    <groupId>org.apache.lucene</groupId>
    <artifactId>lucene-analyzers-common</artifactId>
    <version>6.2.1</version>
</dependency>
<dependency>
    <groupId>org.apache.lucene</groupId>
    <artifactId>lucene-queryparser</artifactId>
    <version>6.2.1</version>
</dependency>
```

Lucene is very modular and it is possible to include only things we need. In our case this is:

- The `core` package: We always need it when using Lucene
- The `analyzers-common` module: This contains common classes for text processing
- The `queryparser`: This is the module used for parsing the query

Lucene provides several types of indexes, including in-memory and filesystem ones. We will use the filesystem one:

```
File index = new File(INDEX_PATH);
FSDirectory directory = FSDirectory.open(index.toPath());
```

Next, we need to define an Analyzer: this is a class that does all the text processing steps, including tokenization, stopwords removal, and normalization.

`StandardAnalyzer` is a basic `Analyzer`, that removes some English stopwords, but does not perform any stemming or lemmatization. It works quite well for English texts, so let's use it for building the index:

```
StandardAnalyzer analyzer = new StandardAnalyzer();
IndexWriter writer = new IndexWriter(directory, new
IndexWriterConfig(analyzer))
```

Now we are ready to index the documents!

Let's take the URLs we crawled through previously and index their content:

```
UrlRepository urls = new UrlRepository();
Path path = Paths.get("data/search-results.txt");
List<String> lines =
        FileUtils.readLines(path.toFile(), StandardCharsets.UTF_8);

for (String line : lines) {
    String[] split = line.split("t");
    String url = split[3];
    Optional<String> html = urls.get(url);
    if (!html.isPresent()) {
        continue;
    }

    org.jsoup.nodes.Document jsoupDoc = Jsoup.parse(html.get());
    Element body = jsoupDoc.body();
    if (body == null) {
        continue;
    }

    Document doc = new Document();
    doc.add(new Field("url", url, URL_FIELD));
    doc.add(new Field("title", jsoupDoc.title(), URL_FIELD));
    doc.add(new Field("content", body.text(), BODY_FIELD));
    writer.addDocument(doc);
}

writer.commit();
writer.close();
directory.close();
```

Let's have a closer look at some things here. First, `UrlRepository` is a class that stores the scraped HTML content for some URLs we created in the Chapter 2, *Data Processing Toolbox*. Given a URL, it returns an `Optional` object, which contains the response if the repository has the data for it; and otherwise it returns an empty `Optional`.

Then we parse the raw HTML with JSoup and extract the title and the text of the body. Now we have the text data, which we put into a Lucene `Document`.

A `Document` in Lucene consists of fields, with each `Field` object storing some information about the document. A `Field` has some properties, such as:

- Whether we store the value in the index or not. If we do, then later we can extract the content.

- Whether we index the value or not. If it is indexed, then it becomes searchable and we can query it.
- Whether it is analyzed or not. If it is, we apply the Analyzer to the content, so we can query individual tokens. Otherwise only the exact match is possible.

These and other properties are kept in the `FieldType` objects.

For example, here is how we specify the properties for `URL_FIELD`:

```
FieldType field = new FieldType();
field.setTokenized(false);
field.setStored(true);
field.freeze();
```

Here we say that we do not want to tokenize it, but want to store the value in the index. The `freeze()` method ensures that once we specify the properties, they no longer can be changed.

And here is how we specify `BODY_FIELD`:

```
FieldType field = new FieldType();
field.setStored(false);
field.setTokenized(true);
field.setIndexOptions(IndexOptions.DOCS_AND_FREQS);
field.freeze();
```

In this case, we only analyze it, but do not store the exact content of the field. This way it is still possible to query it, but since the content is not stored, the field takes less space in the index.

It quite quickly processes our dataset, and after executing it creates an index in the filesystem, which we can query. Let's do it.

```
String userQuery = "cheap used cars";

File index = new File(INDEX_PATH);
FSDirectory directory = FSDirectory.open(index.toPath());
DirectoryReader reader = DirectoryReader.open(directory);
IndexSearcher searcher = new IndexSearcher(reader);

StandardAnalyzer analyzer = new StandardAnalyzer();
AnalyzingQueryParser parser = new AnalyzingQueryParser("content",
analyzer);
Query query = parser.parse(userQuery);

TopDocs result = searcher.search(query, 10);
```

```
ScoreDoc[] scoreDocs = result.scoreDocs;

for (ScoreDoc scored : scoreDocs) {
    int docId = scored.doc;
    float luceneScore = scored.score;
    Document doc = searcher.doc(docId);
    System.out.println(luceneScore + " " + doc.get("url") + " " +
doc.get("title"));
}
```

In this code, we first open the index, then specify the analyzer for processing the query. Using this analyzer, we parse the query, and use the parsed query to extract the top 10 matching documents from the index. We stored the URL and the title, so now we can retrieve this information during the query time and present it to the user.

Natural Language Processing tools

Natural language processing is a field of computer science and computational linguistics that deals with processing texts. As we saw previously, information retrieval uses simple NLP techniques for indexing and retrieving textual information.

But NLP can do more. There are quite a few major NLP tasks, such as text summarization or machine translation, but we will not cover them and only talk about the basic ones:

- **Sentence Splitting**: Given text, we split it into sentences
- **Tokenization:** Given a sentence, split it into individual tokens
- **Lemmatization:** Given a token, we want to find its lemma. For example, for the words *cat* and *cats* the lemma is *cat*.
- **Part-of-Speech tagging (POS Tagging)**: Given a sequence of tokens, the goal is to determine what is the part-of-speech tag for each of them. For example, it means associating a tag VERB with a token like, or a tag NOUN with a token laptop.
- **Named Entity Recognition (NER)**: In a sequence of tokens, find those that correspond to named entities such as cities, countries, and other geographical names, people names, and so on. For example, it should tag Paul McCartney as a person's name, and Germany as a country name.

Let's have a look at one of the libraries that implement these basic methods: Stanford CoreNLP.

Stanford CoreNLP

There are quite a lot of mature NLP libraries in Java. For example, Stanford CoreNLP, OpenNLP, and GATE. Many libraries that we have previously covered have some NLP modules, for example, Smile or JSAT.

In this chapter, we will use Stanford CoreNLP. There is no particular reason, and it should be possible to reproduce the examples in any other library if needed.

Let's start by specifying the following dependencies in our `pom.xml`:

```
<dependency>
  <groupId>edu.stanford.nlp</groupId>
  <artifactId>stanford-corenlp</artifactId>
  <version>3.6.0</version>
</dependency>
<dependency>
  <groupId>edu.stanford.nlp</groupId>
  <artifactId>stanford-corenlp</artifactId>
  <version>3.6.0</version>
  <classifier>models</classifier>
</dependency>
```

There are two dependencies: the first one is for the NLP package itself, and the second one contains the models used by the first module. These models are for English, but there also exist models for other European languages such as German or Spanish.

The main abstraction here is a StanfordCoreNLP class, which acts as a processing pipeline. Inside it specifies a sequence of steps that are applied to the raw text.

Consider the following example:

```
Properties props = new Properties();
props.put("annotators", "tokenize, ssplit, pos, lemma");
StanfordCoreNLP pipeline = new StanfordCoreNLP(props);
```

Here we create a pipeline that takes text, tokenizes it, splits it into sentences, applies the POS model to each token, and then finds its lemma.

This is how we can use it:

```
String text = "some text";

Annotation document = new Annotation(text);
pipeline.annotate(document);
List<Word> results = new ArrayList<>();
```

```
List<CoreLabel> tokens = document.get(TokensAnnotation.class);
for (CoreLabel tokensInfo : tokens) {
    String token = tokensInfo.get(TextAnnotation.class);
    String lemma = tokensInfo.get(LemmaAnnotation.class);
    String pos = tokensInfo.get(PartOfSpeechAnnotation.class);
    results.add(new Word(token, lemma, pos));
}
```

In this code, `Word` is our class, which holds the information about tokens: the surface form (the form which appears in the text), the lemma (the normalized form) and the part of speech.

It is easy to modify the pipeline to add extra steps. For example, if we wish to add NER, then what we do is first we add `NER` to the pipeline:

```
Properties props = new Properties();
props.put("annotators", "tokenize, ssplit, pos, lemma, ner");
StanfordCoreNLP pipeline = new StanfordCoreNLP(props);
```

And then, for each token, extract the associated `NER` tag:

```
String ner = tokensInfo.get(NamedEntityTagAnnotation.class);
```

Still, the preceding code needs some manual cleaning; if we run this, we may notice that it also outputs punctuation and the stopwords. It is easy to fix by adding a few extra checks in the loop:

```
for (CoreLabel tokensInfo : tokens) {
    String token = tokensInfo.get(TextAnnotation.class);
    String lemma = tokensInfo.get(LemmaAnnotation.class);
    String pos = tokensInfo.get(PartOfSpeechAnnotation.class);
    String ner = tokensInfo.get(NamedEntityTagAnnotation.class);

    if (isPunctuation(token) || isStopword(token)) {
        continue;
    }

    results.add(new Word(token, lemma, pos, ner));
}
```

Implementation of the `isStopword` method is easy: we simply check whether the token is in the set of stopwords or not. Checking for punctuation is also not difficult:

```
public static boolean isPunctuation(String token) {
    char first = token.charAt(0);
    return !Character.isAlphabetic(first) && !Character.isDigit(first);
}
```

We just verify that the first character of the String is not alphabetic and not a digit. If it is the case, then it must be a punctuation.

There is another issue with NER, which we might want to fix: it does not concatenate consecutive words of the same class into one token. Consider this example: *My name is Justin Bieber, and I live in New York.* It will produce the following NER tag assignment:

- Justin -> Person
- Bieber -> Person
- New -> Location
- York -> Location
- Other tokens are mapped to O

We can join consecutive tokens labeled with the same NER tag with the following code snippet:

```
String prevNer = "O";

List<List<Word>> groups = new ArrayList<>();
List<Word> group = new ArrayList<>();

for (Word w : words) {
    String ner = w.getNer();
    if (prevNer.equals(ner) && !"O".equals(ner)) {
        group.add(w);
        continue;
    }

    groups.add(group);
    group = new ArrayList<>();
    group.add(w);

    prevNer = ner;
}

groups.add(group);
```

So we simply go through the sequence and see if the current tag is the same as previous tag or not. If it is the case, then we stop one group and start the next one. If we see O, then we always assume it's the next group. After that, we just need to filter empty groups and join the text fields into one, if needed.

While it does not seem a big deal for persons, it may be important for geographical names like New York: these tokens together have an entirely different meaning from separate tokens New and York, so treating them as a single token may be useful for IR systems.

Next, we will see how we can leverage NLP tools such as Stanford CoreNLP in Apache Lucene.

Customizing Apache Lucene

Apache Lucene is an old and very powerful search library. It was written back in 1999, and since then a lot of users not only have adopted it but also created many different extensions for this library.

Still, sometimes the built-in NLP capabilities of Lucene are not enough, and a specialized NLP library is needed.

For example, if we would like to include POS tags along with tokens, or find Named Entities, then we need something such as Stanford CoreNLP. It is not very difficult to include such external specialized NLP libraries in the Lucene workflow, and here we will see how to do it.

Let's use the StanfordNLP library and the tokenizer we have implemented in the previous section. We can call it `StanfordNlpTokenizer`, with one method `tokenize`, where we will put the code for tokenization we previously wrote.

We can use this class to tokenize the content of the crawled HTML data. As we did previously, we extract the text from HTML using JSoup, but now, instead of putting the title and the body directly to the document, we first preprocess it ourselves using the CoreNLP pipeline. We can do it by creating the following utility method, and then using it for tokenizing the title and the body:

```
public static String tokenize(StanfordNlpTokenizer tokenizer, String text)
{
    List<Word> tokens = tokenizer.tokenize(text);
    return tokens.stream()
                .map(Word::getLemma)
                .map(String::toLowerCase)
                .collect(Collectors.joining(" "));
}
```

Note that here we use the lemma, not the token itself, and at the end we again put everything back together to a String.

With this modification, we can use `WhitespaceAnalyzer` from Lucene. As opposed to `StandardAnalyzer`, it is very simple and all it does is split the text by a whitespace character. In our case, the String is already prepared and processed by CoreNLP, so Lucene indexes the content in the desired form.

The full modified version will look like this:

```
Analyzer analyzer = new WhitespaceAnalyzer();
IndexWriter writer =
        new IndexWriter(directory, new IndexWriterConfig(analyzer));
StanfordNlpTokenizer tokenizer = new StanfordNlpTokenizer();

for (String line : lines) {
    String[] split = line.split("t");
    String url = split[3];
    Optional<String> html = urls.get(url);
    if (!html.isPresent()) {
        continue;
    }

    org.jsoup.nodes.Document jsoupDoc = Jsoup.parse(html.get());
    Element body = jsoupDoc.body();
    if (body == null) {
        continue;
    }

    String titleTokens = tokenize(tokenizer, jsoupDoc.title());
    String bodyTokens = tokenize(tokenizer, body.text());

    Document doc = new Document();
    doc.add(new Field("url", url, URL_FIELD));
    doc.add(new Field("title", titleTokens, URL_FIELD));
    doc.add(new Field("content", bodyTokens, BODY_FIELD));
    writer.addDocument(doc);
}
```

 It is possible to use Lucene's `StandardAnalyzer` for some fields, and `WhitespaceAnalyzer` with customized preprocessing for others. For that, we need to use `PerFieldAnalyzerWrapper`, where we can specify a specific `Analyzer` for each field.

This gives us a lot of flexibility in how we preprocess and analyze texts, but it does not let us change the ranking formula: the formula which Lucene uses for ordering the documents. Later in this chapter, we will also see how to do this, but first we will look at how to use machine learning in text analysis.

Machine learning for texts

Machine learning plays an important role in text processing. It allows to better understand the information hidden in the text, and extract the useful knowledge hidden there. We are already familiar with machine learning models from the previous chapters, and, in fact, we have even used some of them for texts already, for example, POS tagger and NER from Stanford CoreNLP are all machine learning based models.

In `Chapters 4`, *Supervised Learning - Clasfication and Regression* and `Chapter 5`, *Unsupervised Learning - Clustering and Dimensionality Reduction* we covered supervised and unsupervised machine learning problems. When it comes to text, both play an important role in helping to organize the texts or extract useful pieces of information. In this section, we will see how to apply them to text data.

Unsupervised learning for texts

As we know, unsupervised machine learning deals with cases when no information about labels is provided. For texts, it means just letting it process a lot of text data with no extra information about the content. Still, it often may be useful, and now we will see how to use both dimensionality reduction and clustering for texts.

Latent Semantic Analysis

Latent Semantic Analysis (**LSA**), also known as **Latent Semantic Indexing** (**LSI**), is an application of unsupervised dimensionality reduction techniques to textual data.

The problems that LSA tries to solve are the problems of:

- Synonymy: This means multiple words having the same meaning
- Polysemy: This means one word having multiple meanings

Shallow term-based techniques such as Bag of Words cannot solve these problems because they only look at the exact raw form of terms. For instance, words such as help and assist will be assigned to different dimensions of the Vector Space, even though they are very close semantically.

To solve these problems, LSA moves the documents from the usual Bag of Words Vector Space to some other Semantic Space, in which words, close in meaning, correspond to the same dimension, and the values of polysemous words are split across dimensions.

This is achieved by looking at the term-term co-occurrence matrix. The assumption is the following: if two words are often used in the same context, then they are synonymous, and vice versa, if a word is polysemous, it will be used in different contexts. Dimensionality reduction techniques can detect such co-occurrence patterns, and compress them into a vector space of smaller dimensions.

One such Dimensionality Reduction technique is **Singular Value Decomposition (SVD)**. If X is a document-term matrix, such as the matrix we get from our `CountVectorizer`, then the SVD of X is:

$$XV = US$$

The terms in the preceding equation are explained as follows:

- V is the basis for terms that is computed on the term-term co-occurrence matrix X^TX
- U is the basis for documents that is computed on the document-document co-occurrence matrix XX^T

So, by applying a Truncated SVD to X, we reduce the dimensionality of a term-term co-occurrence matrix X^TX, and then can use this new reduced basis V for representing our documents.

Our document matrix is stored in `SparseDataset`. If you remember, we have already used SVD on such objects: first, we transformed the SparseDataset into a column-based `SparseMatrix`, and then applied the SVD to it:

```
SparseMatrix matrix = data.toSparseMatrix();
SingularValueDecomposition svd =
SingularValueDecomposition.decompose(matrix, n);
double[][] termBasis = svd.getV();
```

And then the next step is to project our matrix onto this new term basis. We already did this in the previous chapter using the following method:

```
public static double[][] project(SparseDataset dataset, double[][] Vd) {
    CompRowMatrix X = asRowMatrix(dataset);
    DenseMatrix V = new DenseMatrix(Vd);
    DenseMatrix XV = new DenseMatrix(X.numRows(), V.numColumns());
    X.mult(V, XV);
    return to2d(XV);
}
```

Here, `asRowMatrix` converts the `SparseDataset` into a `CompRowMatrix` from MTJ, and `to2d` converts the dense matrix from MTJ to a two-dimensional array of doubles.

Once we project the original data into the LSA space, it is no longer normalized. We can fix that by implementing the following method:

```
public static double[][] l2RowNormalize(double[][] data) {
    for (int i = 0; i < data.length; i++) {
        double[] row = data[i];
        ArrayRealVector vector = new ArrayRealVector(row, false);
        double norm = vector.getNorm();
        if (norm != 0) {
            vector.mapDivideToSelf(norm);
            data[i] = vector.getDataRef();
        }
    }

    return data;
}
```

Here, we apply length normalization to each row of the input matrix, and for that we use `ArrayRealVector` from Apache Commons Math.

For convenience, we can create a special class for LSA. Let's call it `TruncatedSVD`, which will have the following signature:

```
public class TruncatedSVD {
    void fit(SparseDataset data);
    double[][] transform(SparseDataset data);
}
```

It has the following methods:

- `fit` learns the new basis for term
- `transform` reduces the dimensionality of the data by projecting it into the learned basis
- The constructor should have two parameters: n, the desired dimensionality and whether the result should be normalized or not

We can apply LSA to our IR system: now, instead of the cosine similarity in the Bag of Words space, we go to the LSA space and compute the cosine there. For this, we first need to map documents to this space during the indexing time, and later, during the query time, we perform the same transformation on the user queries. Then, computing the cosine is just a matrix multiplication.

So, let's first take the code we used previously:

```
List<List<String>> documents = Files.lines(path, StandardCharsets.UTF_8)
        .map(line -> TextUtils.tokenize(line))
        .map(line -> TextUtils.removeStopwords(line))
        .collect(Collectors.toList());

int minDf = 5;
CountVectorizer cv = new CountVectorizer(minDf);
cv.fit(documents);
SparseDataset docVectors = cv.transform(documents);
```

Now, we map `docVectors` to the LSA space using the `TruncatedSVD` class we just created:

```
int n = 150;
boolean normalize = true;
TruncatedSVD svd = new TruncatedSVD(n, normalize);
svd.fit(docVectors);
double[][] docsLsa = svd.transform(docVectors);
```

And we repeat the same with the query:

```
List<String> query = TextUtils.tokenize("cheap used cars");
query = TextUtils.removeStopwords(query);
SparseDataset queryVectors =
vectorizer.transfrom(Collections.singletonList(query));
double[] queryLsa = svd.transform(queryVectors)[0];
```

Like previously, we wrap the query into a list, and then extract the first row of the result. Here, however, we have a dense vector, not sparse. Now, what is left is computing the similarity, which is just a matrix-vector multiplication:

```
DenseMatrix X = new DenseMatrix(docsLsa);
DenseVector v = new DenseVector(vector);
DenseVector result = new DenseVector(X.numRows());
X.mult(v, result);
double[] scores = result.getData();
```

After executing it, the scores array will contain the similarities, and we can use the ScoredIndex class for ordering the documents by this score. This is quite useful, so let's put this into a utility method:

```
public static List<ScoredIndex> wrapAsScoredIndex(double[] scores, double
minScore) {
    List<ScoredIndex> scored = new ArrayList<>(scores.length);

    for (int idx = 0; idx < scores.length; idx++) {
        double score = scores[idx];
```

```
        if (score >= minScore) {
            scored.add(new ScoredIndex(idx, score));
        }
    }

    Collections.sort(scored);
    return scored;
}
```

Finally, we take the first elements from the list and present them to the user, like we did previously.

Text clustering

In `Chapter 5`, *Unsupervised Learning - Clustering and Dimensionality Reduction*, we covered dimensionality reduction and clustering. We already discussed how to use dimensionality reduction for texts, but have not yet spoken about clustering.

Text clustering is also a useful technique for understanding what is a collection of documents. When we want to cluster texts, the goal is similar to non-text cases: we want to find groups of documents such that they have a lot in common: for example, the documents within such group should be on the same topic. In some cases, this can be useful for IR systems. For example, if a topic is ambiguous, we may want to group the search engine results.

K-means is a simple, yet powerful clustering algorithm, and it works quite well for texts. Let's use the crawled texts, and try to find some topics among them using *K*-means. First, we load the documents and vectorize them. We will use the *K*-Means implementation from Smile, which, if you remember, does not work with sparse matrices, so we also need to reduce the dimensionality. We will use LSA for that.

```
List<List<String>> documents = ... // read the crawl data

int minDf = 5;
CountVectorizer cv = new CountVectorizer(minDf);
cv.fit(documents);

SparseDataset docVectors = cv.transform(documents);
int n = 150;
boolean normalize = true;
TruncatedSVD svd = new TruncatedSVD(n, normalize);
svd.fit(docVectors);

double[][] docsLsa = svd.transform(docVectors);
```

The data is prepared, so we can apply *K*-means:

```
int maxIter = 100;
int runs = 3;
int k = 100;
KMeans km = new KMeans(docsLsa, k, maxIter, runs);
```

Here, k, as you should remember from the previous chapter, is the number of clusters we want to find. The choice of K here is quite arbitrary, so feel free to experiment and choose any other value of K.

Once it has finished, we can have a look at the resulting centroids. These centroids are, however, in the LSA space, and not in the original term space. To bring them back, we need to invert the LSA tranformation.

To go from the original space to the LSA space, we used the matrix formed by the terms basis. Thus, to do the inverse transformation, we need the inverse of that matrix. Since the basis is orthonormal, the inverse is the same as the transpose, and we will use this for inverting the LSA tranformation. This is how it looks in the code:

```
double[][] centroids = km.centroids();
double[][] termBasis = svd.getTermBasis();
double[][] centroidsOriginal = project(centroids, t(termBasis));
```

The following is how the t method computes the transpose:

```
public static double[][] t(double[][] M) {
    Array2DRowRealMatrix matrix = new Array2DRowRealMatrix(M, false);
    return matrix.transpose().getData();
}
```

And the project method just computes the matrix-matrix multiplication.

Now, when the centroids are in the original space, we find the most important terms of each of them.

For that, we just take a centroid and see what the largest dimensions are:

```
List<String> terms = vectorizer.vocabulary();
for (int centroidId = 0; centroidId < k; centroidId++) {
    double[] centroid = centroidsOriginal[centroidId];
    List<ScoredIndex> scored = wrapAsScoredIndex(centroid, 0.0);
    for (int i = 0; i < 20; i++) {
        ScoredIndex scoredTerm = scored.get(i);
        int position = scoredTerm.getIndex();
        String term = terms.get(position);
        System.out.print(term + ", ");
```

```
    }
    System.out.println();
}
```

Here, terms is the list that contains the names of dimensions from the `CountVectorizer,` and `wrapAsScoredIndex` is the function we wrote previously; it takes an array of doubles, creates a list of `ScoredIndex` objects, and sorts it.

When you run it, you may see something similar to these clusters:

Cluster 1	Cluster 2	Cluster 3
Blood pressure hypotension low symptoms heart causes health disease treatment	hp printer printers printing laserjet support officejet print ink software	cars car toyota ford honda used bmw chevrolet vehicle nissan

We just took the first three clusters, and they clearly make sense. There also are some clusters which make less sense, which suggests that the algorithm could be tuned further: we can adjust *K* in *K*-Means and the number of dimensions for LSA.

Word embeddings

So far, we have covered how to apply dimensionality reduction and clustering to textual data. There is another type of unsupervised Learning, which is specific to text: word embeddings. You have probably heard about **Word2Vec,** which is one such algorithm.

The problem Word embeddings tries to solve is how to embed words into low-dimensional vector space such that semantically close words are close in this space, and different words are far apart.

For example, cat and dog should be rather close there, but laptop and sky should be quite far apart.

Here, we will implement a Word Embedding algorithm based on the co-occurrence matrix. It builds upon the ideas of LSA: there we could represent the terms by the documents they contain. So, if two words are contained in the same documents, they should be related. Document, however, is quite a broad context for a word, so we can narrow it down to a sentence, or to a few words before and after the word of interest.

For example, consider the following sentences:

We use Java for Data Science because we like Java. Java is good for enterprise development.

Then, we tokenize the text, split it into sentences, remove stopwords, and get the following:

- "we", "use", "java", "data", "science", "we", "like", "java"
- "java", "good", "enterprise", "development"

Now, suppose that for each word here we want to see what are the two words before and the two words after. This will give us the context in which each of the words is used. For this example, it will be:

- we -> use, java
- use -> we; java, data
- java -> we, use; data, science
- data -> use, java; science, we
- java -> we, like
- java -> good, enterprise
- good -> java; enterprise, development
- enterprise -> java, good; development
- development -> good, enterprise

Then, we can build a co-occurrence matrix, where we will put 1 each time a word occurs in the context of another word. So, for "we", we will add +1 to "use" and "java", and so on.

By the end, each cell will say how many times a word w_1 (from the rows of the matrix) occurred in the context of another word w_2 (from the columns of the matrix). Next, if we reduce the dimensionality of this matrix with SVD, we already get a good improvement over the plain LSA approach.

But we could go futher and replace the counts with **Pointwise Mutual Information** (**PMI**).

PMI is a measure of dependency between two random variables. It initially comes from the information theory, but it is often used in computational linguistics for measuring the degree of associations between two words. It is defined in the following way:

$$\text{PMI}(w, v) = \log\left[p(w, v) \ / \ p(w)p(v)\right]$$

It checks if two words w and v co-occur by chance or not. If they happen to co-occur by chance, then the joint probability *p(w, v)* should be equal to the product of marginal probabilities *p(w) p(v)*, so PMI is 0. But if there is indeed association between two words, PMI gets values higher than 0, such that the higher the values, the stronger the association.

We typically estimate these probabilities by going through a body of text and counting:

- For marginal probabilities, we just count how many times the token occurs
- For join probabilities, we look at the co-occurrence matrix

We use the following formulas:

- `p(w) = c(w) / N`, where `c(w)` is the number of times `w` occurs in the body, and `N` is the total number of tokens
- `p(w, v) = c(w, v) / N`, where `c(w, v)` is the value from the co-occurrence matrix and `N` is the number of tokens as well

In practice, however, small values of `c(w, v)`, `c(w)`, and `c(v)` can distort the probabilities, so they are often smoothed by adding some small number λ:

- `p(w) = [c(w) + λ] / [N + Kλ]`, where `K` is the number of unique tokens in the corpus
- `p(w, v) = [c(w, v) + λ] / [N + Kλ]`

If we replace the PMI formula from the preceding equation, we get the following one:

$$PMI(w, v) = log\ [c(w, v) + λ] + log\ [N + Kλ] - log\ [c(w) + λ] - log\ [c(v) + λ]$$

So what we can do is just replace the counts in the co-occurrence matrix with PMI and then compute the SVD of this matrix. In this case, the resulting embeddings will be of better quality.

Now, let's implement this. First, you may have noticed that we need to have the sentences, and previously we just had a stream of tokens, with no detection of sentence boundaries. As we know, Stanford CoreNLP can do it, so let's create a pipeline:

```
Properties props = new Properties();
props.put("annotators", "tokenize, ssplit, pos, lemma");
StanfordCoreNLP pipeline = new StanfordCoreNLP(props);
```

We will use the sentence splitter for detecting the sentences, and then we will take the word's lemma instead of the surface form.

But let's first create some useful classes. Previously, we used `List<List<String>>` to say that we pass a collection of documents, and each document is a sequence of tokens. Now, when we split each document into sentences, and then each sentence into tokens, it becomes `List<List<List<String>>>`, which is a bit hard to understand. We can replace this with some meaningful classes, such as `Document` and `Sentence`:

```
public class Document {
    private List<Sentence> sentences;
    // getter, setter and constructor is omitted
}

public class Sentence {
    private List<String> tokens;
    // getter, setter and constructor is omitted
}
```

 Create such small classes whenever possible. Even though it may seem verbose at the beginning, it greatly helps when it comes to reading the code afterwards and understanding the intention.

Now, let's use them for tokenizing a document. We can create a `Tokenizer` class with the following method:

```
public Document tokenize(String text) {
    Annotation document = new Annotation(text);
    pipeline.annotate(document);

    List<Sentence> sentencesResult = new ArrayList<>();
    List<CoreMap> sentences = document.get(SentencesAnnotation.class);

    for (CoreMap sentence : sentences) {
        List<CoreLabel> tokens = sentence.get(TokensAnnotation.class);
        List<String> tokensResult = new ArrayList<>();

        for (CoreLabel tokensInfo : tokens) {
            String token = tokensInfo.get(TextAnnotation.class);
            String lemma = tokensInfo.get(LemmaAnnotation.class);
            if (isPunctuation(token)
                    || isStopword(token)
                    || lemma.length() <= 2) {
                continue;
            }

            tokensResult.add(lemma.toLowerCase());
        }
```

```
    if (!tokensResult.isEmpty()) {
        sentencesResult.add(new Sentence(tokensResult));
    }
}

return new Document(sentencesResult);
}
```

So here we apply the sentence splitter to the text, and then, for each sentence, collect the tokens. We have already seen `isPunctuation` and `isStopword` methods - here they have the same implementation as previously.

Then we can use the crawled HTML dataset again, and apply the tokenizer on the content extracted with JSoup. We will omit this part for brevity. Now, we are ready to build the co-occurrence matrix from this data.

The first step, as in `CountVectorizer`, is to apply the document frequency filter to discard infrequent tokens, and then build a map that associates a token with some integer: the column number of the resulting sparse matrix. We know how to do it already, so we can skip this part.

Then, to estimate `p(w)` and `p(v)`, we need to know the number of times each token occurs:

```
Multiset<String> counts = HashMultiset.create();
for (Document doc : documents) {
    for (Sentence sentence : doc.getSentences()) {
        counts.addAll(sentence.getTokens());
    }
}
```

Now, we can proceed to calculating the co-occurrence matrix. For that, we can use the `Table` class from Guava:

```
Table<String, String, Integer> coOccurrence = HashBasedTable.create();
for (Document doc : documents) {
    for (Sentence sentence : doc.getSentences()) {
        processWindow(sentence, window, coOccurrence);
    }
}
```

Here, we define the `processWindow` function with the following content:

```
List<String> tokens = sentence.getTokens();

for (int idx = 0; idx < tokens.size(); idx++) {
    String token = tokens.get(idx);
```

```
            Map<String, Integer> tokenRow = coOccurrence.row(token);

    for (int otherIdx = idx - window;
            otherIdx <= idx + window;
            otherIdx++) {

        if (otherIdx < 0
                || otherIdx >= tokens.size()
                || otherIdx == idx) {
            continue;
        }

        String other = tokens.get(otherIdx);
        int currentCnt = tokenRow.getOrDefault(other, 0);
        tokenRow.put(other, currentCnt + 1);
    }
}
```

Here we slide a window of a specified size over each sentence of the document. Then, for a word in the center of this window, we look at the words before and after, and for each one of them increase the co-occurrence count by 1.

The next step is to create a matrix with PMI values from this data. Like we did previously, we will use the `SparseDataset` class from Smile to keep these values:

```
int vocabularySize = vocabulary.size();

double logTotalNumTokens = Math.log(counts.size() + vocabularySize *
smoothing);
SparseDataset result = new SparseDataset(vocabularySize);

for (int rowIdx = 0; rowIdx < vocabularySize; rowIdx++) {
    String token = vocabulary.get(rowIdx);
    double logMainTokenCount = Math.log(counts.count(token) + smoothing);
    Map<String, Integer> tokenCooc = coOccurrence.row(token);

    for (Entry<String, Integer> otherTokenEntry : tokenCooc.entrySet()) {
        String otherToken = otherTokenEntry.getKey();
        double logOtherTokenCount = Math.log(counts.count(otherToken) +
smoothing);
        double logCoOccCount = Math.log(otherTokenEntry.getValue() +
smoothing);

        double pmi = logCoOccCount + logTotalNumTokens
                - logMainTokenCount - logOtherTokenCount;

        if (pmi > 0) {
            int colIdx = tokenToIndex.get(otherToken);
```

```
                result.set(rowIdx, colIdx, pmi);
            }
        }

    }
```

In this code, we just apply the PMI formula to the co-occurrence counts we have. Finally, we perform SVD of this matrix, and for that we just use the `TruncatedSVD` class we created previously.

Now, we can see if the embedding we trained make sense. To do this, we can select some terms and, for each, find the most similar ones. This can be achieved in the following way:

- First, for a given token, we look up its vector representation
- Then, we compute the similarity of this token with the rest of the vectors. As we know, this can be done by matrix-vector multiplication
- Finally, we sort the results of the multiplication by score, and show the tokens with the highest score.

By now we have done the exact same procedure a few times, so we can skip the code. Of course, it is available in the code bundle for the chapter.

But let's anyway have a look at the results. We have selected a few words: **cat**, **germany** and **laptop**, and the following words are the most similar ones, according to the embeddings we just trained:

Cat	Germany	Laptop
0.835 pet	0.829 country	0.882 notebook
0.812 dog	0.815 immigrant	0.869 ultrabook
0.796 kitten	0.813 united	0.866 desktop
0.793 funny	0.808 states	0.865 pro
0.788 puppy	0.802 brazil	0.845 touchscreen
0.762 animal	0.789 canada	0.842 lenovo
0.742 shelter	0.777 german	0.841 gaming
0.727 friend	0.776 australia	0.836 tablet
0.727 rescue	0.760 europe	0.834 asus
0.726 picture	0.759 foreign	0.829 macbook

Even though it's not ideal, the result still makes sense. It can be improved further by training these embeddings on a lot more text data, or fine-tuning the parameters such as the dimensionality of SVD, minimal document frequency, and the amount of smoothing.

 When training word embeddings, getting more data is always a good idea. Wikipedia is a good source of textual data; it is available in many languages, and they regularly publish dumps at `https://dumps.wikimed` `ia.org/`. If Wikipedia is not enough, you can use *Common Crawl* (`http` `://commoncrawl.org/`), where they crawl everything on the Internet and make it available to anyone for free. We will also talk about Common Crawl in `Chapter 9`, *Scaling Data Science*.

Finally, there are a lot of pretrained word embeddings available on the Internet.

For example, you can have a look at the collection here: `https://github.com/3Top/word2v` `ec-api`. It is quite easy to load embeddings from there.

To do this, let's first create a class to store the vectors:

```
public class WordEmbeddings {
    private final double[][] embeddings;
    private final List<String> vocabulary;
    private final Map<String, Integer> tokenToIndex;
    // constructor and getters are omitted

    List<ScoredToken> mostSimilar(String top, int topK, double
minSimilarity);
    Optional<double[]> representation(String token);
}
```

This class has the following fields and methods:

- `embeddings`: This is the array which stores the vectors
- `vocabulary`: This is the list of all the tokens
- `tokenToIndex`: This is the mapping from a token to the index at which the vector is stored
- `mostSimilar`: This returns top K other tokens most similar to the provided one
- `representation`: This returns a vector representation for a term or Optional.absent if there is no vector for it

Of course, we can put the PMI-based embeddings there. But let's see how we can load the existing GloVe and Word2Vec vectors from the preceding link.

The text file format for storing the vector is quite similar for both Word2Vec and GloVe, so we can cover only one of them. GloVe is a bit simpler, so let's use it as follows:

- First, download the pretrained embeddings from `http://nlp.stanford.edu/data/glove.6B.zip`
- Unpack it; there are several files trained on the same corpus of different dimensionality
- Let's use `glove.6B.300d.txt`

The storage format is straightforward; on each line, there is a token followed by a sequence of numbers. The numbers are obviously the embedding vector for the token. Let's read them:

```
List<Pair<String, double[]>> pairs =
        Files.lines(file.toPath(), StandardCharsets.UTF_8)
            .parallel()
            .map(String::trim)
            .filter(StringUtils::isNotEmpty)
            .map(line -> parseGloveTextLine(line))
            .collect(Collectors.toList());

List<String> vocabulary = new ArrayList<>(pairs.size());
double[][] embeddings = new double[pairs.size()][];

for (int i = 0; i < pairs.size(); i++) {
    Pair<String, double[]> pair = pairs.get(i);
    vocabulary.add(pair.getLeft());
    embeddings[i] = pair.getRight();
}

embeddings = l2RowNormalize(embeddings);
WordEmbeddings result = new WordEmbeddings(embeddings, vocabulary);
```

Here, we parse each line of the text file, then create the vocabulary list and normalize the length of the vectors. The `parseGloveTextLine` has the following content:

```
List<String> split = Arrays.asList(line.split(" "));
String token = split.get(0);
double[] vector = split.subList(1, split.size()).stream()
        .mapToDouble(Double::parseDouble).toArray();
Pair<String, double[]> result = ImmutablePair.of(token, vector);
```

Here, `ImmutablePair` is an object from Apache Commons Lang.

Let's take the same words and have a look at their neighbors using these GloVe embeddings. This is the result:

Cat	Germany	Laptop
- 0.682 dog	- 0.749 german	- 0.796 laptops
- 0.682 cats	- 0.663 austria	- 0.673 computers
- 0.587 pet	- 0.646 berlin	- 0.599 phones
- 0.541 dogs	- 0.597 europe	- 0.596 computer
- 0.490 feline	- 0.586 munich	- 0.580 portable
- 0.488 monkey	- 0.579 poland	- 0.562 desktop
- 0.473 horse	- 0.577 switzerland	- 0.547 cellphones
- 0.463 pets	- 0.575 germans	- 0.546 notebooks
- 0.461 rabbit	- 0.559 denmark	- 0.544 pcs
- 0.459 leopard	- 0.557 france	- 0.529 cellphone

The results indeed make sense, and, in some cases, it is better than the embeddings we trained ourselves with.

As we mentioned, the text format for word2vec vectors is pretty similar to the GloVe ones, so only minor modifications are needed for reading them. There is, however, a binary format for storing word2vec embeddings. It is a bit more complex, but if you would like to know how to read it, have a look at the code bundle for this chapter.

Later in this chapter, we will see how we can apply word embeddings to solve supervised learning problems.

Supervised learning for texts

Supervised machine learning methods are also quite useful for text data. Like in the usual settings, here we have the label information, which we can use to understand the information within texts.

A very common example of such application of supervised learning to texts is spam detection: every time you hit the spam button in your e-mail client, this data is collected and then put in a classifier. Then, this classifier is trained to tell apart spam versus nonspam e-mails.

In this section, we will look into how to use Supervised methods for text on two examples: first, we will build a model for sentiment analysis, and then we will use a ranking classifier for reranking search results.

Text classification

Text Classification is a problem where given a collection of texts and labels, it trains a model that can predict these labels for new unseen text. So the settings here are usual for supervised learning, except that now we have text data.

There are many possible classification problems, as follows:

- **Spam detection**: This predicts whether an e-mail is spam or not
- **Sentiment analysis**: This predicts whether the sentiment of the text is positive or negative
- **Language detection**: Given a text, this detects its language

The general workflow for text classification is similar in almost all cases:

- We tokenize and vectorize the text
- Then we fit a linear classifier treating each token as a feature

As we know that if we vectorize the text, the resulting vector is quite sparse. This is why it is a good idea to use linear models: they are very fast and can easily deal with sparsity and high dimensionality of the text data.

So let's solve one of these problems.

For example, we can take a sentiment analysis problem, and build a model, which predicts the polarity of texts, that is, whether the text is positive or negative.

We can take the data from here: `http://ai.stanford.edu/~amaas/data/sentiment/`. This dataset contains 50.000 labeled movie reviews extracted from IMDB, and the authors provide a predefined train-test split. To store the reviews from there, we can create a class for it:

```
public class SentimentRecord {
    private final String id;
    private final boolean train;
    private final boolean label;
    private final String content;
    // constructor and getters omitted
}
```

We will not go into details of the code for reading the data from the archive, but, as usual, you are welcome to check the code bundle.

As for the model, we will use LIBLINEAR--as you already know from `Chapter 4`, *Supervised Learning - Classification and Regression*. It is a library with fast implementation of linear classifiers such as logistic regression and Linear SVM.

Now, let's read the data:

```
List<SentimentRecord> data = readFromTagGz("data/aclImdb_v1.tar.gz");

List<SentimentRecord> train = data.stream()
        .filter(SentimentRecord::isTrain)
        .collect(Collectors.toList());

List<List<String>> trainTokens = train.stream()
        .map(r -> r.getContent())
        .map(line -> TextUtils.tokenize(line))
        .map(line -> TextUtils.removeStopwords(line))
        .collect(Collectors.toList());
```

Here, we read the data from the archive, and then tokenize the train data. Next, we vectorize the texts:

```
int minDf = 10;
CountVectorizer cv = new CountVectorizer(minDf);
cv.fit(trainTokens);
SparseDataset trainData = cv.transform(trainTokens);
```

So far, nothing new. But now we need to convert `SparseDataset` into the LIBLINEAR format. Let's create a couple of utility methods for this:

```
public static Feature[][] wrapX(SparseDataset dataset) {
    int nrow = dataset.size();
    Feature[][] X = new Feature[nrow][];

    int i = 0;
    for (Datum<SparseArray> inrow : dataset) {
        X[i] = wrapRow(inrow);
        i++;
    }

    return X;
}


public static Feature[] wrapRow(Datum<SparseArray> inrow) {
```

```
SparseArray features = inrow.x;

int nonzero = features.size();
Feature[] outrow = new Feature[nonzero];
Iterator<Entry> it = features.iterator();

for (int j = 0; j < nonzero; j++) {
    Entry next = it.next();
    outrow[j] = new FeatureNode(next.i + 1, next.x);
}

return outrow;
}
```

The first method, wrapX, takes a SparseDataset and creates a two-dimensional array of Feature objects. This is the LIBLINEAR's format for storing the data. The second method, wrapRow, takes one particular row of SparseDataset, and wraps it into a one-dimensional array of Feature objects.

Now, we need to extract the label information and create an instance of the Problem class, which describes the data:

```
double[] y = train.stream().mapToDouble(s -> s.getLabel() ? 1.0 :
0.0).toArray();
Problem problem = new Problem();
problem.x = wrapX(dataset);
problem.y = y;
problem.n = dataset.ncols() + 1;
problem.l = dataset.size();
```

Then, we define the parameters and train the model:

```
Parameter param = new Parameter(SolverType.L1R_LR, 1, 0.001);
Model model = Linear.train(problem, param);
```

Here, we specify a Logistic Regression model with L1 regularization and the cost parameter C=1.

Linear classifiers such as logistic regression or SVM with L1 regularization are very good for approaching high sparsity problems such as Text Classification. The L1 penalty makes sure the model converges very fast, and, additionally, it forces the solution to be sparse: that is, it performs feature selection and only keeps the most informative words.

For predicting the probability, we can create another utility method, which takes a model and a test dataset, and returns a one-dimensional array of probabilities:

```
public static double[] predictProba(Model model, SparseDataset dataset) {
    int n = dataset.size();
    double[] results = new double[n];
    double[] probs = new double[2];
    int i = 0;

    for (Datum<SparseArray> inrow : dataset) {
        Feature[] row = wrapRow(inrow);
        Linear.predictProbability(model, row, probs);
        results[i] = probs[1];
        i++;
    }

    return results;
}
```

Now we can test the model. So we take the test data, tokenize and vectorize it, and then invoke the predictProba method for checking the output. Finally, we can evaluate the performance using some evaluation metric such as AUC. In this particular case, the AUC is 0.89, which is reasonably good performance for this dataset.

Learning to rank for information retrieval

Learning to rank is a family of algorithms that deal with ordering data. This family is a part of supervised machine learning; to order the data, we need to know which items are more important and need to be shown first.

Learning to rank is often used in the context of building search engines; based on some relevance evaluations, we build a model that tries to rank relevant items higher than nonrelevant ones. In the unsupervised ranking case, such as cosine on TF-IDF weights, we typically have only one feature, by which we order the documents. However, there could be a lot more features, which we may want to include in the model and let it combine them in the best possible way.

There are several types of learning to rank models. Some of them are called Point-wise-- they are applied to each document individually and consider them in isolation from the rest of the training data. Even though this is a strict assumption, these algorithms are easy to implement and they work well in practice. Typically, it amounts to using either classification or a regression model, and then order the items by the score.

Let's get back to our running example of building the search engine and include more features into it. Previously, it was unsupervised; we just ranked the items by one feature, the cosine. But we can add more features and make it a supervised learning problem.

However, for that, we need to know the labels. We already have the positive labels: for a query we know about 30 relevant documents. But we do not know the negative labels: the search engine, which we used, returns only the relevant pages. So we need to get negative examples, and then it will be possible to train a binary classifier which will tell relevant pages apart from irrelevant.

There is a technique we can use to obtain the negative data, and it is called negative sampling. This idea is based on the assumption that most of the documents in the corpus are not relevant, so if we randomly sample some of them from there and say that they are not relevant, we will be right most of the time. If a sampled document turns to be relevant, then nothing bad happens; this would be just a noisy observation which should not affect the overall result.

So, we do the following:

- First, we read the ranking data and group the documents there based on the query
- Then, we split the queries into two non-overlapping groups: one for training and one for validation
- Next, within each group, we take a query and randomly sample 9 negative examples. These URLs from the negative queries are assigned the negative label
- Finally, we train a model based on these labeled document/query pairs

 At the negative sampling step, it is important that for training we do not take negative examples from the validation group and vice versa. If we sample only within the train/validation group, then we can be sure that our model generalizes well to unseen queries and documents.

Negative sampling is quite easy to implement, so let's do it:

```
private static List<String> negativeSampling(String positive, List<String> collection,
                int size, Random rnd) {
    Set<String> others = new HashSet<>(collection);
    others.remove(positive);
    List<String> othersList = new ArrayList<>(others);
    Collections.shuffle(othersList, rnd);
    return othersList.subList(0, size);
}
```

The idea is the following: first, we take the entire collection of queries, and remove the one we are considering currently. Then, we shuffle this collection and take the top *N* ones from there.

Now that we have both positive and negative examples, we need to extract features, which we will put into the model. Let's create a `QueryDocumentPair` class, which will contain the information about the user query as well as the data about the document:

```
public class QueryDocumentPair {
    private final String query;
    private final String url;
    private final String title;
    private final String bodyText;
    private final String allHeaders;
    private final String h1;
    private final String h2;
    private final String h3;
    // getters and constructor omitted
}
```

The objects of this class can be created by parsing the HTML content with JSoup and extracting the title, the text of the body, all the header text together (h1-h6), and h1, h2, h3 headers separately.

We will use these fields for computing the features.

For example, we can compute the following ones:

- Bag-of-word TF-IDF similarity between the query and all other text fields
- LSA similarity between the query and all other text fields
- Embeddings similarity between the query and the title and h1, h2, and h3 headers.

We already know how to compute the first two types of features:

- We vectorize each of the fields separately using `CountVectorizer` and use the transform method to vectorize the query
- For LSA, we use the `TruncatedSVD` class in the same way; we train it on the text fields and then apply it to the query
- Then, we compute the cosine similarity between the text fields and the query in both Bag of Words and LSA spaces

However, we have not covered the last one here, using word embeddings. The idea is as follows:

- For query, get the vector for each token and put them together into a matrix
- For title (or other text field), do the same
- Compute the similarity of each query vector with each title vector via matrix multiplication
- Look at the distribution of similarities and take some characteristics of this distribution such as min, mean, max, and standard deviation. We can use these values as features
- Also, we can take the average query vector and the average title vector and compute the similarity between them

Let's implement this. First, create a method for getting the vectors for a collection of tokens:

```
public static double[][] wordsToVec(WordEmbeddings we, List<String> tokens)
{
    List<double[]> vectors = new ArrayList<>(tokens.size());
    for (String token : tokens) {
        Optional<double[]> vector = we.representation(token);
        if (vector.isPresent()) {
            vectors.add(vector.get());
        }
    }

    int nrows = vectors.size();
    double[][] result = new double[nrows][];
    for (int i = 0; i < nrows; i++) {
        result[i] = vectors.get(i);
    }

    return result;
}
```

Here, we use the `WordsEmbeddings` class we created previously, and then for each token we look up its representation, and if it's present, we put it into a matrix.

Then, getting all the similarities is just a multiplication of the two embedding matrices:

```
private static double[] similarities(double[][] m1, double[][] m2) {
    DenseMatrix M1 = new DenseMatrix(m1);
    DenseMatrix M2 = new DenseMatrix(m2);
    DenseMatrix M1M2 = new DenseMatrix(M1.numRows(), M2.numRows());
    M1.transBmult(M2, M1M2);
    return M1M2.getData();
```

```
    }
```

As we know, MTJ stores the values of a matrix column-wise in a one-dimensional data array, and previously, we converted it to a two-dimensional array. In this case, we don't really need to do it, so we take these values as is.

Now, given a list of queries, and a list of tokens from some other field (for example, title), we compute the distribution features:

```
int size = query.size();

List<Double> mins = new ArrayList<>(size);
List<Double> means = new ArrayList<>(size);
List<Double> maxs = new ArrayList<>(size);
List<Double> stds = new ArrayList<>(size);

for (int i = 0; i < size; i++) {
    double[][] queryEmbed = wordsToVec(glove, query.get(i));
    double[][] textEmbed = wordsToVec(glove, text.get(i));
    double[] similarities = similarities(queryEmbed, textEmbed);

    DescriptiveStatistics stats = new DescriptiveStatistics(similarities);
    mins.add(stats.getMin());
    means.add(stats.getMean());
    maxs.add(stats.getMax());
    stds.add(stats.getStandardDeviation());
}
```

Of course, here we could add even more features like 25th or 75th percentiles, but these four features are enough for now. Note that sometimes either queryEmbed or textEmbed can be empty and we need to handle this case by adding multiple NaN instances to each list.

We also mentioned another useful feature, the similarity between the average vectors. We compute it in a similar manner:

```
List<Double> avgCos = new ArrayList<>(size);
for (int i = 0; i < size; i++) {
    double[] avgQuery = averageVector(wordsToVec(glove, query.get(i)));
    double[] avgText = averageVector(wordsToVec(glove, text.get(i)));
    avgCos.add(dot(avgQuery, avgText));
}
```

Here, the dot is the inner product between two vectors, and averageVector is implemented in the following way:

```
private static double[] averageVector(double[][] rows) {
    ArrayRealVector acc = new ArrayRealVector(rows[0], true);
```

```
for (int i = 1; i < rows.length; i++) {
    ArrayRealVector vec = new ArrayRealVector(rows[0], false);
    acc.combineToSelf(1.0, 1.0, vec);
}

double norm = acc.getNorm();
acc.mapDivideToSelf(norm);
return acc.getDataRef();
}
```

Once we have computed all these features, we can put them into an array of doubles and use it for training a classifier. There are many possible models we can choose from.

For example, we can use the Random Forest classifier from Smile: typically, tree-based methods are quite good at discovering complex interactions between features, and these methods work well for Learning to Rank tasks.

There is another thing we have not yet discussed: how to evaluate the ranking results. There are special evaluation metrics for ranking models, such as **Mean Average Precision** (**MAP**) or **Normalized Discounted Cumulative Gain** (**NDCG**), but for our current case AUC is more than sufficient. Recall that one possible interpretation of AUC is that it corresponds to the probability that a randomly-chosen positive example will be ranked higher than a randomly chosen negative one.

So, AUC fits quite well to this task, and in our experiments, a random forest model achieves the AUC of 98%. In this section, we omitted some code, but, as usual, the full code is available in the code bundle, and you can go through the feature extraction pipeline in more detail.

Reranking with Lucene

In this chapter, we already mentioned that Lucene can be customized, and we already took a look at how to do preprocessing outside of Lucene and then seamlessly integrate the results in the Lucene workflow.

When it comes to reranking search results, the situation is more or less similar. The common approach to this is taking the Lucene ranking as is and retrieve the top 100 (or more) results. Then we take these already retrieved documents and apply the ranking model to this for reordering.

If we have such a reranking model, we need to make sure that we store all the data we used for training. In our case, it was a `QueryDocumentPair` class from which we extracted the relevance features. So let's create an index:

```
FSDirectory directory = FSDirectory.open(index);
WhitespaceAnalyzer analyzer = new WhitespaceAnalyzer();
IndexWriter writer = new IndexWriter(directory, new
IndexWriterConfig(analyzer));

List<HtmlDocument> docs = // read documents for indexing

for (HtmlDocument htmlDoc : docs.) {
    String url, title, bodyText, ... // extract the field values
    Document doc = new Document();
    doc.add(new Field("url", url, URL_FIELD));
    doc.add(new Field("title", title, TEXT_FIELD));
    doc.add(new Field("bodyText", bodyText, TEXT_FIELD));
    doc.add(new Field("allHeaders", allHeaders, TEXT_FIELD));
    doc.add(new Field("h1", h1, TEXT_FIELD));
    doc.add(new Field("h2", h2, TEXT_FIELD));
    doc.add(new Field("h3", h3, TEXT_FIELD));

    writer.addDocument(doc);
}

writer.commit();
writer.close();
directory.close();
```

In this code, `HtmlDocument` is a class which stores the details about the documents-- their title, body, header, and so on. We iterate over all our documents and put this information into Lucene's index.

In this example, all the fields are stored, because, later on, during query time, we will need to retrieve these values and use them for computing the features.

So, the index is built, and now, let's query it:

```
RandomForest rf = load("project/random-forest-model.bin");

FSDirectory directory = FSDirectory.open(index);
DirectoryReader reader = DirectoryReader.open(directory);
IndexSearcher searcher = new IndexSearcher(reader);

WhitespaceAnalyzer analyzer = new WhitespaceAnalyzer();
AnalyzingQueryParser parser = new AnalyzingQueryParser("bodyText",
analyzer);
```

```
String userQuery = "cheap used cars";
Query query = parser.parse(userQuery);

TopDocs result = searcher.search(query, 100);

List<QueryDocumentPair> data = wrapResults(userQuery, searcher, result);
double[][] matrix = extractFeatures(data);
double[] probs = predict(rf, matrix);

List<ScoredIndex> scored = wrapAsScoredIndex(probs);
for (ScoredIndex idx : scored) {
    QueryDocumentPair doc = data.get(idx.getIndex());
    System.out.printf("%.4f: %s, %s%n", idx.getScore(), doc.getTitle(),
doc.getUrl());
}
```

In this code, we first read the model we previously trained and saved, and then we read the index. Next, a user gives a query, we parse it, and retrieve the top 100 results from the index. All the values we need are stored in the index, so we get them and put them into `QueryDocumentPair`+--this is what happens inside the `wrapResults` method. Then we extract the features, apply the random forest model, and use the scores for reranking the results before presenting them to the user.

At the feature extraction step, it is very important to follow the exact same procedure we used for training. Otherwise, the model results may be meaningless or misleading. The best way of achieving this is creating a special method for extracting features and use it for both training the model and during the query time.

If you need to return more than 100 results, you can perform reranking for the top 100 entires returned by Lucene, but keep the original order for 100 plus entries. In reality, users rarely go past the first page, so the probability of reaching the 100th entry is pretty less, so we usually do not need to bother with reordering the documents there.

Let's take a closer look at the content of the `wrapResults` method:

```
List<QueryDocumentPair> data = new ArrayList<>();

for (ScoreDoc scored : result.scoreDocs) {
    int docId = scored.doc;
    Document doc = searcher.doc(docId);

    String url = doc.get("url");
    String title = doc.get("title");
    String bodyText = doc.get("bodyText");
    String allHeaders = doc.get("allHeaders");
```

```
    String h1 = doc.get("h1");
    String h2 = doc.get("h2");
    String h3 = doc.get("h3");

    QueryDocumentPair pair = new QueryDocumentPair(userQuery,
            url, title, bodyText, allHeaders, h1, h2, h3);
    data.add(pair);
}
```

Since all the fields are stored, we can get them from the index and build the `QueryDocumentPair` objects. Then we just apply the exact same procedure for feature extraction and put them into our model.

With this, we have created a search engine based on Lucene and then used a machine learning model for reranking the query results. There is a lot of room for further improvements: it can be adding more features or getting more training data, or it can be trying to use a different model. In the next chapter, we will talk about XGBoost, which also can be used for Learning to Rank tasks.

Summary

In this chapter, we covered a lot of ground in the information retrieval and NLP fields, including the basics of IR and how to apply machine learning to text. While doing this, we implemented a naive search engine first, and then used a learning to rank approach on top of Apache Lucene for an industrial-strength IR model.

In the next chapter, we will look at Gradient Boosting Machines, and at XGBoost, an implementation of this algorithm. This library provides state-of-the-art performance for many Data Science problems, including classification, regression, and ranking.

7
Extreme Gradient Boosting

By now we should have become quite familiar with machine learning and data science in Java: we have covered both supervised and unsupervised learning and also considered an application of machine learning to textual data.

In this chapter, we continue with supervised machine learning and will discuss a library which gives state-of-the-art performance in many supervised tasks: XGBoost and Extreme Gradient Boosting. We will look at familiar problems such as predicting whether a URL ranks for the first page or not, performance prediction, and ranking for the search engine, but this time we will use XGBoost to solve the problem.

The outline of this chapter is as follows:

- Gradient Boosting Machines and XGBoost
- Installing XGBoost
- XGBoost for classification
- XGBoost for regression
- XGBoost for learning to rank

By the end of this chapter, you will learn how to build XGBoost from the sources and use it for solving data science problems.

Gradient Boosting Machines and XGBoost

Gradient Boosting Machines (**GBM**) is an ensembling algorithm. The main idea behind GBM is to take some base model and then fit this model, over and over, to the data, gradually improving the performance. It is different from Random Forest models because GBM tries to improve the results at each step, while random forest builds multiple independent models and takes their average.

The main idea behind GBM can be best illustrated with a Linear Regression example. To fit several linear regressions to data, we can do the following:

1. Fit the base model to the original data.
2. Take the difference between the target value and the prediction of the first model (we call it the residuals of Step 1) and use this for training the second model.
3. Take the difference between the residuals of step 1 and predictions of step 2 (this is the residuals of Step 2) and fit the 3rd model.
4. Continue until you train N models.
5. For predicting, sum up the predictions of all individual models.

So, as you can see, at each step of the algorithm, the model tries to improve the results of the previous step, and by the end, it takes all the models and combines their prediction into the final one.

Essentially, any model can be used as the base model, not only Linear Regression. For example, it could be Logistic Regression or Decision Tree. Typically, tree-based models are very good and show excellent performance on a variety of problems. When we use trees in GBM, the overall model is typically called **Gradient Boosted Trees**, and depending on the type of the trees, it can be **Gradient Boosted Regression Trees** or **Gradient Boosted Classification Trees**.

Extreme Gradient Boosting, **XGBoost**, or **XGB** for short, is an implementation of Gradient Boosting Machines, and it provides a few base models, including decision trees. The tree-based XGBoost models are very powerful: they do not make any assumptions about the dataset and the distribution of values in its features, they naturally handle missing values, and they are extremely fast and can efficiently utilize all the available CPUs.

XGBoost can achieve excellent performance and can squeeze as much as possible from the data. If you know https://www.kaggle.com/, a website for hosting data science competitions, then you have probably already heard about XGBoost. It is the library the winners very often use in their solutions. Of course, it performs just as well outside of Kaggle and helps many Data Scientists in their daily job.

The library is originally written in C++, but there exist bindings for other languages like R and Python. Quite recently, a wrapper for Java was created as well, and in this chapter, we will see how to use it in our Java applications. This wrapper library is called **XGBoost4j,** and it is implemented via **Java Native Interface (JNI)** bindings, so it uses C++ underneath. But before we can use it, we need to be able to build it and install it. Now we will see how it can be done.

Installing XGBoost

As we have already mentioned, XGBoost is written in C++, and there is a Java library that allows using XGBoost in Java via JNI. Unfortunately, at the time of writing, XGBoost4J is not available on Maven Central, which means that it needs to be built locally and then published to the local Maven repository. There are plans to release the library to the central repository, and you can see the progress at `https://github.com/dmlc/xgboost/issues/1807`.

Even when it is released to Maven Central, it is still useful to know how to build it to get the bleeding edge version with the latest changes and bugfixes. So, let's see how to build the XGBoost library itself and then how to build the Java wrapper for it. For that, you can follow the official instruction from `https://xgboost.readthedocs.io/en/latest/build.html`, and here we will give an unofficial summary.

XGBoost mostly targets Linux systems, so building it on Linux is trivial:

```
git clone --recursive https://github.com/dmlc/xgboost
cd xgboost
make -j4
```

By executing the previous commands, we installed the base XGBoost library, but now we need to install the XGBoost4J bindings. To do so, perform the following sequence of steps:

- First, make sure you have the `JAVA_HOME` environment variable set and that it points to your JDK
- Then, go to the `jvm-packages` directory
- Finally, run `mvn -DskipTests install` here

The last command builds the XGBoost4J JNI bindings, then compiles the Java code and publishes everything to the local Maven repository.

Now, all we need to do for using XGBoost4J in our projects is to include the following dependency:

```
<dependency>
  <groupId>ml.dmlc</groupId>
  <artifactId>xgboost4j</artifactId>
  <version>0.7</version>
</dependency>
```

The installation process for OS X is pretty similar. However, when it comes to Windows, it is more complex.

To build it for Windows, we need to first download the 64-bit GCC compilers from `https://sourceforge.net/projects/mingw-w64/`. When installing, it is important to select `x86_64` architecture, and not `i686`, as only 64-bit platforms are supported by XGBoost. If, for some reason, the installer does not work, we can directly download the `x86_64-6.2.0-release-posix-seh-rt_v5-rev1.7z` archive with binaries from `https://goo.gl/CVcb8d` and then just unpack them.

 When building XGBoost on Windows, it is important to avoid directory names with spaces there. It is therefore best to create a folder in the root, for example, `C:/soft`, and perform all the installations from there.

Next, we clone XGBoost and `make` it. Here we assume that you use the Git Windows console:

```
git clone --recursive https://github.com/dmlc/xgboost
PATH=/c/soft/mingw64/bin/:$PATH
alias make='mingw32-make'
cp make/mingw64.mk config.mk
make -j4
```

Finally, we need to build the XGBoost4J JNI binaries. You need the content of your JDK. However, there is a problem in Windows: by default, JDK is installed to the `Program Files` folder, which has a space in it, and this will cause problems during installation. One possible solution is to copy the JDK to some other place.

After doing this, we are ready to build the library:

```
export JAVA_HOME=/c/soft/jdk1.8.0_102
make jvm
cd jvm-packages
mvn -DskipTests install
```

If your Maven complains about the style and aborts the build, you can disable it by passing the `-Dcheckstyle.skip` flag:

```
mvn -DskipTests -Dcheckstyle.skip install
```

After successfully performing this step, the XGBoost4J library should be published to the local maven repository and we can use the same dependency that we used previously.

To test if a library is built correctly, try to execute this line of code:

```
Class<Booster> boosterClass = Booster.class;
```

If you see that the code terminates correctly, then you are ready to go. However if you get `UnsatisfiedLinkError` with a message similar to `xgboost4j.dll: Can't find dependent libraries`, then make sure that the `mingw64/bin` folder is on the system `PATH` variable.

XGBoost in practice

After we have successfully built and installed the library, we can use it for creating machine learning models, and in this chapter we will cover three cases: binary classification, regression, and learning to rank models. We will also talk about the familiar use cases: predicting whether a URL is on the first page or search engine results, predicting the performance of a computer, and ranking for our own search engine.

XGBoost for classification

Now let's finally use it for solving a classification problem!

In `Chapter 4`, *Supervised Learning - Classification and Regression*, we tried to predict whether a URL is likely to appear on the first page of search results or not. Previously, we created a special object for keeping the features:

```
public class RankedPage {
    private String url;
    private int position;
    private int page;
    private int titleLength;
    private int bodyContentLength;
    private boolean queryInTitle;
    private int numberOfHeaders;
    private int numberOfLinks;
    public boolean isHttps();
    public boolean isComDomain();
    public boolean isOrgDomain();
    public boolean isNetDomain();
    public int getNumberOfSlashes();
}
```

As you can see, there are a number of features, but none of them really involved text. If you remember, with these features we achieved around 0.58 AUC on a held-out test set.

As a first step, let's try to reproduce this result with XGBoost. Because this is a binary classification, we set the objective parameter to `binary:logistic`, and since the last time we used AUC for evaluation, we will stick to this choice and set `eval_metric` to `auc` as well. We set the parameters via a map:

```
Map<String, Object> params = new HashMap<>();
params.put("objective", "binary:logistic");
params.put("eval_metric", "logloss");
params.put("nthread", 8);
params.put("seed", 42);
params.put("silent", 1);

// default values:
params.put("eta", 0.3);
params.put("gamma", 0);
params.put("max_depth", 6);
params.put("min_child_weight", 1);
params.put("max_delta_step", 0);
params.put("subsample", 1);
params.put("colsample_bytree", 1);
params.put("colsample_bylevel", 1);
params.put("lambda", 1);
params.put("alpha", 0);
params.put("tree_method", "approx");
```

Here, most of the parameters are set to their default values, with the exception of objective, `eval_metric`, `nthread`, `seed`, and `silent`.

As you see, XGBoost is a very configurable implementation of the Gradient Boosting Machines algorithm, and there are a lot of parameters that we can change. We will not include all the parameters here; you can refer to the official documentation at `https://gith ub.com/dmlc/xgboost/blob/master/doc/parameter.md`for the full list. In this chapter, we will only use tree-based methods, so let's review some of their parameters:

Parameter name	Range	Description
nthread	1 and more	This is the number of threads to use when building the trees
eta	from 0 to 1	This is the weight of each model in the ensemble
max_depth	1 and more	This is the maximal depth of each tree
min_child_weight	1 and more	This is the minimal number of observations per leaf
subsample	from 0 to 1	This is the fraction of observations to be used at each step

colsample_bytree	from 0 to 1	This is the fraction of features to be used at each step
objective		This defines the task (regression or classification)
eval_metric		This is the evaluation metric for the task
seed	integer	This sets the seed for reproducibility
silent	0 or 1	Here, 1 turns off the debugging output during training

Then, we read the data and create the train, validation, and test sets. We already have special functions for this, which we will use here as well:

```
Dataset dataset = readData();

Split split = dataset.trainTestSplit(0.2);
Dataset trainFull = split.getTrain();
Dataset test = split.getTest();

Split trainSplit = trainFull.trainTestSplit(0.2);
Dataset train = trainSplit.getTrain();
Dataset val = trainSplit.getTest();
```

Previously, we applied the Standardization (or Z-Score transformation) to our data. For tree-based algorithms, including XGBoost, this is not required: these methods are insensitive to such monotone transformations, so we can skip this step.

Next, we need to wrap our dataset into XGBoost's internal format: DMatrix. Let's create a utility method for this:

```
public static DMatrix wrapData(Dataset data) throws XGBoostError {
    int nrow = data.length();
    double[][] X = data.getX();
    double[] y = data.getY();

    List<LabeledPoint> points = new ArrayList<>();

    for (int i = 0; i < nrow; i++) {
        float label = (float) y[i];
        float[] floatRow = asFloat(X[i]);
        LabeledPoint point = LabeledPoint.fromDenseVector(label, floatRow);
        points.add(point);
    }

    String cacheInfo = "";
    return new DMatrix(points.iterator(), cacheInfo);
}
```

Now we can use it for wrapping the datasets:

```
DMatrix dtrain = XgbUtils.wrapData(train);
DMatrix dval = XgbUtils.wrapData(val);
```

XGBoost gives us a convenient way to monitor the performance of our model via the so-called watchlist. In essence, this is analogous to learning curves, where we can see how the evaluation metric evolves at each step. If, during training, we see that the values of training and evaluation metrics diverge significantly, then it may indicate that we are likely to overfit. Likewise, if at some step the validation metric starts decreasing while the train metric values keep increasing, then we overfit.

A watchlist is defined via a map where we associate some name with every dataset we are interested in:

```
Map<String, DMatrix> watches = ImmutableMap.of("train", dtrain, "val",
dval);
```

Now we are ready to train an XGBoost model:

```
int nrounds = 30;
IObjective obj = null;
IEvaluation eval = null;
Booster model = XGBoost.train(dtrain, params, nrounds, watches, obj, eval);
```

It is possible to provide custom objective and evaluation functions in XGBoost, but since we only use the standard ones, these parameters are set to null.

As we discussed, the training process can be monitored via a watchlist, and this is what you will see during the training process: at each step it will compute the evaluation function on the provided datasets and output the values to the console:

```
[0]     train-auc:0.735058     val-auc:0.533165
[1]     train-auc:0.804517     val-auc:0.576641
[2]     train-auc:0.842617     val-auc:0.561298
[3]     train-auc:0.860178     val-auc:0.567264
[4]     train-auc:0.875294     val-auc:0.570171
[5]     train-auc:0.888918     val-auc:0.575836
[6]     train-auc:0.896271     val-auc:0.573969
[7]     train-auc:0.904762     val-auc:0.577094
[8]     train-auc:0.907462     val-auc:0.580005
[9]     train-auc:0.911556     val-auc:0.580033
[10]    train-auc:0.922488     val-auc:0.575021
[11]    train-auc:0.929859     val-auc:0.579274
[12]    train-auc:0.934084     val-auc:0.580852
[13]    train-auc:0.941198     val-auc:0.577722
[14]    train-auc:0.951749     val-auc:0.582231
```

```
[15]      train-auc:0.952837      val-auc:0.579925
```

If, during training, we want to build a lot of trees, then digesting the text output from the console is hard, and it often helps to visualize these curves. In our case, however, we only had 30 iterations, so it is possible to make some judgment of the performance. If we take a careful look, we may notice that in step 8 the validation score stopped increasing, while the train score was still getting better and better. The conclusion that we can make from this is that at some point it starts overfitting. To avoid that, we can only use the first nine trees when making predictions:

```
boolean outputMargin = true;
int treeLimit = 9;
float[][] res = model.predict(dval, outputMargin, treeLimit);
```

Note two things here:

- If we set `outputMargin` to false, the un-normalized values will be returned, not probabilities. Setting it to true will apply the logistic transformation to the values, and it will make sure that the results look like probabilities.
- The results are a two-dimensional array of floats, not a one-dimensional array of doubles.

Let's write a utility function for transforming these results into doubles:

```
public static double[] unwrapToDouble(float[][] floatResults) {
    int n = floatResults.length;
    double[] result = new double[n];
    for (int i = 0; i < n; i++) {
        result[i] = floatResults[i][0];
    }
    return result;
}
```

Now we can use other methods we developed previously, for example, a method for checking AUC:

```
double[] predict = XgbUtils.unwrapToDouble(res);
double auc = Metrics.auc(val.getY(), predict);
System.out.printf("auc: %.4f%n", auc);
```

If we do not specify the number of trees in predict, then it uses all the available trees and performs the normalization of values by default:

```
float[][] res = model.predict(dval);
double[] predict = unwrapToDouble(res);
double auc = Metrics.auc(val.getY(), predict);
System.out.printf("auc: %.4f%n", auc);
```

In the previous chapters, we have created some code for K-Fold cross-validation. We can use it here as well:

```
int numFolds = 3;
List<Split> kfold = trainFull.kfold(numFolds);
double aucs = 0;

for (Split cvSplit : kfold) {
    DMatrix dtrain = XgbUtils.wrapData(cvSplit.getTrain());

    Dataset validation = cvSplit.getTest();
    DMatrix dval = XgbUtils.wrapData(validation);
    Map<String, DMatrix> watches = ImmutableMap.of("train", dtrain, "val",
dval);

    Booster model = XGBoost.train(dtrain, params, nrounds, watches, obj,
eval);
    float[][] res = model.predict(dval);
    double[] predict = unwrapToDouble(res);

    double auc = Metrics.auc(validation.getY(), predict);
    System.out.printf("fold auc: %.4f%n", auc);
    aucs = aucs + auc;
}

aucs = aucs / numFolds;
System.out.printf("cv auc: %.4f%n", aucs);
```

However, XGBoost has built-in capabilities for performing Cross-Validation: all we need to do is to provide DMatrix, and then it will split the data and run the evaluation automatically. Here is how we can use it:

```
DMatrix dtrainfull = wrapData(trainFull);
int nfold = 3;
String[] metric = {"auc"};
XGBoost.crossValidation(dtrainfull, params, nrounds, nfold, metric, obj,
eval);
```

And we will see the following evaluation log:

```
[0]     cv-test-auc:0.556261    cv-train-auc:0.714733
[1]     cv-test-auc:0.578281    cv-train-auc:0.762113
[2]     cv-test-auc:0.584887    cv-train-auc:0.792096
[3]     cv-test-auc:0.592273    cv-train-auc:0.824534
[4]     cv-test-auc:0.593516    cv-train-auc:0.841793
[5]     cv-test-auc:0.593855    cv-train-auc:0.856439
[6]     cv-test-auc:0.593967    cv-train-auc:0.875119
[7]     cv-test-auc:0.588910    cv-train-auc:0.887434
[8]     cv-test-auc:0.592887    cv-train-auc:0.897417
[9]     cv-test-auc:0.589738    cv-train-auc:0.906296
[10]    cv-test-auc:0.588782    cv-train-auc:0.915271
[11]    cv-test-auc:0.586081    cv-train-auc:0.924716
[12]    cv-test-auc:0.586461    cv-train-auc:0.935201
[13]    cv-test-auc:0.584988    cv-train-auc:0.940725
[14]    cv-test-auc:0.586363    cv-train-auc:0.945656
[15]    cv-test-auc:0.585908    cv-train-auc:0.951073
```

After we chose the best parameters (the number of trees in this case), we can retrain the model on the entire train part of the data and then evaluate it on the test:

```
int bestNRounds = 9;
Map<String, DMatring> watches = Collections.singletonMap("dtrainfull",
dtrainfull);

Booster model = XGBoost.train(dtrainfull, params, bestNRounds, watches,
obj, eval);

DMatrix dtest = XgbUtils.wrapData(test);
float[][] res = model.predict(dtest);
double[] predict = XgbUtils.unwrapToDouble(res);

double auc = Metrics.auc(test.getY(), predict);
System.out.printf("final auc: %.4f%n", auc);
```

Finally, we can save the model and use it afterwards:

```
Path path = Paths.get("xgboost.bin");
try (OutputStream os = Files.newOutputStream(path)) {
    model.saveModel(os);
}
```

Reading the saved model is also simple:

```
Path path = Paths.get("xgboost.bin");
try (InputStream is = Files.newInputStream(path)) {
    Booster model = XGBoost.loadModel(is);
}
```

 These models are compatible with other XGBoost bindings. So, we can train a model in Python or R, and then import it into Java - or the other way round.

Here, we used only the default parameters, which are often not ideal. Let's look at how we can modify them to achieve the best performance.

Parameter tuning

So far we have discussed three ways to perform Cross-Validation with XGBoost: hold-out dataset, manual K-Fold, and XGBoost K-Fold. Any of these ways can be used for selecting the best performance.

The implementations from XGBoost are typically better-suited for this task because they can show the performance at each step, and the training process can be manually stopped once you see that the learning curves diverge too much.

If your dataset is relatively large (for example, more that 100k examples), then simply selecting a hold-out dataset may be the best and fastest option. On the other hand, if your dataset is smaller, it may be a good idea to perform the *K*-Fold Cross-Validation.

Once we have decided on the validation scheme, we can start tuning the model. Since XGBoost has a lot of parameters, it is quite a complex problem because it is not computationally feasible to try all the possible combinations. There are, however, a few approaches that may help to achieve reasonably good performance.

The general approach is to change one parameter at a time and then run the training process with a watchlist. When doing so, we closely monitor the validation values and take a note of the largest ones. Finally, we select the combination of parameters, which gives the best validation performance. If two combinations give comparable performance, then we should opt for the simpler one (for example, less deep, with more instances in leaves, and so on).

Here is one such algorithm for tuning the parameters:

1. For the start, select a very large value for the number of trees, like 2,000 or 3,000. Never grow all these trees and stop the training process when you see that the validation scores stop growing or start decreasing.
2. Take the default parameters and change one at a time.
3. If your dataset is quite small, it may make sense to pick a smaller `eta` at the beginning, for example, 0.1. If the dataset is big enough, then the default value is fine.
4. First, we tune the `depth` parameter. Train the model with the default value (6), then try with small value (3) and large value (10). Depending on which one performs better, move in the appropriate direction.
5. Once the tree depth is settled, try changing the `subsample` parameter. First, try the default value (1) and then try decreasing it to 0.8, 0.6, and 0.4, and then move it to the appropriate direction. Typically, values around 0.6-0.7 work reasonably well.
6. Next, tune `colsample_bytree`. The approach is the same as for subsample, and values around 0.6-0.7 also work quite well.
7. Now, we tune `min_child_weight`. You can try values such as 10, 20, 50, and then move to the appropriate direction.
8. Finally, set `eta` to some small value (such as 0.01, 0.05, or 0.1 depending on the size of the dataset) and see what is the iteration number where the validation performance stops increasing. Use this number for selecting the number of iterations for the final model.

There are alternative ways of doing this. For example:

- Initialize `depth` to 10, `eta` to 0.1, and `min_child_weight` to 5
- As previously, first find the best `depth` by trying smaller and larger values
- Then, tune the `subsample` parameter
- After that, tune `min_child_weight`
- The last parameter to tune is `colsample_bytree`
- Finally, we set `eta` to a smaller number and watch the validation performance to select the number of trees

These are simple heuristics and do not touch many available parameters, but they can, nonetheless, give a reasonably good model. You can also tune the regularization parameters such as `gamma`, `alpha`, and `beta`. For example, for high `depth` values (more than 10), you may want to increase the `gamma` parameter a bit and see what happens.

Unfortunately, none of these algorithms gives a 100% guarantee to find the best solution, but you should try them and find the one you personally like the most - which probably be a combination of these ones, or maybe even something completely different.

 If you do not have a lot of data and do not want to tune the parameters manually, then try setting the parameters randomly, repeat it multiple times, and select the best model based on Cross-Validation. This is called Random Search Parameter Optimization: it does not require hand tuning and often works well in practice.

It may seem very overwhelming at the beginning, so do not worry. After doing it several times, you will develop some intuition as to how these parameters depend on each other and what is the best way to tune them.

Text features

In the previous chapter, we learned a lot of things that could be applied to text data and used some of the ideas when building the search engine. Let's take these features, include them into our model, and see how our AUC changes.

Recall that we previously created these features:

- Cosine similarity in the TF-IDF space between the query and the text fields of the documents, such as the title, the body content, and the h1, h2, and h3 headers
- LSA similarity between the query and all other text fields

We also used GloVe features in the previous chapter, but we will skip them here.In addition we won't include the implementation of the previous features in this chapter. For information on how to do it, refer to Chapter 6, *Working with Text - Natural Language Processing and Information Retrieval*.

Once we have added the features, we can play with parameters a bit. For example, we can end up using these parameters:

```
Map<String, Object> params = XgbUtils.defaultParams();
params.put("eval_metric", "auc");
params.put("colsample_bytree", 0.5);
params.put("max_depth", 3);
params.put("min_child_weight", 30);
params.put("subsample", 0.7);
params.put("eta", 0.01);
```

Here, XgbUtils.defaultParams() is a helper function, which creates a map with some parameters set to their default values, and then we can modify some of them. For example, since the performance is not very good and it is easy to overfit here, we grow smaller trees of depth 3 and ask for at least 30 observations in leaf nodes. Finally, we set the learning rate parameter eta to a small value because the dataset is not very large.

With these features, we can now achieve the AUC of 64.4%. This is very far from good performance, but it's a 5% improvement over the previous version with no features, which is a considerable step forward.

To avoid repetition, we have omitted a lot of code. If you feel a bit lost, you are always welcome to check the chapter's code bundle for details.

Feature importance

Finally, we can also see which features contribute most to the model, which are less important, and order our features according to their performance. XGBoost implements one such feature's important measure called **FScore,** which is the number of times a feature is used by the model.

To extract FScore, we first need to create a feature map: a file that contains the names of the features:

```
List<String> featureNames = columnNames(dataframe);
String fmap = "feature_map.fmap";
try (PrintWriter printWriter = new PrintWriter(fileName)) {
    for (int i = 0; i < featureNames.size(); i++) {
        printWriter.print(i);
        printWriter.print('t');
        printWriter.print(featureNames.get(i));
        printWriter.print('t');
        printWriter.print("q");
        printWriter.println();
    }
}
```

In this code, we first call a function, columnNames (not present here), which extracts the column names from a joinery dataframe. Then, we create a file where at each line we first print the feature name, and then a letter q, which means that the feature is quantitative and not an i - indicator.

Then, we call a method called `getFeatureScore`, which takes the feature map file and returns the feature's importance in a map. After getting it, we can sort the entries of the map according to their values, and this will produce a list of features ranked by their importance:

```
Map<String, Integer> scores = model.getFeatureScore(fmap);
Comparator<Map.Entry<String, Integer>> byValue =
Map.Entry.comparingByValue();
scores.entrySet().stream().sorted(byValue.reversed()).forEach(System.out::p
rintln);
```

For the classification model with text features, it will produce the following output:

```
numberOfLinks=17
queryBodyLsi=15
queryTitleLsi=14
bodyContentLength=13
numberOfHeaders=10
queryBodySimilarity=10
urlLength=7
queryTitleSimilarity=6
https=3
domainOrg=1
numberOfSlashes=1
```

We see that these new features are quite important to the model. We also see that features such as `domainOrg` or `numberOfSlashes` are rarely used, and many of the features we included are not even on this list. This means that we can safely exclude these features from our model and re-train the model without them.

 FScore is not the only feature-importance measure available for tree-based methods, but the XGBoost library provides only this score. There are external libraries such as XGBFI (`https://github.com/Far0n/xgbfi`), which can use the model dump for calculating metrics such as Gain, Weighted FScore, and others, and often these scores are more informative.

XGBoost is good not only for classification purposes, but also shines when it comes to Regression. Next, we will see how to use XGBoost for it.

XGBoost for regression

Gradient Boosting is quite a general model: it can deal with both classification and regression tasks. To use it to solve the regression problem all we need to do is to change the objective and the evaluation metric.

For binary classification, we used the `binary:logistic` objective, but for regression, we just change it to `reg:linear`. When it comes to evaluation, there are the following built-in evaluation metrics:

- Root-Means-Square Error (set `eval_metric` to `rmse`)
- Mean Absolute Deviation (set `eval_metric` to `mae`)

Apart from these changes, the other parameters for tree-based models are exactly the same! We can follow the same approach for tuning the parameters, except that now we will monitor a different metric.

In `Chapter 4`, *Supervised Learning - Classification and Regression*, we used the matrix multiplication performance data for illustrating the regression problem. Let's take the same dataset again, and this time use XGBoost for building the model.

To speed things up, we can take the reduced dataset from `Chapter 5`, *Unsupervised Learning - Clustering and Dimensionality Reduction*. However, in `Chapter 6`, *Working with Text - Natural Language Processing and Information Retrieval*, we have created a special class for SVD: `TruncatedSVD`. So, let's use it for reducing the dimensionality of this dataset:

```
Dataset dataset = ... // read the data
StandardizationPreprocessor preprocessor =
StandardizationPreprocessor.train(dataset);
dataset = preprocessor.transform(dataset);

Split trainTestSplit = dataset.shuffleSplit(0.3);
Dataset allTrain = trainTestSplit.getTrain();
Split split = allTrain.trainTestSplit(0.3);
Dataset train = split.getTrain();
Dataset val = split.getTest();

TruncatedSVD svd = new TruncatedSVD(100, false)
svd.fit(train);

train = dimred(train, svd);
val = dimred(val, svd);
```

You should remember from `Chapter 5`, *Unsupervised Learning - Clustering and Dimensionality Reduction* , that if we are going to reduce the dimensionality of the dataset with PCA via SVD, we need to standardize the data before that, and the following is what happens right after we read the data. We do the usual train-validation-test split and reduce the dimensionality of all the datasets. The `dimred` function just wraps calling the `transform` method from SVD and then it puts the results back to a `Dataset` class.

Now, let's use XGBoost:

```
DMatrix dtrain = XgbUtils.wrapData(train);
DMatrix dval = XgbUtils.wrapData(val);
Map<String, DMatrix> watches = ImmutableMap.of("train", dtrain, "val",
dval);
IObjective obj = null;
IEvaluation eval = null;

Map<String, Object> params = XgbUtils.defaultParams();
params.put("objective", "reg:linear");
params.put("eval_metric", "rmse");
int nrounds = 100;

Booster model = XGBoost.train(dtrain, params, nrounds, watches, obj, eval);
```

Here, we wrap our datasets into `DMatrix`, then create a watchlist, and finally set the `objective` and `eval_metric` parameters to the appropriate ones. Now we can train the model.

Let's look at the watchlist output (for brevity, we will only show every 10th record here):

```
[0]     train-rmse:21.223036    val-rmse:18.009176
[9]     train-rmse:3.584128     val-rmse:5.860992
[19]    train-rmse:1.430081     val-rmse:5.104758
[29]    train-rmse:1.117103     val-rmse:5.004717
[39]    train-rmse:0.914069     val-rmse:4.989938
[49]    train-rmse:0.777749     val-rmse:4.982237
[59]    train-rmse:0.667336     val-rmse:4.976982
[69]    train-rmse:0.583321     val-rmse:4.967544
[79]    train-rmse:0.533318     val-rmse:4.969896
[89]    train-rmse:0.476646     val-rmse:4.967906
[99]    train-rmse:0.422991     val-rmse:4.970358
```

We can see that the validation error stopped decreasing around the 50th tree and then started increasing again. So, let's limit the model to 50 trees and apply this model to the test data:

```
DMatrix dtrainall = XgbUtils.wrapData(allTrain);
watches = ImmutableMap.of("trainall", dtrainall);
nrounds = 50;
model = XGBoost.train(dtrainall, params, nrounds, watches, obj, eval);
```

Then, we can apply this model to the test data and see the final performance:

```
Dataset test = trainTestSplit.getTest();
double[] predict = XgbUtils.predict(model, test);
double testRmse = rmse(test.getY(), predict);
System.out.printf("test rmse: %.4f%n", testRmse);
```

Here, `XgbUtils.predict` converts a dataset into `DMatrix`, then calls the predict method and finally converts the array of floats into doubles. After executing the code, we will see the following:

```
test rmse: 4.2573
```

Recall that previously it was around 15, so with XGBoost it is more than three times better than with a linear regression!

Note that in the original dataset there are categorical variables, and when we use One-Hot-Encoding (via the `toModelMatrix` method from the joinery data frame), the resulting matrix is sparse. In addition, we then compress this data with PCA. However, XGBoost can also deal with sparse data, so let's use this example to illustrate how to do it.

In *Chapter 5*, *Unsupervised Learning - Clustering and Dimensionality Reduction*, we created a class for performing One-Hot-Encoding: we used it for converting categorical variables into an object of the `SparseDataset` class from Smile. Now we can use this method for creating such `SparseDataset`, and then for constructing a `DMatrix` object for XGBoost from it.

So, let's create a method for converting `SparseDataset` into `DMatrix`:

```
public static DMatrix wrapData(SparseDataset data) {
    int nrow = data.size();
    List<LabeledPoint> points = new ArrayList<>();

    for (int i = 0; i < nrow; i++) {
        Datum<SparseArray> datum = data.get(i);
        float label = (float) datum.y;
        SparseArray array = datum.x;

        int size = array.size();
        int[] indices = new int[size];
        float[] values = new float[size];

        int idx = 0;
        for (Entry e : array) {
            indices[idx] = e.i;
            values[idx] = (float) e.x;
            idx++;
        }
```

```
        LabeledPoint point =
                LabeledPoint.fromSparseVector(label, indices, values);
        points.add(point);
    }

    String cacheInfo = "";
    return new DMatrix(points.iterator(), cacheInfo);
}
```

Here, the code is pretty similar to what we used for dense matrices, but now we call the `fromSparseVector` factory method instead of `fromDenseVector`. To use it, we convert each row of `SparseDataset` into an array of indexes and array of values and then use them to create a `LabeledPoint` instance, which we use to create a `DMatrix` instance.

After converting it, we run the XGBoost model on it:

```
SparseDataset sparse = readData();
DMatrix dfull = XgbUtils.wrapData(sparse);

Map<String, Object> params = XgbUtils.defaultParams();
params.put("objective", "reg:linear");
params.put("eval_metric", "rmse");

int nrounds = 100;
int nfold = 3;
String[] metric = {"rmse"};
XGBoost.crossValidation(dfull, params, nrounds, nfold, metric, null, null);
```

When we run this, we see that RMSE reaches 17.549534 and never goes down after that. This is expected, since we a small subset of features; these features are all categorical and not all of them are very informative. Still, this serves as a good illustration of how we can use XGBoost for sparse datasets.

Apart from Classification and Regression, XGBoost also provides special support for creating ranking models, and now we will see how we can use it.

XGBoost for learning to rank

Our search engine has become quite powerful. Previously, we used Lucene for the fast retrieval of documents and then used a machine learning model for reordering them. By doing this, we were solving a ranking problem. After being given a query and a collection of documents, we need to order all the documents such that the ones that are the most relevant to the query have the highest rank.

Previously, we approached this problem as a classification: we built a binary classification model to separate relevant and non-relevant documents, and we used the probability of a document being relevant for sorting. This approach works reasonably well in practice, but has a limitation: it only considers one element at a time and keeps other documents in complete isolation. In other words, when deciding whether a document is relevant, we look only at the features of this particular document and do not look at the features of other documents.

What we can do instead is to look at the positions of the documents in relation to each other. Then, for each query, we can form a group of documents, which we consider to this particular query, and optimize the ranking within all such groups.

LambdaMART is the name of a model that uses this idea. It looks at the pairs of documents and considers the relative order of the documents within the pair. If the order is wrong (an irrelevant document ranks higher than a relevant one), then the model introduces a penalty, and during training we want to make this penalty as small as possible.

MART in LambdaMART stands for **Multiple Additive Regression Trees**, so it is a tree-based method. XGBoost also implements this algorithm. To use it, we set the objective to `rank:pairwise` and then we set the evaluation measure to one of the following:

- `ndcg`: This stands for Normalized Discounted Cumulative Gain
- `ndcg@n`: NDCG at N is the first N elements of the list and evaluates NDCG on it
- `map`: This stands for Mean Average Precision
- `map@n`: This is MAP evaluated at the first N elements of each group

For our purposes, it is not important to know in detail what these metrics do; for now, it is enough to know that the higher the value of a metric, the better it would be. However, there is an important difference between these two metrics: MAP can only deal with binary (0/1) labels, but NDCG can work with ordinal (0, 1, 2, ...) labels.

When we built a classifier, we only had two labels: positive (`1`) and negative (`0`). It may make sense to extend the labels to include more degrees of relatedness. For example, we can assign the labels in the following fashion:

- First, 3 URLs get a relevance of 3
- Other URLs on the first page get a relevance of 2
- The remaining relevant URLs on the second and third page get a relevance of 1
- And all non-relevant documents are labeled with 0

As we have mentioned, NDCG can deal with such ordinal labels, so we will use it for evaluation. To implement this relevance assignment, we can take the `RankedPage` class we used previously and create the following method:

```
private static int relevanceLabel(RankedPage page) {
    if (page.getPage() == 0) {
        if (page.getPosition() < 3) {
            return 3;
        } else {
            return 2;
        }
    }

    return 1;
}
```

We can use this method for all the documents within one query, and for all the other documents, we just assign a relevance of 0. Apart from this method, the remaining code for creating and extracting features stays the same, so for brevity, we will omit the code.

Once the data is prepared, we wrap `Dataset` it into `DMatrix`. When doing this, we need to specify the groups, and within each we will optimize the ranking. In our case, we group the data by the query.

XGBoost expects the objects belonging to the same group to be in a consecutive order, so it needs an array of group sizes. For example, suppose in our dataset we have 12 objects: 4 from group 1, 3 from group 2, and 5 from group 3:

qid	1	1	1	1	2	2	2	3	3	3	3	3
size	4				3			5				

Then, the size array should contain the sizes of these groups: `[4, 3, 5]`.

Here, `qid` is the ID of a query: an integer, which we put in association with each query:

qid	query	url
1	adidas basketball shoes	http://www.adidas.com/us/men-basketball-shoes
1	adidas basketball shoes	http://www.adidas.com/us/basketball
1	adidas basketball shoes	http://www.eastbay.com/adidas/Basketball/Shoes/_-_/N-x8Z1e1Zne
2	angry birds	https://www.angrybirds.com/
2	angry birds	http://chrome.angrybirds.com/
2	angry birds	http://www.youtube.com/channel/UCYC2wjLop-S6Ld4raeoUVNA
2	angry birds	http://www.rovio.com/index.php?page=angry-birds
3	animal shelter	http://www.animalshelter.org/
3	animal shelter	https://www.petfinder.com/animal-shelters-and-rescues
3	animal shelter	https://www.animalhouseshelter.com/pets/berlin/
3	animal shelter	https://www.petfinder.com/
3	animal shelter	http://www.adoptapet.com/adoption_rescue/80291.html

Let's first create a utility function for calculating the size arrays:

```
private static int[] groups(List<Integer> queryIds) {
    Multiset<Integer> groupSizes = LinkedHashMultiset.create(queryIds);
    return groupSizes.entrySet().stream().mapToInt(e ->
e.getCount()).toArray();
}
```

This method takes in a list of query IDs and then it counts how many times each ID is present there. For that, we use `LinkedHashMultiset` - a multiset from Guava. This particular implementation of the multiset remembers the order in which the elements were inserted, so when getting back the counts the order is preserved.

Now we can specify the group sizes for both datasets:

```
DMatrix dtrain = XgbUtils.wrapData(trainDataset);
int[] trainGroups = queryGroups(trainFeatures.col("queryId"));
dtrain.setGroup(trainGroups);

DMatrix dtest = XgbUtils.wrapData(testDataset);
int[] testGroups = queryGroups(testFeatures.col("queryId"));
dtest.setGroup(testGroups);
```

And we are ready to train a model:

```
Map<String, DMatrix> watches = ImmutableMap.of("train", dtrain, "test",
dtest);
IObjective obj = null;
IEvaluation eval = null;

Map<String, Object> params = XgbUtils.defaultParams();
```

```
params.put("objective", "rank:pairwise");
params.put("eval_metric", "ndcg@30");

int nrounds = 500;
Booster model = XGBoost.train(dtrain, params, nrounds, watches, obj, eval);
```

Here, we change the objective to `rank:pairwise`, because we are interested in solving the ranking problem.We also set the evaluation metrics to `ndcg@30`, which means that we want to look only at NDCG of the first 30 documents, and do not really care about the documents we have after 30. The reason for this is that the users of search engines rarely look at the second and third pages of the search results, and it is very unlikely that they will look past the third page, and so we only consider the first three pages of the search results. That is, we are interested only in the top 30 documents, so we only look at NDCG at 30.

As we did previously, we start with default parameters and go through the same parameter tuning procedure as we do for classification or regression.

We can tune it a bit, for example, using the following parameters:

```
Map<String, Object> params = XgbUtils.defaultParams();
params.put("objective", "rank:pairwise");
params.put("eval_metric", "ndcg@30");
params.put("colsample_bytree", 0.5);
params.put("max_depth", 4);
params.put("min_child_weight", 30);
params.put("subsample", 0.7);
params.put("eta", 0.02);
```

With this set of parameters, we see that the best NDCG@30 of 0.632 for the hold-out data is reached at about the 220th iteration, so we should not grow more than 220 trees.

Now we can save the model with XGBoost model dumper and use it in Lucene. For that, we need to use the same code as we did previously with almost no changes; the only thing we need to change is the model. That is, the only difference is that instead of loading a random forest model, we need to load the XGBoost model. After that, we just follow the same procedure: we retrieve the top 100 documents with Lucene and rerank them with the new XGBoost model.

Therefore, with XGBoost, we are able to take into consideration the relative order of documents within each query group, and use this information to improve the model further.

Summary

In this chapter, we learned about Extreme Gradient Boosting --an implementation of Gradient Boosting Machines. We learned how to install the library and then we applied to solve a variety of supervised learning problems: classification, regression, and ranking.

XGBoost shines when the data is structured: when it is possible to extract good features from our data and put these features into a tabular format. However, in some cases, the data is quite hard to structure. For example, when dealing with images or sounds, a lot of effort is needed to extract useful features. But we do not necessarily have to do the feature extraction ourselves, instead, we can use Neural Network models which can learn the best features themselves.

In the next chapter, we will look at deeplearning4j--a deep learning library for Java.

8
Deep Learning with DeepLearning4J

In the previous chapter, we covered **Extreme Gradient Boosting** (**XGBoost**)--a library that implements the gradient boosting machine algorithm. This library provides state-of-the-art performance for many supervised machine learning problems. However, XGBoost only shines when the data is already structured and there are good handmade features.

The feature engineering process is usually quite complex and requires a lot of effort, especially when it comes to unstructured information such as images, sounds, or videos. This is the area where deep learning algorithms are usually superior to others, including XGBoost; they do not need hand-crafted features and are able to learn the structure of the data themselves.

In this chapter, we will look into a deep learning library for Java--DeepLearning4J. This library allows us to easily specify complex neural network architectures that are able to process unstructured data such as images. In particular, we will look into Convolutional Neural Networks--a special kind of neural network that is well-suited for images.

This chapter will cover the following:

- ND4J--the engine behind DeepLearning4J
- Simple neural networks for handwritten digit recognition
- Deep networks with convolutional layers for digit recognition
- A model for classifying images with dogs and cats

By the end of this chapter, you will learn how to run DeepLearning4J, apply it to image recognition problems, and use AWS and GPUs to speed it up.

Neural Networks and DeepLearning4J

Neural Networks are typically good models that give a reasonable performance on structured datasets, but they might not necessarily be better than others. However, when it comes to dealing with unstructured data, most often they are the best.

In this chapter, we will look into a Java library for designing Deep Neural Networks, called DeepLearning4j. But before we do this, we first will look into its *backend*--ND4J, which does all the number crunching and heavy lifting.

ND4J - N-dimensional arrays for Java

DeepLearning4j relies on ND4J for preforming linear algebra operations such as matrix multiplication. Previously, we covered quite a few such libraries, for example, Apache Commons Math or Matrix Toolkit Java. Why do we need yet another linear algebra library?

There are two reasons for this. First, these libraries usually deal only with vectors and matrices, but for deep learning we need tensors. A **tensor** is a generalization of vectors and matrices to multiple dimensions; we can see vectors as one-dimensional tensors and matrices as two-dimensional ones. For deep learning, this is important because we have images, which are three-dimensional; not only do they have height and width, but also multiple channels.

Another quite important reason for ND4J is its GPU support; all the operations can be executed on the graphical processors, which are designed to handle a lot of complex linear algebra operations in parallel, and this is extremely helpful for speeding up the training of neural networks.

So, before going into DeepLearning4j, let's quickly go over some basics of ND4J, even if it is not so important to know the specifics of how Deep Neural Networks are implemented, it can be useful for other purposes.

As usual, we first need to include the dependency on the pom file:

```
<dependency>
  <groupId>org.nd4j</groupId>
  <artifactId>nd4j-native-platform</artifactId>
  <version>0.7.1</version>
</dependency>
```

This will download the CPU version for Linux, MacOS, or Windows, depending on your platform. Note that for Linux you might need to have OpenBLAS installed. It is usually very easy, for example, for Ubuntu Linux, you can install it by executing the following command:

```
sudo apt-get install libopenblas-dev
```

After including the library to the `pom` file and installing dependencies, we are ready to start using it.

 ND4J's interface is heavily inspired by NumPy, a numerical library for Python. If you already know NumPy, you will quickly recognize familiarities in ND4J.

Let's begin by creating ND4J arrays. Suppose, we want to create a `5 x 10` array filled with ones (or with zeros). This is quite simple, for that, we can use the *ones* and *zeros* utility methods from the `Nd4j` class:

```
INDArray ones = Nd4j.ones(5, 10);
INDArray zeros = Nd4j.zeros(5, 10);
```

If we already have an array of doubles, then wrapping them into `Nd4j` is easy:

```
Random rnd = new Random(10);
double[] doubles = rnd.doubles(100).toArray();
INDArray arr1d = Nd4j.create(doubles);
```

When creating an array, we can specify the resulting shape. Suppose we want to take this array with `100` elements and put it into a `10 x 10` matrix. All we need to do is specify the shape when creating the array:

```
INDArray arr2d = Nd4j.create(doubles, new int[] { 10, 10 });
```

Alternatively, we can reshape the array after creating it:

```
INDArray reshaped = arr1d.reshape(10, 10);
```

Any array of any dimensionality can be reshaped into a one-dimensional array with the `reshape` method:

```
INDArray reshaped1d = reshaped.reshape(1, -1);
```

Note that we use -1 here; this way we ask ND4J to automatically infer the right number of elements.

If we have a two-dimensional Java array of doubles, then there is a special syntax for wrapping them into ND4J:

```
double[][] doubles = new double[3][];
doubles[0] = rnd.doubles(5).toArray();
doubles[1] = rnd.doubles(5).toArray();
doubles[2] = rnd.doubles(5).toArray();
INDArray arr2d = Nd4j.create(doubles);
```

Likewise, we can create a three-dimensional ND4J array from doubles:

```
double[] doubles = rnd.doubles(3 * 5 * 5).toArray();
INDArray arr3d = Nd4j.create(doubles, new int[] { 3, 5, 5 });
```

So far, we used Java's `Random` class for generating random numbers, but we can use ND4J's method for this:

```
int seed = 0;
INDArray rand = Nd4j.rand(new int[] { 5, 5 }, seed);
```

What is more, we can specify a distribution from which we will sample the values:

```
double mean = 0.5;
double std = 0.2;
INDArray rand = Nd4j.rand(new int[] { 3, 5, 5 }, new
NormalDistribution(mean, std));
```

As we mentioned previously, three-dimensional tensors are useful for representing images. Typically, an image is a three-dimensional array where the dimensions are the number of `channels * height * width`, and the values typically range from 0 to 255.

Let's generate an image-like array of size 2 * 5 with three channels:

```
double[] picArray = rnd.doubles(3 * 2 * 5).map(d -> Math.round(d *
255)).toArray();
INDArray pic = Nd4j.create(picArray).reshape(3, 2, 5);
```

If we print this array, we will see something like the following:

```
[[[51.00, 230.00, 225.00, 146.00, 244.00],
  [64.00, 147.00, 25.00, 12.00, 230.00]],
 [[145.00, 160.00, 57.00, 202.00, 143.00],
  [170.00, 91.00, 181.00, 94.00, 92.00]],
 [[193.00, 43.00, 248.00, 211.00, 27.00],
  [68.00, 139.00, 115.00, 44.00, 97.00]]]
```

Here, the output is first grouped by channels, and inside we have the pixel value information of each channel separately. To get a specific channel only, we can use the `get` method:

```
for (int i = 0; i < 3; i++) {
    INDArray channel = pic.get(NDArrayIndex.point(i));
    System.out.println(channel);
}
```

Alternatively, if we are interested in all the rows of the 0th channels with columns from 2nd to 3rd, we can use the `get` method for accessing this specific part of the array in this way:

```
INDArray slice = pic.get(NDArrayIndex.point(0), NDArrayIndex.all(),
NDArrayIndex.interval(2, 4));
System.out.println(slice);
```

The following is the output:

```
[[225.00, 146.00],
 [25.00, 12.00]]
```

This library has a lot more things such as dot product, matrix multiplication, and so on. This functionality is quite similar to what we have already covered in detail for analogous libraries, so we will not repeat ourselves here.

Now, let's start with neural networks!

Neural networks in DeepLearning4J

After learning some basics of ND4J, we are now ready to start using DeepLearning4j and create neural networks with it.

As you probably know already, neural networks are models where we stack individual neurons in layers. During the prediction phase, each neuron gets some input, processes it, and forwards the results to the next layer. We start from the input layer, which receives the raw data, and gradually push the values forward to the output layer, which will contain the prediction of the model for the given input.

A neural network with one hidden layer might look like this:

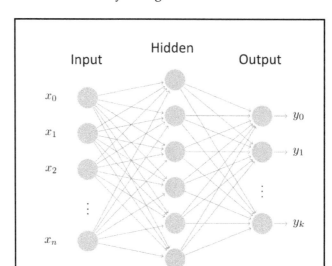

DeepLearning4J allows us to easily design such networks. If we take the network from the preceding figure and try to implement it with DeepLearning4j, we might end up with the following:

```
DenseLayer input = new DenseLayer.Builder().nIn(n).nOut(6).build();
nnet.layer(0, input);
OutputLayer output = new OutputLayer.Builder().nIn(6).nOut(k).build();
nnet.layer(1, output);
```

As you see, it is not difficult to read and understand. So, let's use it; for that, we first need to specify its dependency to the `pom.xml` file:

```
<dependency>
    <groupId>org.deeplearning4j</groupId>
    <artifactId>deeplearning4j-core</artifactId>
    <version>0.7.1</version>
</dependency>
```

Note that the versions of DeepLearning4j and ND4J must be the same.

For the illustration, we will use the MNIST dataset; this dataset contains images of handwritten digits from 0 to 9, and the goal is to predict the depicted number given in the image:

This dataset is quite a famous one; creating a model to recognize the digits often serves as a *Hello World* for neural networks and deep learning.

This chapter starts with a simple network with only one inner layer. Since all the images are 28 * 28 pixels, the input layer should have 28 * 28 neurons (the pictures are grayscale, so there is only one channel). To be able to input the pictures into the network, we first need to *unwrap* it into a one-dimensional array:

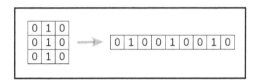

As we already know, with ND4J, this is very easy to do; we just invoke reshape(1, -1). However, we do not need to do it; DeepLearning4J will handle it automatically and reshape the input for us.

Next, we create an inner layer, and we can start with 1,000 neurons there. Since there are 10 digits, the number of neurons in the output layer should be equal to 10.

Now, let's implement this network in DeepLearning4J. Since MNIST is a very popular dataset, the library already provides a convenient loader for it, so all we need to do is use the following code:

```
int batchSize = 128;
int seed = 1;
DataSetIterator mnistTrain = new MnistDataSetIterator(batchSize, true,
seed);
DataSetIterator mnistTest = new MnistDataSetIterator(batchSize, false,
seed);
```

For the training part, there are 50,000 labeled examples, and there are 10,000 testing examples. To iterate over them, we use DeepLearning4j's abstraction-- `DataSetIterator`. What it does here is takes the entire dataset, shuffle it, and then chunks it into batches of 128 pictures.

The reason we prepare batches is that neural networks are typically trained with **Stochastic Gradient Descent (SGD)**, and the training happens in batches; we take a batch, train a model on it, update the weights, and then take the next batch. Taking one batch and training a model on it is called an **iteration**, and iterating over all available training batches is called an **epoch**.

After getting the data, we can specify the training configuration of our network:

```
NeuralNetConfiguration.Builder config = new
NeuralNetConfiguration.Builder();
config.seed(seed);
config.optimizationAlgo(OptimizationAlgorithm.STOCHASTIC_GRADIENT_DESCENT);
config.learningRate(0.005);
config.regularization(true).l2(0.0001);
```

In this code, we say that we want to use SGD for training with a learning rate of 0.005 and L2 regularization of 0.0001. SGD is a reasonable default and you should stick to it.

The learning rate is the most important training configuration parameter. If we set it too high, then the training procedure will diverge, and if it is too small--it will take a lot of time before converging. For selecting the optimal learning rate, we typically run the training procedure for values such as 0.1, 0.01, 0.001, ..., 0.000001 and see when the neural network stops diverging.

Another thing we used here was L2 regularization. L1 and L2 regularization work in exactly the same way as in linear models such as logistic regression--they help to avoid overfitting by making the weights smaller, and L1 ensures the sparsity of the solution.

However, there are regularization strategies specific to neural networks--dropout and dropconnect, which *mute* a random part of the net at each training iteration. We can specify them for the entire network in the configuration:

```
config.dropOut(0.1);
```

But the preferable way is to specify them per layer--we will see later how to do it.

Once we are done with the training configuration, we can continue with specifying the architecture of the net, that is, things such as its layers and the number of neurons in each.

For that we get an object of the `ListBuilder` class:

```
ListBuilder architecture = config.list();
```

Now, let's add the first layer:

```
DenseLayer.Builder innerLayer = new DenseLayer.Builder();
innerLayer.nIn(28 * 28);
innerLayer.nOut(1000);
innerLayer.activation("tanh");
innerLayer.weightInit(WeightInit.UNIFORM);
architecture.layer(0, innerLayer.build());
```

As we previously discussed, the number of neurons in the input layer should be equal to the size of the image, which is 28 times 28. Since the inner layer has 1,000 neurons, the output of this layer is 1,000.

Additionally, we specify here the activation function and the weight initialization strategy.

The activation function is the nonlinear transformation, which is applied to each neuron's output. There can be several activation functions:

Activation	Plot
linear: no activation	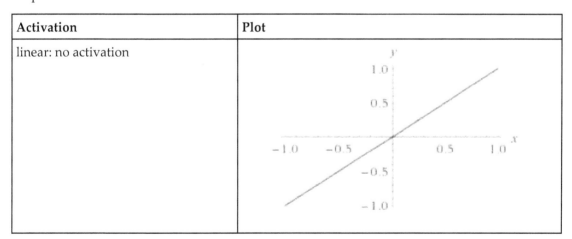

sigmoid: `[0, 1]` range	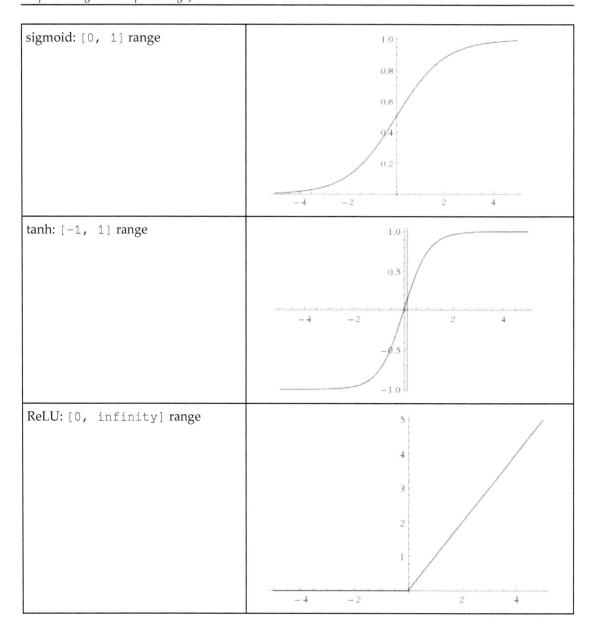
tanh: `[-1, 1]` range	
ReLU: `[0, infinity]` range	

Leaky ReLU: `[-infinity, infinity]`	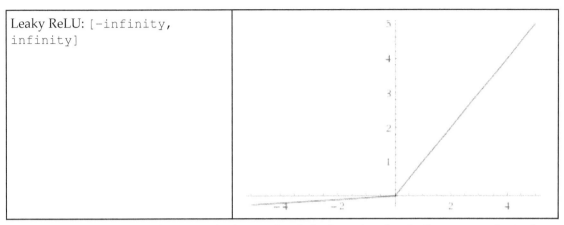

For this example, we used `tanh`, which was the default option for shallow networks in the pre-deep-learning era. However, for deep networks, ReLU activations should typically be preferred because they solve the vanishing gradient problem.

 Vanishing gradient is a problem that occurs during the training of neural networks. For training, we calculate the gradient--the direction which we need to follow, and update the weights based on that. This problem occurs when we use `sigmoid` or `tanh` activations in deep networks--the first layers (processed last during optimization) have a very small gradient and do not get updated at all.

However, ReLU also sometimes has a problem, called **dying ReLU**, which can be solved using other activation functions such as LeakyReLU.

 If the input to the ReLU function is negative, then the output is exactly zero, which means that in many cases the neuron is not activated. What is more, while training the derivative, in this case, is is zero, so following the gradient may never update the weights. This is known as the **dying ReLU** problem, many neurons never get activated and die. This problem can be solved using the LeakyReLU activation, instead of always outputting zero for negative values, it outputs something very small, so the gradient can still be calculated.

Another thing we specified here is the weight initialization. Typically, before we train a network, we need to initialize the parameters, and some initializations work better than others, but, as usual, this is case-specific and often we need to try several methods before settling on a particular one.

Weight initialization method	Comment
WeightInit.ZERO	Here, all the weights are set to zero. This is not recommended.
WeightInit.UNIFORM	Here, weights are set to uniform values in [-a, a] range, where a depends on the number neurons.
WeightInit.XAVIER	This is the Gaussian distribution with variance, which depends on the number of neurons. If in doubt, use this initialization.
WeightInit.RELU	This is the Gaussian distribution with higher variance than in XAVIER. It helps with the Dying ReLU problem.
WeightInit.DISTRIBUTION	This lets you specify any distribution from which the weights will be sampled. In this case, the distribution is set this way: `layer.setDist(new NormalDistribution(0, 0.01));`.
others	There are other weight initialization strategies, see the JavaDocs of the WeightInit class.

The UNIFORM and XAVIER methods are usually good starting points; try them first and see if they produce good results. If not, then try to experiment and choose some other methods.

If you experience the dying ReLU problem, then it is best to use the WeightInit.RELU initialization method. Otherwise, use WeightInit.XAVIER.

Next, we specify the output layer:

```
architecture.layer(1, outputLayer.build());
```

For the output layer, we need to specify the `loss` function--the function we want to optimize with the network during training. There are multiple options, but the most common ones are as follows:

- `LossFunction.NEGATIVELOGLIKELIHOOD`, which is `LogLoss`. Use this for classification.
- `LossFunction.MSE`, which is Mean Squared Error. Use it for regression.

You might have noticed that here we used a different activation function--softmax, and we have not covered this activation previously. This is a generalization of the `sigmoid` function to multiple classes. If we have a binary classification problem, and we want to predict only one value, the probability of belonging to the positive class, then we use a `sigmoid`. But if our problem is multiclass, or we output two values for the binary classification problem, then we need to use softmax. If we solve the regression problem, then we use the linear activation function.

Output activation	When to use
`sigmoid`	Binary classification
`softmax`	Multiclass classification
`linear`	Regression

Now, when we have established the architecture, we can build the network from it:

```
MultiLayerNetwork nn = new MultiLayerNetwork(architecture.build());
nn.init();
```

It is often useful to monitor the training progress and see the scores as the model train, and for that we can use `ScoreIterationListener`--it subscribes to the model, and after each iteration it outputs the new training score:

```
nn.setListeners(new ScoreIterationListener(1));
```

Now we are ready to train the network:

```
int numEpochs = 10;
for (int i = 0; i < numEpochs; i++) {
    nn.fit(mnistTrain);
}
```

Here, we train the network for 10 epochs, that is, we iterate over the entire training dataset 10 times, and if you remember, each epoch consists of a number of 128-sized batches.

Once the training is done, we can evaluate the performance of the model on the test. For this purpose, we create a special object of type `Evaluation`, and then we iterate over the batches of the test set, and apply the model to each batch. Every time we do this, we update the `Evaluation` object, which keeps track of the overall performance.

Once the training is done, we can evaluate the performance of the model. For this we create a special object of type `Evaluation`, and then iterate over the validation dataset and apply the model to each batch. The results are recorded by the `Evaluation` class, and in the end we can see the result:

```
while (mnistTest.hasNext()) {
    DataSet next = mnistTest.next();
    INDArray output = nn.output(next.getFeatures());
    eval.eval(next.getLabels(), output);
}

System.out.println(eval.stats());
```

If we run it for 10 epochs, it will produce this:

```
Accuracy:       0.9
Precision:      0.8989
Recall:         0.8985
F1 Score:       0.8987
```

So the performance is not very impressive, and to improve it, we can modify the architecture, for example, by adding another inner layer:

```
DenseLayer.Builder innerLayer1 = new DenseLayer.Builder();
innerLayer1.nIn(numrow * numcol);
innerLayer1.nOut(1000);
innerLayer1.activation("tanh");
innerLayer1.dropOut(0.5);
innerLayer1.weightInit(WeightInit.UNIFORM);
architecture.layer(0, innerLayer1.build());

DenseLayer.Builder innerLayer2 = new DenseLayer.Builder();
innerLayer2.nIn(1000);
innerLayer2.nOut(2000);
innerLayer2.activation("tanh");
innerLayer2.dropOut(0.5);
innerLayer2.weightInit(WeightInit.UNIFORM);
architecture.layer(1, innerLayer2.build());

LossFunction loss = LossFunction.NEGATIVELOGLIKELIHOOD;
OutputLayer.Builder outputLayer = new OutputLayer.Builder(loss);
outputLayer.nIn(2000);
```

```
outputLayer.nOut(10);
outputLayer.activation("softmax");
outputLayer.weightInit(WeightInit.UNIFORM);
architecture.layer(2, outputLayer.build());
```

As you can see, here we added an extra layer with `2000` neurons between the first layer and the output layer. We also added dropout to each layer for regularization purposes.

With this setup, we can achieve slightly better accuracy:

```
Accuracy:       0.9124
Precision:      0.9116
Recall:         0.9112
F1 Score:       0.9114
```

Of course, the improvement is only marginal, and the network is far from being well-tuned. To improve it, we can use the ReLU activation, Nesterov's updater with momentum around 0.9, and XAVIER's weight initialization. This should give an accuracy higher than 95%. In fact, you can find a very well-tuned network in the examples from the official DeepLearning4j repository; look for the class named `MLPMnistSingleLayerExample.java`.

In our example, we used classical neural network; they are rather shallow (that is, they do not have many layers), and all the layers are fully connected. While for small-scale problems this might be good enough, typically it is better to use Convolutional Neural Networks for image recognition tasks, these networks take into account the image structure and can achieve better performance.

Convolutional Neural Networks

As we have already mentioned several times, neural networks can do the feature engineering part themselves, and this is especially useful for images. Now we will finally see this in action. For that we will use Convolutional Neural Networks, they are a special kind of neural networks that uses special convolutional layers. They are very well suited for image processing.

In the usual neural networks, the layers are fully connected, meaning that each neuron of a layer is connected to all the neurons from the previous layer. For `28 x 28` images such as digits from MNIST, this is not a big deal, but it starts to be a problem for larger images. Imagine that we need to process images of size `300 x 300`; in this case, the input layer will have 90,000 neurons. Then, if the next layer also has 90,000 neurons, then there will be `90000 x 90000` connections between these two layers, which is clearly a lot.

In images, however, only a small area of each pixel is important. So the preceding problem can be solved by considering only a small neighborhood for each pixel, and this is exactly what convolutional layers do; inside, they keep a set of *filters* of some small size. Then, we slide a window over the image and calculate the similarity of the content within the window to each of the filters:

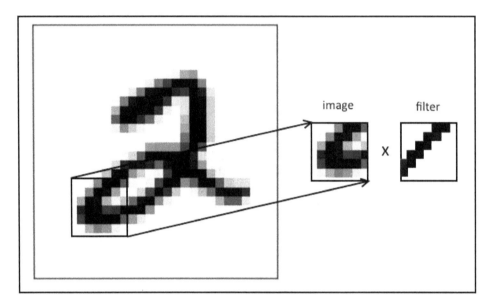

The filters are the neurons in these convolutional layers, and they are learned during training phase, in a way similar to the usual fully-connected case.

When we slide a window over an image, we calculate the similarity of the content to the filter, which is the dot product between them. For each window, we write the results to the output. We say the filter is activated when the area under consideration is similar to the filter. Clearly, if it is similar, the dot product will tend to produce higher values.

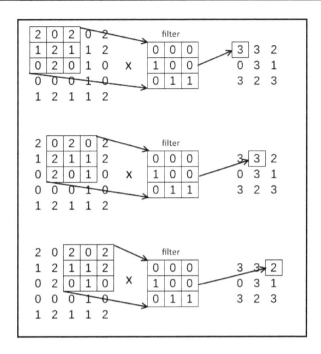

Since images usually have multiple channels, we actually deal with volumes (or 3D tensors) of dimensionality **number of channels** times **height** times **width**. When an image goes through a convolutional layer, each filter is applied in turn, and as the output, we have the volume of dimensionality **number of filters** times **height** times **width**. When we stack such layers on top of each other, we get a sequence of volumes:

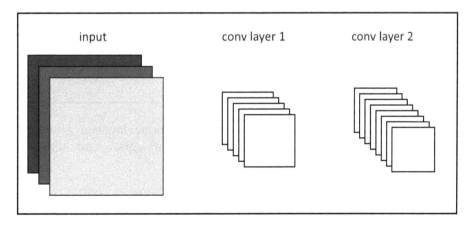

Apart from convolutional layers, another layer type is important for convolutional networks--the downsampling layer, or the pooling layer. The purpose of this layer is to reduce the dimensionality of the input, and usually each side is reduced by the factor of 2, so in total, the dimensionality is reduced 4 times. Usually, we use max pooling, which keeps the maximal value when downsampling:

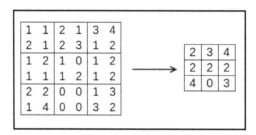

The reason we do this is to decrease the number of parameters our network has, it makes the training a lot faster.

When such a layer gets a volume, it only changes the height and the width but does not change the number of filters. Typically, we put the pooling layers after convolutional layers, and often organize the architecture such that two convolutional layers are followed by one pooling layer:

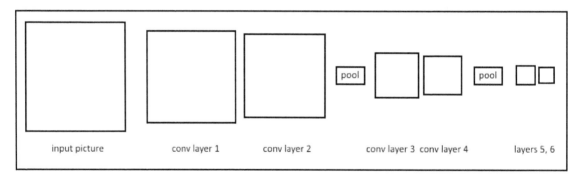

Then, at some point, after we have added enough convolutional layers, we switch to fully-connected layers, the same type of layer we have in usual networks. And then, in the end, we have the output layer, as we did previously.

Let's continue with the MNIST example, but this time let's train a Convolutional Neural Network to recognize digits. For this task, there is a famous architecture called LeNet (created by researcher Yann LeCun), so let's implement it. We will base our example on the official DeepLearning4j example available in their repository.

The architecture is as follows:

- 5 x 5 convolutional layer with 20 filters
- Max pooling
- 5 x 5 convolutional layer with 50 filters
- Max pooling
- Fully connected layers with 500 neurons
- Output layer with softmax

So there are six layers in this network.

Like we did previously, first, we specify the training configuration of the network:

```
NeuralNetConfiguration.Builder config = new
NeuralNetConfiguration.Builder();
config.seed(seed);
config.regularization(true).l2(0.0005);
config.learningRate(0.01);
config.weightInit(WeightInit.XAVIER);
config.optimizationAlgo(OptimizationAlgorithm.STOCHASTIC_GRADIENT_DESCENT);
config.updater(Updater.NESTEROVS).momentum(0.9);
```

There is almost nothing new here, except for `Updater`;we use Nesterov's update with momentum set to `0.9`. The purpose of this is faster convergence.

Now we can create the architecture:

```
ListBuilder architect = config.list();
```

First, the convolutional layer:

```
ConvolutionLayer cnn1 = new ConvolutionLayer.Builder(5, 5)
        .name("cnn1")
        .nIn(nChannels)
        .stride(1, 1)
        .nOut(20)
        .activation("identity")
        .build();
architect.layer(0, cnn1);
```

Here, in the Builder's constructor, we specify the dimensionality of the filter, which is 5 x 5. Then the `nIn` parameter is set to the number of channels in the input pictures, which is 1 for MNIST, they are all gray scale images. The `nOut` parameter specifies the number of filters this layer has. The stride parameter specifies the step at which we slide the window over the image, and typically it is set to 1. Finally, the layer does not use any activation.

The next layer in the architecture is the pooling layer:

```
SubsamplingLayer pool1 = new SubsamplingLayer.Builder(PoolingType.MAX)
        .name("pool1")
        .kernelSize(2, 2)
        .stride(2, 2)
        .build();
architect.layer(1, pool1);
```

When we create this layer, we first specify the way we want to downsample, and we use `MAX` since we are interested in max pooling. There are other options such as `AVG` average, and `SUM`, but they are not used very frequently in practice.

This layer has two parameters--the `kernelSize` parameter, which is the size of the window we slide over the picture, and the stride parameter, which is the step we take when sliding the window. Typically, these values are set to 2.

Then we add the next convolutional layer and a pooling layer for it:

```
ConvolutionLayer cnn2 = new ConvolutionLayer.Builder(5, 5)
        .name("cnn2")
        .stride(1, 1)
        .nOut(50)
        .activation("identity")
        .build();
architect.layer(2, cnn2);
SubsamplingLayer pool2 = new SubsamplingLayer.Builder(PoolingType.MAX)
        .name("pool2")
        .kernelSize(2, 2)
        .stride(2, 2)
        .build();
architect.layer(3, pool2);
```

Finally, we create the fully-connected layer and the output layer:

```
DenseLayer dense1 = new DenseLayer.Builder()
        .name("dense1")
        .activation("relu")
        .nOut(500)
        .build();
architect.layer(4, dense1);
```

```
OutputLayer output = new
OutputLayer.Builder(LossFunction.NEGATIVELOGLIKELIHOOD)
        .name("output")
        .nOut(outputNum)
        .activation("softmax")
        .build();
architect.layer(5, output);
```

For the last two layers, there is nothing new for us, we do not use any new parameters.

Finally, before training, we need to tell the optimizer that the input is a picture, and this is done by specifying the input type:

```
architect.setInputType(InputType.convolutionalFlat(height, width,
nChannels));
```

With this, we are ready to begin the training:

```
for (int i = 0; i < nEpochs; i++) {
    model.fit(mnistTrain);
    Evaluation eval = new Evaluation(outputNum);

    while (mnistTest.hasNext()) {
        DataSet ds = mnistTest.next();
        INDArray out = model.output(ds.getFeatureMatrix(), false);
        eval.eval(ds.getLabels(), out);
    }

    System.out.println(eval.stats());
    mnistTest.reset();
}
```

For this architecture, the accuracy the network can achieve after one epoch is 97%, which is significantly better than our previous attempts. But after training it for 10 epochs, the accuracy is 99%.

Deep learning for cats versus dogs

While MNIST is a very good dataset for educational purpose, it is quite small. Let's take a look at a different image recognition problem: given a picture, we want to predict if there is a cat on the image or a dog.

For this, we will use the dataset with dogs and cats pictures from a competition run on kaggle, and the dataset can be downloaded from `https://www.kaggle.com/c/dogs-vs-cats`.

Let's start by first reading the data.

Reading the data

For the dogs versus cats competition, there are two datasets; training, with 25,000 images of dogs and cats, 50% each, and testing. For the purposes of this chapter, we only need to download the training dataset. Once you have downloaded it, unpack it somewhere.

The filenames look like the following:

```
dog.9993.jpg        cat.10000.jpg
dog.9994.jpg        cat.10001.jpg
dog.9995.jpg        cat.10002.jpg
```

The label (`dog` or `cat`) is encoded into the filename.

As you know, the first thing we always do is to split the data into training and validation sets. Since all we have here is a collection of files, we just get all the filenames and then split them into two parts--training and validation.

For that we can use this simple script:

```
File trainDir = new File(root,  "train");
double valFrac = 0.2;
long seed = 1;

Iterator<File> files = FileUtils.iterateFiles(trainDir, new String[] {
```

```
        "jpg" }, false);
    List<File> all = Lists.newArrayList(files);
    Random random = new Random(seed);
    Collections.shuffle(all, random);

    int trainSize = (int) (all.size() * (1 - valFrac));
    List<File> train = all.subList(0, trainSize);
    copyTo(train, new File(root, "train_cv"));

    List<File> val = all.subList(trainSize, all.size());
    copyTo(val, new File(root, "val_cv"));
```

In the code, we use the `FileUtils.iterateFiles` method from Apache Commons IO to iterate over all `.jpg` files in the training directory. Then we put all these files into a list, shuffle it, and split them into 80% and 20% parts.

The `copyTo` method just copies the files into the specified directory:

```
    private static void copyTo(List<File> pics, File dir) {
        for (File pic : pics) {
            FileUtils.copyFileToDirectory(pic, dir);
        }
    }
```

Here, the `FileUtils.copyFileToDirectory` method also comes from Apache Commons IO.

There are a number of things we need to do to use the data for training a network. They are as follows:

- Getting the paths to each picture
- Getting the label (`dog` or `cat` from the filename)
- Resizing the input so every picture has the same size
- Applying some normalization to the image
- Creating `DataSetIterator` from it

Getting the paths to each picture is easy and we already know how to do it, we can use the same method from Commons IO as we did previously. But now we need to get `URI` for each file as DeepLearning4j dataset iterators expect the file's `URI`, and not the file itself. For that we create a helper method:

```
    private static List<URI> readImages(File dir) {
        Iterator<File> files = FileUtils.iterateFiles(dir,
                                    new String[] { "jpg" }, false);
        List<URI> all = new ArrayList<>();
```

```
        while (files.hasNext()) {
            File next = files.next();
            all.add(next.toURI());
        }

        return all;
    }
```

Getting the class name (dog or cat) from the filename is done by implementing the PathLabelGenerator interface:

```
    private static class FileNamePartLabelGenerator implements
    PathLabelGenerator {

        @Override
        public Writable getLabelForPath(String path) {
            File file = new File(path);
            String name = file.getName();
            String[] split = name.split(Pattern.quote("."));
            return new Text(split[0]);
        }

        @Override
        public Writable getLabelForPath(URI uri) {
            return getLabelForPath(new File(uri).toString());
        }
    }
```

Inside we just split the filename by . and then take the first element of the result.

Finally, we create a method, which takes in a list of URI and creates a DataSetIterator:

```
    private static DataSetIterator datasetIterator(List<URI> uris)
                        throws IOException {
        CollectionInputSplit train = new CollectionInputSplit(uris);
        PathLabelGenerator labelMaker = new FileNamePartLabelGenerator();

        ImageRecordReader trainRecordReader = new ImageRecordReader(HEIGHT,
    WIDTH, CHANNELS, labelMaker);
        trainRecordReader.initialize(train);

        return new RecordReaderDataSetIterator(trainRecordReader, BATCH_SIZE,
    1, NUM_CLASSES);
    }
```

This method uses some constants, which we initialize with the following values:

```
HEIGHT = 128;
WIDTH = 128;
CHANNELS = 3;
BATCH_SIZE = 30;
NUM_CLASSES = 2;
```

The `ImageRecordReader` will use the `HEIGHT` and `WIDTH` parameters to resize the images into the specified form, and if it is grayscale, it will artificially create RGB channels for it. The `BATCH_SIZE` specifies how many images we will consider at once during training.

In linear models, normalization plays an important role and helps the model converge faster. For neural networks as well, this is the case, so we need to normalize the image. For this, we can use a special built-in class `ImagePreProcessingScaler`. `DataSetIterator` can have a preprocessor, so we put this scaler there:

```
DataSetIterator dataSet = datasetIterator(valUris);
ImagePreProcessingScaler preprocessor = new ImagePreProcessingScaler(0, 1);
dataSet.setPreProcessor(preprocessor);
```

With this, the data preparation is done and we can proceed to create the model.

Creating the model

For the model's architecture, we will use a variation of the VGG network. This architecture is taken from a publicly available script from the forums (`https://www.kaggle.com/jeffd 23/dogs-vs-cats-redux-kernels-edition/catdognet-keras-convnet-starter`) and here we will adapt this example to DeepLearning4j.

VGG is a model that took 2nd place in the image net 2014 challenge, and it uses only 3 x 3 and 2 x 2 convolutional filters.

It is always a good idea to use the existing architectures, as it solves a lot of time--coming up with a good architecture on your own is a challenging task.

The architecture we will use is as follows:

- Two layers of 3 x 3 convolution with 32 filters
- Max pooling
- Two layers of 3 x 3 convolution with 64 filters
- Max pooling
- Two layers of 3 x 3 convolution with 128 filters
- Max pooling
- A fully connected layer with 512 neurons
- A fully connected layer with 256 neurons
- The output layer with softmax activation

For our example, we will use ReLU activation for all the convolution and fully-connected layers. To avoid the dying ReLU problem, we will use the `WeightInit.RELU` weight initialization scheme. In our experiments, without using it, the network tends to produce the same result no matter what input it receives.

So, first we start with the configuration:

```
NeuralNetConfiguration.Builder config = new
NeuralNetConfiguration.Builder();
config.seed(SEED);
config.weightInit(WeightInit.RELU);
config.optimizationAlgo(OptimizationAlgorithm.STOCHASTIC_GRADIENT_DESCENT);
config.learningRate(0.001);
config.updater(Updater.RMSPROP);
config.rmsDecay(0.99);
```

Some of the parameters should already be quite familiar by now, but there are two new things here--the `RMSPROP` updater and the `rmsDecay` parameter. Using them allows us to adaptively change the learning rate as we train. At the beginning, the learning rate is larger and we take bigger steps toward the minimum, but as we train and approach the minimum, it decreases the learning rate and we take smaller steps.

The learning rate was selected by trying different values such as 0.1, 0.001 and 0.0001 and watching when the network stops diverging. This is easy to spot because when diverging the training error varies a lot and then starts outputting Infinity or `NaN`.

Now we specify the architecture.

First, we create the convolutional layers and the pooling layers:

```
int l = 0;
ListBuilder network = config.list();

ConvolutionLayer cnn1 = new ConvolutionLayer.Builder(3, 3)
        .name("cnn1")
        .stride(1, 1)
        .nIn(3).nOut(32)
        .activation("relu").build();
network.layer(l++, cnn1);

ConvolutionLayer cnn2 = new ConvolutionLayer.Builder(3, 3)
        .name("cnn2")
        .stride(1, 1)
        .nIn(32).nOut(32)
        .activation("relu").build();
network.layer(l++, cnn2);

SubsamplingLayer pool1 = new SubsamplingLayer.Builder(PoolingType.MAX)
        .kernelSize(2, 2)
        .stride(2, 2)
        .name("pool1").build();
network.layer(l++, pool1);

ConvolutionLayer cnn3 = new ConvolutionLayer.Builder(3, 3)
        .name("cnn3")
        .stride(1, 1)
        .nIn(32).nOut(64)
        .activation("relu").build();
network.layer(l++, cnn3);

ConvolutionLayer cnn4 = new ConvolutionLayer.Builder(3, 3)
        .name("cnn4")
        .stride(1, 1)
        .nIn(64).nOut(64)
        .activation("relu").build();
network.layer(l++, cnn4);

SubsamplingLayer pool2 = new SubsamplingLayer.Builder(PoolingType.MAX)
        .kernelSize(2, 2)
        .stride(2, 2)
        .name("pool2").build();
network.layer(l++, pool2);

ConvolutionLayer cnn5 = new ConvolutionLayer.Builder(3, 3)
        .name("cnn5")
        .stride(1, 1)
```

```
        .nIn(64).nOut(128)
        .activation("relu").build();
network.layer(l++, cnn5);

ConvolutionLayer cnn6 = new ConvolutionLayer.Builder(3, 3)
        .name("cnn6")
        .stride(1, 1)
        .nIn(128).nOut(128)
        .activation("relu").build();
network.layer(l++, cnn6);

SubsamplingLayer pool3 = new SubsamplingLayer.Builder(PoolingType.MAX)
        .kernelSize(2, 2)
        .stride(2, 2)
        .name("pool3").build();
network.layer(l++, pool3);
```

There should be nothing new for us here. And then we create the fully-connected layers and the output:

```
DenseLayer dense1 = new DenseLayer.Builder()
        .name("ffn1")
        .nOut(512).build();
network.layer(l++, dense1);

DenseLayer dense2 = new DenseLayer.Builder()
        .name("ffn2")
        .nOut(256).build();
network.layer(l++, dense2);

OutputLayer output = new
OutputLayer.Builder(LossFunction.NEGATIVELOGLIKELIHOOD)
        .name("output")
        .nOut(2)
        .activation("softmax").build();
network.layer(l++, output);
```

Finally, as previously, we specify the input size:

```
network.setInputType(InputType.convolutionalFlat(HEIGHT, WIDTH, CHANNELS));
```

Now, we create the model from this architecture and specify the score listener for train monitoring purposes:

```
MultiLayerNetwork model = new MultiLayerNetwork(network.build())
ScoreIterationListener scoreListener = new ScoreIterationListener(1);
model.setListeners(scoreListener);
```

As for training, it happens in exactly the same was as we did previously--we train the model for a few epochs:

```
List<URI> trainUris = readImages(new File(root, "train_cv"));
DataSetIterator trainSet = datasetIterator(trainUris);
trainSet.setPreProcessor(preprocessor);

for (int epoch = 0; epoch < 10; epoch++) {
    model.fit(trainSet);
}

ModelSerializer.writeModel(model, new File("model.zip"), true);
```

In the end, we also save the model into a ZIP archive with three files inside--the coefficients of the model, the configuration (both parameters and the architecture) in a `.json` file, and the configuration for the updater--in case we would like to continue training the model in the future (the last parameter `true` tells us to save it and with `false` we cannot continue training).

Here, however, the performance monitoring is pretty primitive, we only watch the training error and do not look at the validation error at all. Next, we will look at more options for performance monitoring.

Monitoring the performance

What we did for monitoring previously was adding the listener, which outputs the training score of the model after each iteration:

```
MultiLayerNetwork model = new MultiLayerNetwork(network.build())
ScoreIterationListener scoreListener = new ScoreIterationListener(1);
model.setListeners(scoreListener);
```

This will give you some idea of the performance of the model, but only on the training data, but we typically need more than that--at least the performance on the validation set would be useful to know to see if we start overfitting or not.

So, let's read the validation dataset:

```
DataSetIterator valSet = datasetIterator(valUris);
valSet.setPreProcessor(preprocessor);
```

For training, previously we just took the dataset iterator and passed it to the fit function. We can improve this process by taking all the training data, shuffling it before each epoch, and chunking it into parts, with each chunk being equal to 20 batches. After the training on each chunk is finished, we can iterate over the validation set and see the current validation performance of the model.

In code, it looks like this:

```
for (int epoch = 0; epoch < 20000; epoch++) {
    ArrayList<URI> uris = new ArrayList<>(trainUris);
    Collections.shuffle(uris);
    List<List<URI>> partitions = Lists.partition(uris, BATCH_SIZE * 20);

    for (List<URI> set : partitions) {
        DataSetIterator trainSet = datasetIterator(set);
        trainSet.setPreProcessor(preprocessor);
        model.fit(trainSet);
        showTrainPredictions(trainSet, model);
        showLogloss(model, valSet, epoch);
    }

    saveModel(model, epoch);
}
```

So here we take the `URI`, shuffle them, and partition them into lists of 20 batches. For partitioning, we use the `Lists.partition` method from Google Guava. From each such partition, we create a dataset iterator and use it for training the model, and then, after each chunk, we look at the validation score to make sure the network is not overfitting.

Also, it is helpful to see what the network predicts for the data it was just trained on, especially to check if the network is learning anything. We do this inside the `showTrainPredictions` method. If the predictions are different for different inputs, then it is a good sign. Also, you may want to see how close the predictions are to the actual labels.

Additionally, we save the model at the end of each epoch, in case something goes wrong, we can train the process. If you noticed, we set the number of epochs to a high number, so at some point we can just stop the training (for example, when we see from the logs that we start overfitting), and just take the last good model.

Let's see how these methods are implemented:

```
private static void showTrainPredictions(DataSetIterator trainSet,
            MultiLayerNetwork model) {
    trainSet.reset();
    DataSet ds = trainSet.next();
    INDArray pred = model.output(ds.getFeatureMatrix(), false);
    pred = pred.get(NDArrayIndex.all(), NDArrayIndex.point(0));
    System.out.println("train pred: " + pred);
}
```

The `showLogLoss` method is simple, but a bit verbose because of the iterators. It does the following:

- Go over all batches in the validation dataset
- Record the prediction and the true label for each batch
- Put all predictions together in a single double array and does the same with the actual labels
- Calculate the log loss using the code we wrote in `Chapter` 4, *Supervised Learning - Classification and Regression*.

For brevity, we will omit the exact code here, but you are welcome to check the code bundle.

Saving the model is simple, and we already know how to do it. Here we just add some extra information to the filename about the epoch number:

```
private static void saveModel(MultiLayerNetwork model, int epoch) throws
IOException {
    File locationToSave = new File("models", "cats_dogs_" + epoch +
".zip");
    boolean saveUpdater = true;
    ModelSerializer.writeModel(model, locationToSave, saveUpdater);
}
```

Now, when we have a lot of information to monitor, it becomes quite difficult to comprehend everything from the logs. To make life easier for us, DeepLearning4j comes with a special graphical dashboard for monitoring.

This is how the dashboard looks:

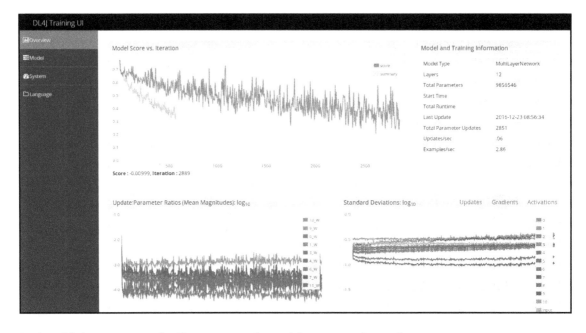

Let's add this to our code. First, we need to add an extra dependency to our pom:

```
<dependency>
  <groupId>org.deeplearning4j</groupId>
  <artifactId>deeplearning4j-ui_2.10</artifactId>
  <version>0.7.1</version>
</dependency>
```

It is written in Scala, which is why there is the _2.10 suffix at the end, it tells us that this version is written in Scala 2.10. Since we are using it from Java, it does not matter for us, so we can take any version we want.

Next, we can create the instance of the UI server, and create a special listener for the network, which will subscribe to the network's updates:

```
UIServer uiServer = UIServer.getInstance();
StatsStorage statsStorage = new InMemoryStatsStorage();
uiServer.attach(statsStorage);
StatsListener statsListener = new StatsListener(statsStorage);
```

And we use it in the same way we used `ScoreIterationListener`, we add it to the model via the `setListeners` method:

```
MultiLayerNetwork model = createNetwork();
ScoreIterationListener scoreListener = new ScoreIterationListener(1);
model.setListeners(scoreListener, statsListener);
```

With these changes, when we run the code, it starts the UI server, which we can see if we open the browser and go to `http://localhost:9000`; this will show the dashboard from the preceding code.

These charts are quite useful. The most useful one is the chart showing the model score at each iteration. This is the training score, the same one we see in the logs from `ScoreIterationListener`, which looks like this:

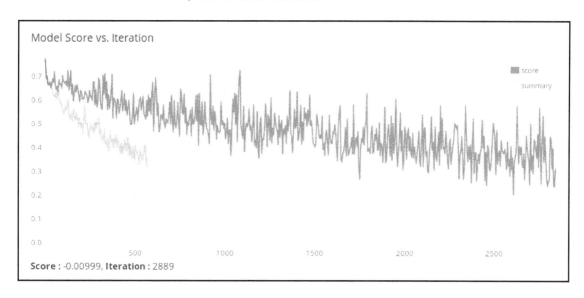

Based on this chart, we can understand how the model behaves during the training-- whether the training process is stable, or whether the model is learning anything at all. Ideally, we should see the downward trend as shown in the preceding screenshot. If there is no decrease in the score, then maybe there is something wrong with the network configuration, for example, the learning rate is too small, not good weight initialization or too much regularization. If there is an increase in the score, then the most likely problem is too large learning rate.

The other charts also allow to monitor the training process. The parameter ratios chart shows the changes in the parameters between each iterations, on the logarithmic scale (that is, -3.0 corresponds to 0.001 change between iterations). If you see that the change is too low, for example, below -6.0, then, probably, the network is not learning anything.

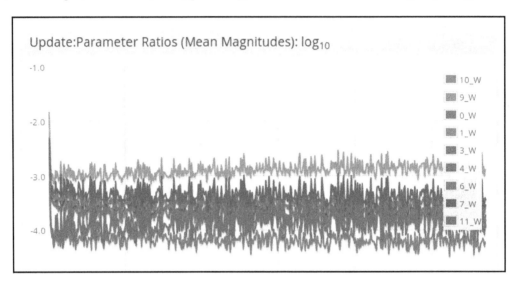

Finally, there is a chart that shows the standard deviations of all activations. The reason we may need this is to detect the so-called *vanishing* and *exploding* activations:

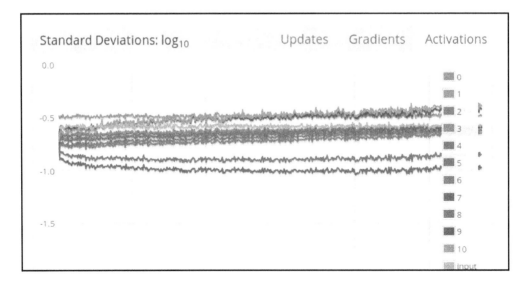

The **vanishing activation** problem is related to the **vanishing gradient** problem. For some activations, a change in input results is almost no change in the output, and the gradient is almost zero, so the neuron is not updated, so its activation *vanishes*. The exploding activation is the opposite, the activation score keeps growing until it reaches infinity.

In this interface, we can also see the full network on the **Models** tab. Here is a part of our model:

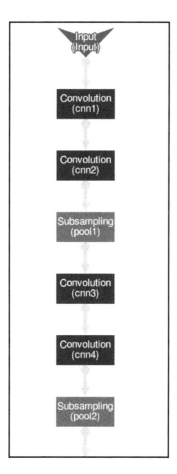

If we click on each individual layer, we can see some charts for this specific layer.

With these tools, we can closely monitor the performance of the model and adapt the training process and our parameters when we see that something unusual happens.

Data augmentation

For this problem, we have only 25, 000 training examples. For a deep learning model, this amount of data is usually not enough to capture all the details. No matter how sophisticated our network is and how much time we spent tuning it, at some point 25, 000 examples will not be enough to improve the performance further.

Often, getting more data is very expensive or not possible at all. But what we can do is generating more data from the data we already have, and this is called **data augmentation**. Usually, we generate new data by doing some of the following transformations:

- Rotating the image
- Flipping the image
- Randomly cropping the image
- Switching the color channels (for example, changing the red and blue channels)
- Changing color saturation, constrast, and brightness
- Adding noise

In this chapter, we will look at the first three transformations--rotation, flipping, and cropping. To do them, we will use `Scalr`--a library for image manipulation. Let's add it to the pom file:

```
<dependency>
  <groupId>org.imgscalr</groupId>
  <artifactId>imgscalr-lib</artifactId>
  <version>4.2</version>
</dependency>
```

It is very simple and only extends the standard Java API, in the same sense as Apache Commons Lang does--by providing useful utility methods around the standard functionality.

For rotation and flipping, we just use the `Scalr.rotate` method:

```
File image = new File("cat.10000.jpg");
BufferedImage src = ImageIO.read(image);
Rotation rotation = Rotation.CW_90;
BufferedImage rotated = Scalr.rotate(src, rotation);
File outputFile = new File("cat.10000_cw_90.jpg");
ImageIO.write(rotated, "jpg", outputFile);
```

As you see, this is pretty easy to use and quite intuitive. All we need to do is pass a `BufferedImage` and the desired `Rotation`. `Rotation` is an enum with the following values:

- `Rotation.CW_90`: This involves clockwise rotation by 90 degrees
- `Rotation.CW_180`: This involves clockwise rotation by 180 degrees
- `Rotation.CW_270`: This involves clockwise rotation by 270 degrees
- `Rotation.FLIP_HORZ`: This involves flipping the image horizontally
- `Rotation.FLIP_VERT`: This involves flipping the image vertically

Cropping is also not difficult, and it's done via the `Scalr.crop` method, which takes in four parameters--the position where the crop starts (x and y coordinates) and the size of the crop (height and width). For our problem what we can do is randomly select a coordinate in the top left corner of the image, and then randomly select the height and the width of the crop. We can do it this way:

```
int width = src.getWidth();
int x = rnd.nextInt(width / 2);
int w = (int) ((0.7 + rnd.nextDouble() / 2) * width / 2);

int height = src.getHeight();
int y = rnd.nextInt(height / 2);
int h = (int) ((0.7 + rnd.nextDouble() / 2) * height / 2);

if (x + w > width) {
    w = width - x;
}

if (y + h > height) {
    h = height - y;
}

BufferedImage crop = Scalr.crop(src, x, y, w, h);
```

Here, we first randomly select the x and y coordinates and then select the width and the height. In the code, we select the weight and the height such that they are at least 35% of the image--but can go up to 60% of the image. Of course, you are free to play with these parameters and change them to whatever makes more sense.

Then we also check if we do not overcome the image boundaries, that is, the crop always stays within the image; and finally we call the `crop` method. Optionally, we can also rotate or flip the cropped image at the end.

So, for all the files, it may look like this:

```
for (File f : all) {
    BufferedImage src = ImageIO.read(f);
    for (Rotation rotation : Rotation.values()) {
        BufferedImage rotated = Scalr.rotate(src, rotation);
        String rotatedFile = f.getName() + "_" + rotation.name() + ".jpg";
        File outputFile = new File(outputDir, rotatedFile);
        ImageIO.write(rotated, "jpg", outputFile);

        int width = src.getWidth();
        int x = rnd.nextInt(width / 2);
        int w = (int) ((0.7 + rnd.nextDouble() / 2) * width / 2);

        int height = src.getHeight();
        int y = rnd.nextInt(height / 2);
        int h = (int) ((0.7 + rnd.nextDouble() / 2) * height / 2);

        if (x + w > width) {
            w = width - x;
        }

        if (y + h > height) {
            h = height - y;
        }

        BufferedImage crop = Scalr.crop(src, x, y, w, h);
        rotated = Scalr.rotate(crop, rotation);

        String cropppedFile = f.getName() + "_" + x + "_" + w + "_" +
                    y + "_" + h + "_" + rotation.name() + ".jpg";

        outputFile = new File(outputDir, cropppedFile);
        ImageIO.write(rotated, "jpg", outputFile);
    }
}
```

In this code, we iterate over all training files, and then we apply all the rotations to the image itself and to a random crop from this image. This code should generate 10 new images from each source image. For example, for the following image of a cat, there will be 10 images generated as follows:

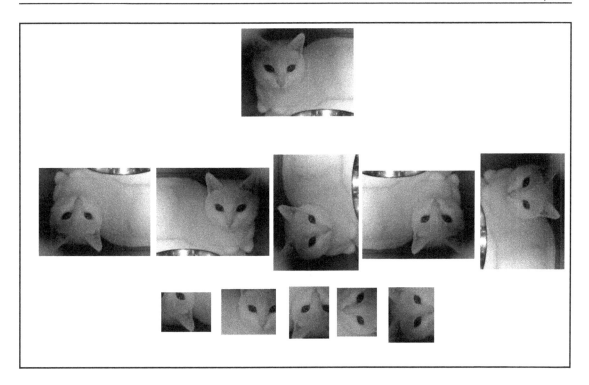

We only briefly listed the possible augmentations, and if you remember, the last one was *adding random noise*. This is typically easy to implement, so here are some ideas as to what you can do:

- Replace some pixel values with 0 or with some random value
- Add or subtract the same small number from all the values
- Generate some Gaussian noise with a small variance and add it to all the channels
- Add the noise only to a part of the image
- Invert a part of the image
- Add a filled square of some random color to the image; the color could have the alpha channel (that is, it could somewhat transparent) or not
- Apply strong JPG encoding to the image

With this, you can virtually generate an infinite number of data samples for training. Of course, you probably will not need so many samples, but by using these techniques, you can augment any image dataset and considerably improve the performance of the model trained on this data.

Running DeepLearning4J on GPU

As we mentioned previously, DeepLearning4j relies on ND4J for numerical calculations. ND4J is an interface, and there are multiple possible implementations. So far, we have used the one based on OpenBLAS, but there are other ones. We also mentioned that ND4J can utilize a **Graphics Processing Unit** (**GPU**), which is a lot faster than CPUs for typical Linear Algebra operations used in neural networks such as matrix multiplication. To use it, we need to get the CUDA ND4J backend.

 CUDA is an interface used for executing the computations on NVidia's GPUs, and it supports a wide range of graphical cards. Internally, ND4J uses CUDA to run numerical computations on GPUs.

If you have previously executed all the code on the CPU via BLAS, you must have noticed how slow it is. Switching the ND4J backend to CUDA should considerably improve the performance by several orders of magnitude.

This is done by including the following dependency to the pom file:

```
<dependency>
  <groupId>org.nd4j</groupId>
  <artifactId>nd4j-cuda-7.5</artifactId>
  <version>0.7.1</version>
</dependency>
```

This dependency assumes that you have CUDA 7.5 installed.

For CUDA 8.0, you should replace 7.5 with 8.0: both CUDA 7.5 and CUDA 8.0 are supported by ND4J.

If you already have a GPU with all the drivers installed, just adding this dependency is enough to use the GPU for training the networks, and when you do this, you will see a great performance boost.

What is more, you can use the UI dashboard to monitor the GPU memory usage, and if you see that it is low, you can try to utilize it better, for example, by increasing the batch size. You can find this chart on the **System** tab:

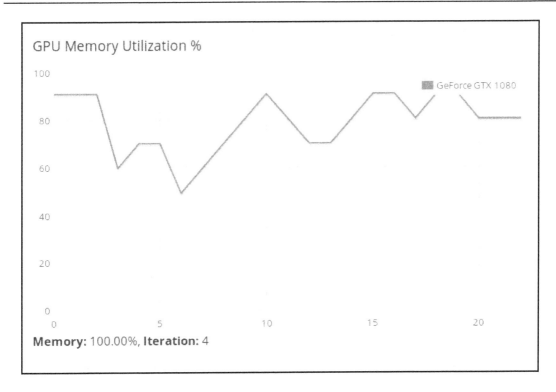

If you do not have a GPU, but do not want to wait while your CPU is crunching numbers, you can easily rent a GPU computer. There are cloud providers such as Amazon AWS who allow you to instantly get a server with a GPU even just for a few hours.

If you have never rented a server on Amazon AWS, we have prepared simple instructions on how to get started with training there.

Before renting a server, let's first prepare everything that we need; the code and the data.

For data, we just take all the files (including the augmented ones) and put them into a single archive file:

```
zip -r all-data.zip  train_cv/  val_cv/
```

Then, we need to build the code such that we also have all the .jar files with dependencies laying nearby. This is done with maven-dependency-plugin, a plugin for Maven. We have used this plugin previously in Chapter 3, *Exploratory Data Analysis*, so we will omit the XML configuration that we need to add to our pom.xml file.

Now we use Maven to compile our code and put this into a `.jar` file:

```
mvn package
```

In our case, the project is called `chapter-08-dl4j`, so executing the package goal with Maven creates a `chapter-08-dl4j-0.0.1-SNAPSHOT.jar` file in the `target` folder. But since we also use the dependency plugin, it creates a `libs` folder, where you can find all the dependencies. Let's put everything into a single `.zip` file:

```
zip -r code.zip chapter-08-dl4j-0.0.1-SNAPSHOT.jar libs/
```

After performing the preparation steps, we will have two ZIP files, `all-data.zip` and `code.zip`.

Now, when we have prepared the program and the data, we can go to `aws.amazon.com` and sign into the console or create an account if you don't have one yet. When you are in, select **EC2**, which will bring you to the EC2 dashboard. Next, you can select the region you are interested in. You can either select something geographically close or the cheapest one. Usually, N. Virginia and US West Oregon are quite cheap compared to others.

Then, find the **Launch Instance** button and click on it.

If you need a GPU computer only for a few hours, you can choose to create a spot instance--they are cheaper than the usual instances, but their price is dynamic, and at some point, such an instance can die if somebody else is willing to pay more for the instance you are using. When starting it, you can set a price threshold, and if you choose something like $1 there, the instance should last for a long time.

When creating an instance, it is possible to use an existing AMI, an image of a system with some software preinstalled. The best option here is to look for CUDA, which will give you the official NVidia CUDA 7.5 image, but you are free to choose any other image you want.

Note that some of the AMIs are not free, be careful when choosing. Also, choose the AMI provider you can trust, as sometimes there could be malicious images, which will use the computational resources for something else than your task. If in doubt, use the official NVidia image, or create an image yourself from scratch.

Once you select the image, you can choose the instance type. For our purposes, the `g2.2.xlarge` instance is enough, but there are larger and more powerful ones if you wish.

Next, you need to select the storage type; we don't need anything and can skip this step. But the next is important, here we set up the security rules. Since the UI dashboard runs on port 9,000, we need to open it, so it is accessible from the outside world. We can then add a custom TCP rule and write `9000` there.

After this step, we are done and can proceed to launching the instance before reviewing the details.

Next, it will ask you to specify the key pair (`.pem`) for ssh to the instance, and you can create and download a new one if you don't have any. Let's create a key pair named `dl4j` and save it to the home folder.

Now, the instance is launched and ready to use. To access it, go to the dashboard and find the public DNS of the instance, this is the name you can use for accessing the server from your machine. Let's put this into an environment variable:

```
EC2_HOST=ec2-54-205-18-41.compute-1.amazonaws.com
```

From now on, we will assume you are using a bash shell on Linux, but it should work well in MacOS or Windows with cygwin or MinGW.

Now, we can upload the `.jar` file we previously built along with the data. For that, we will use `sftp`. Connecting the `sftp` client using the `pem` file is done this way:

```
sftp -o IdentityFile=~/dl4j.pem ec2-user@$EC2_HOST
```

Note that you should be in the folder with the data and the program archive. Then you can upload them by executing the following commands:

```
put code.zip
put all-data.zip
```

The data is uploaded, so now we can apply `ssh` to the instance to run the program:

```
ssh -i "~/dl4j.pem" ec2-user@$EC2_HOST
```

The first thing we do is to unpack the archives:

```
unzip code.zip
unzip all-data.zip
```

 If for some reason you do not have any free space left in the home folder, run the `df -h` command to see if there are any places with free space. There must be other disks with available space, where you can store the data.

By now we have unpacked everything and are ready to execute the code. But if you use the CUDA 7.5 AMI from NVidia, it only has Java 7 support. Since we used Java 8 for writing the code, we need to install Java 8:

```
sudo yum install java-1.8.0-openjdk.x86_64
```

We do not want the execution to stop when we leave the ssh session, so it is best to create screen there (or you can use tmux if you prefer):

```
screen -R dl4j
```

Now we run the code there:

```
java8 -cp chapter-08-dl4j.jar:libs/* chapter08.catsdogs.VggCatDog ~/data
```

Once you see that the model started training, you can detach the screen by pressing *Ctrl + A* followed by D. Now you can close the terminal and use the UI to watch the training process. To do it, just put EC2_HOST:9000 to your browser, where EC2_HOST is the public DNS of the instance.

This is it, now you just need to wait for some time until your model converges.

There could be some problem along the way.

If it says that it cannot find openblas binaries, then you have several options. You can either remove the dl4j-native JARS from the libs folder, or you can install openblas. The first option might be preferrable because we don't need to use the CPU anyways.

Another issue you can potentially run into is a missing NVCC executable, which is needed for dj4j's CUDA 7.5 library. Solving it is easy, you just need to add the path to CUDA's binaries to the PATH variable:

```
PATH=/usr/local/cuda-7.5/bin:$PATH
```

Summary

In this chapter, we looked at how we can use deep learning in Java applications, learned the basics of the DeepLearning4j library, and then tried to apply it to an image recognition problem where we wanted to classify images to dogs and cats.

In the next chapter, we will cover Apache Spark--a library for distributing data science algorithms across a cluster of machines.

9
Scaling Data Science

So far we have covered a lot of material about data science, we learned how to do both supervised and unsupervised learning in Java, how to perform text mining, use XGBoost and train Deep Neural Networks. However, most of the methods and techniques we used so far were designed to run on a single machine with the assumption that all the data will fit into memory. As you should already know, this is often the case: there are very large datasets that are not possible to process with traditional techniques on a typical hardware.

In this chapter, we will see how to process such datasets--we will look at the tools that allow processing the data across several machines. We will cover two use cases: one is large scale HTML processing from Common Crawl - the copy of the Web, and another is Link Prediction for a social network.

We will cover the following topics:

- Apache Hadoop MapReduce
- Common Crawl processing
- Apache Spark
- Link prediction
- Spark GraphFrame and MLlib libraries
- XGBoost on Apache Spark

By the end of this chapter, you will learnt how to use Hadoop to extracting data from Common Crawl, how to use Apache Spark for link prediction, and how to use XGBoost in Spark.

Apache Hadoop

Apache Hadoop is a set of tools that allows you to scale your data processing pipelines to thousands of machines. It includes:

- **Hadoop MapReduce**: This is a data processing framework
- **HDFS:** This is a distributed filesystem, which allows us to store data on multiple machines
- **YARN:** This is the executor of MapReduce and other jobs

We will only cover MapReduce, as it is the core of Hadoop and it is related to data processing. We will not cover the rest, and we will also not talk about setting up or configuring a Hadoop Cluster as this is slightly beyond scope for this book. If you are interested in knowing more about it, *Hadoop: The Definitive Guide* by *Tom White* is an excellent book for learning this subject in depth.

In our experiments, we will use the local mode, that is, we will emulate the cluster, but still run the code on a local machine. This is very useful for testing, and once we are sure that it works correctly, it can be deployed to a cluster with no changes.

Hadoop MapReduce

As we already said, Hadoop MapReduce is a library, that allows you to process data in a scalable way.

There are two main abstractions in the MapReduce framework: Map and Reduce. This idea originally comes from the functional programming paradigm, where `map` and `reduce` are high-level functions:

- `map`: This takes in a function and a sequence of elements and applies the function to each of the elements in turn. The result is a new sequence.
- `reduce`: This also takes in a function and a sequence, and it uses this function to process the sequence and ultimately return a single element in the end.

In this book, we have already used the map function from the Java Stream API quite extensively, starting with `Chapter 2`, *Data Processing Toolbox*, so you must be quite familiar with it by now.

In Hadoop MapReduce, the `map` and `reduce` functions are a bit different from their predecessors:

- Map takes in an element and returns a number of key-value pairs. It can return nothing, one, or several such pairs, so it is more `flatMap` than `map`
- Then the output is grouped by key via sorting
- Finally, `reduce` takes in a group, and for each group outputs a number of key-value pairs

Typically, MapReduce is illustrated with the word count example: given a text, we want to count how many times each word appeared in the text. The solution is as follows:

- The `map` takes in text, then tokenizes it, and for each token outputs a pair (`token, 1`), where `token` is the key, and `1` is the associated value.
- The `reducer` sums over all ones and this is the final count.

We will implement something similar: instead of just counting words, we will create TF-IDF vectors for each of the tokens in the corpus. But first, we need to get a large amount of text data from somewhere. We will use the Common Crawl dataset, which contains a copy of the Web.

Common Crawl

Common Crawl (`http://commoncrawl.org/`) is a repository of data crawled from the Internet over the last seven years. It is extremely large and, what is more is, it is available for everyone to download and analyze.

Of course, we will not be able to use all of it: even a small fraction is so large that it requires a big and powerful cluster for processing it. In this chapter, will take a few archives from the end of 2016, and extract the text ting TF-IDF.

Downloading the data is not complex and you can find the instructions at `http://commoncrawl.org/the-data/get-started/`. The data is already available in the S3 storage, so AWS users can access it easily. In this chapter, however, we will download a part of Common Crawl via HTTP without using AWS.

At the time of writing, the most recent data is from December 2016, which is located at `s3://commoncrawl/crawl-data/CC-MAIN-2016-50`. As per the instruction, we first need to get all the paths to individual archive files for this month, and they are stored in a `warc.paths.gz` file. So, in our case, we are interested in `s3://commoncrawl/crawl-data/CC-MAIN-2016-50/warc.paths.gz`.

Since we do not plan to use AWS, we need to convert it to a path downloadable via HTTP. For that, we replace `s3://commoncrawl/` with `https://commoncrawl.s3.amazonaws.com`:

```
wget
https://commoncrawl.s3.amazonaws.com/crawl-data/CC-MAIN-2016-50/warc.paths.
gz
```

Let's look at the file:

```
zcat warc.paths.gz | head -n 3
```

You will see a lot of lines like this (the suffixes are omitted for brevity):

```
.../CC-MAIN-20161202170900-00000-ip-10-31-129-80.ec2.internal.warc.gz
.../CC-MAIN-20161202170900-00001-ip-10-31-129-80.ec2.internal.warc.gz
.../CC-MAIN-20161202170900-00002-ip-10-31-129-80.ec2.internal.warc.gz
```

To download it via HTTP, we again need to append `https://commoncrawl.s3.amazonaws.com/` to every line of this file. This is easily achieved with awk:

```
zcat warc.paths.gz
  | head
  | awk '{ print "https://commoncrawl.s3.amazonaws.com/" $0}'
  > files.txt
```

Now we have the first 10 URLs from this file, so we can download them:

```
for url in $(cat files.txt); do
  wget $url;
done
```

To speed things up, we can download the files in parallel with gnu-parallel:

```
cat files.txt | parallel --gnu "wget {}"
```

Now we have downloaded somewhat biggish data: about 10 files of 1GB each. Note that there are about 50,000 lines in the path file, there are approximately 50,000 GBs of data just for December. This is a lot of data, and everybody can use it at any time!

We won't use all of it and will only concentrate on the 10 files we have already downloaded. Let's process them with Hadoop.

The first step is normal: we need to specify the dependencies to Hadoop in the `.pom` file:

```
<dependency>
  <groupId>org.apache.hadoop</groupId>
  <artifactId>hadoop-client</artifactId>
  <version>2.7.3</version>
</dependency>
<dependency>
  <groupId>org.apache.hadoop</groupId>
  <artifactId>hadoop-common</artifactId>
  <version>2.7.3</version>
</dependency>
```

Common Crawl uses WARC for storing the HTML data: this is a special format for storing the crawled data. To be able to process it, we need to add a special library for reading it:

```
<dependency>
  <groupId>org.netpreserve.commons</groupId>
  <artifactId>webarchive-commons</artifactId>
  <version>1.1.2</version>
</dependency>
```

Next, we need to tell Hadoop how to use such files. For this purpose, programmers typically need to provide implementations of `FileRecordReader` and `FileImportFormat` classes. Luckily, there are open source implementations, which we can just copy and paste to our projects. One of them is available at `https://github.com/Smerity/cc-warc-exampl es` in the `org.commoncrawl.warc` package. So we just copy `WARCFileInputFormat` and `WARCFileRecordReader` from there to our project. This code is also included in the code bundle of this book, in case the repository is removed.

With this, we are ready to start coding. First, we need to create a `Job` class: it specifies which mapper and reducer classes will be used to run the job and allows us to configure how this job will be executed. So, let's create an `WarcPreparationJob` class, which extends the `Configured` class and implements the `Tool` interface:

```
public class WarcPreparationJob extends Configured implements Tool {
    public static void main(String[] args) throws Exception {
        int res = ToolRunner.run(new Configuration(),
                new WarcPreparationJob(), args);
        System.exit(res);
    }

    public int run(String[] args) throws Exception {
```

```
        // implementation goes here
    }
}
```

The Java doc for the `Tool` interface is quite informative and describes in detail how such a `Job` class should be implemented: it has overriden the `run` method, where it should specify the input and the output paths as well as the mapper and reducer classes.

We will adapt this code slightly: first, we will have a map-only Job, so we do not need a reducer. Also, since we are working with texts, it is useful to compress the output. So, let's create the `run` method with the following code. First, we create a `Job` class:

```
Job job = Job.getInstance(getConf());
```

Now we will look at the input and its format (WARC in our case):

```
Path inputPath = new Path(args[0]);
FileInputFormat.addInputPath(job, inputPath);
job.setInputFormatClass(WARCFileInputFormat.class);
```

Next, we specify the output, which is gzipped text:

```
Path outputPath = new Path(args[1];
TextOutputFormat.setOutputPath(job, outputPath);
TextOutputFormat.setCompressOutput(job, true);
TextOutputFormat.setOutputCompressorClass(job, GzipCodec.class);
job.setOutputFormatClass(TextOutputFormat.class);
```

Usually, the output is key-value pairs, but since we just want to process WARC and extract the text from there, we only output a key, and no value:

```
job.setOutputKeyClass(Text.class);
job.setOutputValueClass(NullWritable.class);
```

Finally, we specify the mapper class and say that there will be no reducers:

```
job.setMapperClass(WarcPreparationMapper.class);
job.setNumReduceTasks(0);
```

Now, when we have specified the job, we can implement the mapper class-- `WarcPreparationMapper` in our case. This class should extend the `Mapper` class. All mappers should implement the `map` method, so our mapper should have the following outline:

```
public class WarcPreparationMapper extends
        Mapper<Text, ArchiveReader, Text, NullWritable> {
```

```
@Override
protected void map(Text input, ArchiveReader archive, Context context)
        throws IOException, InterruptedException {
    // implementation goes here
}

}
```

The `map` method takes in a WARC `archive` with a collection of records, so we want to process all of them. Thus, we put the following to the `map` method:

```
for (ArchiveRecord record : archive) {
    process(record, context);
}
```

And the process method does the following: it extracts the HTML from the record, then extracts the text from HTML, tokenizes it, and then, finally, writes the results to the output. In code it looks like this:

```
String url = record.getHeader().getUrl();
String html = TextUtils.extractHtml(record);
String text = TextUtils.extractText(html);
List<String> tokens = TextUtils.tokenize(text);
String result = url + "t" + String.join(" ", tokens);
context.write(new Text(result), NullWritable.get());
```

Inside we use three helper functions: `extractHtml`, `extractText`, and `tokenize`. We have already used the last two (`exctractHtml` and `tokenize`) a few times, so we will omit their implementation; refer to `Chapter 6`, *Working with Text - Natural Language Processing and Information Retrieval*.

And the first one, `extractHtml`, contains the following code:

```
byte[] rawData = IOUtils.toByteArray(r, r.available());
String rawContent = new String(rawData, "UTF-8");
String[] split = rawContent.split("(r?n){2}", 2);
String html = split[1].trim();
```

It converts the data from the archive to `String` with UTF-8 encoding (which sometimes might not be ideal because not all pages on the Internet use UTF-8), and then removes the response header and keeps only the remaining HTML.

Finally, to run these classes, we can use the following code:

```
String[] args = { /data/cc_warc", "/data/cc_warc_processed" };
ToolRunner.run(new Configuration(), new WarcPreparationJob(), args);
```

Here we manually specify the "command-line" parameters (the ones that you get in the main method) and pass them to the `ToolRunner` class, which can run Hadoop Jobs in the local model.

 The results may have pornographic content. Since Common Crawl is a copy of the Web, and there are a lot of pornographic websites on the Internet, it is very likely that you will see some pornographic text in the processed results. It is quite easy to filter it out by keeping a special a list of pornographic keywords and discarding all the documents that contain any of these words.

After running this job, you will see that there are plenty of different languages in the results. If we are interested in a specific language, then we can automatically detect the language of a document, and keep only those documents that are in the language we are interested in.

Several Java libraries which can do language detection. One of them is language-detector, which can be included in our project with the following dependency snippet:

```
<dependency>
  <groupId>com.optimaize.languagedetector</groupId>
  <artifactId>language-detector</artifactId>
  <version>0.5</version>
</dependency>
```

Not surprisingly, this library uses machine learning for detecting the language. So, the first thing we need to do to use it is to load the model:

```
List<LanguageProfile> languageProfiles =
        new LanguageProfileReader().readAllBuiltIn();
LanguageDetector detector =
LanguageDetectorBuilder.create(NgramExtractors.standard())
        .withProfiles(languageProfiles)
        .build();
```

And we can use it this way:

```
Optional<LdLocale> result = detector.detect(text);
String language = "unk";
if (result.isPresent()) {
    language = result.get().getLanguage();
}
```

With this, we can just keep the articles in English (or any other language) and discard the rest. So, let's extract the text from the files we downloaded:

```
String lang = detectLanguage(text.get());
if (lang.equals("en")) {
    // process the data
}
```

Here, `detectLanguage` is a method, that contains the code for detecting what is the language of the text: we wrote this code earlier.

Once we have processed the WARC files and extracted the text from them, we can calculate IDF for every token in our corpus. For that, we need to first calculate DF - Document Frequency. This is very similar to the Word Count example:

- First, we need a `mapper` that outputs 1 for each distinct word in the document
- Then the `reducer` sums up all the ones to come up with the final count

This job will process the documents we just parsed from Common Crawl.

Let's create the mapper. It will have the following code in the `map` method:

```
String doc = value.toString();
String[] split = doc.split("t");
String joinedTokens = split[1];
Set<String> tokens = Sets.newHashSet(joinedTokens.split(" "));
LongWritable one = new LongWritable(1);

for (String token : tokens) {
    context.write(new Text(token), one);
}
```

The input to the mapper is a `Text` object (named `value`), which contains the URL and the tokens. We split the tokens and keep only distinct ones using a `HashSet`. Finally, for each distinct token, we write 1.

For calculating IDF, we typically need to know N: the number of documents in our corpus. There are two ways of getting it. First, we can use the counters: create a counter and increment it for each successfully processed document. It is quite easy to do.

The first step is to create a special `enum` with the possible counters we want to use in our application. Since we need to have only one type of counter, we create an `enum` with just one element:

```
public static enum Counter {
    DOCUMENTS;
}
```

The second step is to use the `context.getCounter()` method and increment the counter:

```
context.getCounter(Counter.DOCUMENTS).increment(1);
```

Once the job is over, we can get the value of the counter with this code:

```
Counters counters = job.getCounters();
long count = counters.findCounter(Counter.DOCUMENTS).getValue();
```

But there is another option: we can just pick a large number and use it as the number of documents. It typically does not need to be exact since IDFs of all tokens share the same N.

Now, let's continue with the `reducer`. Since the mapper outputs `Text` and a long (via `LongWritable`), the reducer gets in a `Text` and an iterable over `LongWritable` classes-- this is the token and a bunch of ones. What we can do is just sum over all of them:

```
long sum = 0;
for (LongWritable cnt : values) {
    sum = sum + cnt.get();
}
```

To keep only frequent tokens, we can add a filter, to discard all infrequent words and make the results significantly smaller:

```
if (sum > 100) {
    context.write(key, new LongWritable(sum));
}
```

Then, the code in our `job` class for running it will look like this:

```
job.setInputFormatClass(TextInputFormat.class);
job.setOutputFormatClass(TextOutputFormat.class);
job.setOutputKeyClass(Text.class);
job.setOutputValueClass(LongWritable.class);

job.setMapperClass(DocumentFrequencyMapper.class);
job.setCombinerClass(DocumentFrequencyReducer.class);
job.setReducerClass(DocumentFrequencyReducer.class);
```

Note that we not only set mapper and reducer, but also specify a combiner: this allows us to pre-aggregate some 1's that we output in the mapper and spend less time sorting the data and sending the results around the network.

Finally, to convert a document to TF-IDF, we can create a third job, reduce-less again, which will read the results of the first job (where we processed WARC files) and apply the IDF weighting from the second job.

We expect that the output of the second job should be quite small to fit into memory, so what we can do is send the file to all mappers, read it during the initialization, and then go over the lines of processed WARC and previously.

The main parts of the `job` class are the same: we input and the output is `Text`--the output is compressed and the number of reducer tasks is `0`.

Now we need to send the results of the `df` job to all the mappers. This is done via the cache files:

```
Path dfInputPath = new Path(args[3]);
job.addCacheFile(new URI(dfInputPath.toUri() + "#df"));
```

So here we specify the path to the `df` job results and then put it to the cache file. Note `#df` at the end: this is the alias we will use for accessing the file later.

Inside the mapper, we can read all the results into a map (in the setup method):

```
dfs = new HashMap<>();
File dir = new File("./df");
for (File file : dir.listFiles()) {
    try (FileInputStream is = FileUtils.openInputStream(file)) {
        LineIterator lines = IOUtils.lineIterator(is,
StandardCharsets.UTF_8);
        while (lines.hasNext()) {
            String line = lines.next();
            String[] split = line.split("t");
            dfs.put(split[0], Integer.parseInt(split[1]));
        }
    }
}
```

Here, `df` is the alias we assigned to the results file, and it is actually a folder, not a file. So to get the result, we need to go over each file in the folder, read them line by line, and put the results into a map. Then we can use this dictionary with counts in the map method for applying the IDF weight:

```
String doc = value.toString();
```

```
String[] split = doc.split("t");
String url = split[0];
List<String> tokens = Arrays.asList(split[1].split(" "));
Multiset<String> counts = HashMultiset.create(tokens);
String tfIdfTokens = counts.entrySet().stream()
        .map(e -> toTfIdf(dfs, e))
        .collect(Collectors.joining(" "));
Text output = new Text(url + "t" + tfIdfTokens);
context.write(output, NullWritable.get());
```

Here we take the tokens and use `Multiset` for calculating the Term Frequency. Next, we multiply the TF by IDF inside the `toTfIdf` function:

```
String token = e.getElement();
int tf = e.getCount();
int df = dfs.getOrDefault(token, 100);
double idf = LOG_N - Math.log(df);
String result = String.format("%s:%.5f", token, tf * idf);
```

Here, we get the DF (Document Frequency) for each input entry of `Multiset`, and if the token is not in our dictionary, we assume that it is quite rare, so we assign it the default DF of 100. Next, we calculate IDF and finally `tf*idf`. For calculating IDF, we use `LOG_N`, which is a constant we set to `Math.log(1_000_000)`.

For this example, 1 million was chosen as the number of documents. Even though the real number of documents is smaller (around 5k), it is the same for all the tokens. What is more, if we decide to add more documents to our index, we can still use the same *N* and not worry about re-calculating everything.

This produces the output that looks like this:

```
http://url.com/          flavors:9.21034 gluten:9.21034 specialty:14.28197
salad:18.36156 ...
```

As you must have noticed, the output of each job is saved to the disk. If we have multiple jobs, like we did, we need to read the data, process it, and save it back. I/O is quite costly, so some of these steps are intermediate and we do not need to save the results. In Hadoop there is no way to avoid this, which is why it is pretty slow sometimes and gives a lot of I/O overhead.

Luckily, there is another library that solves this problem: Apache Spark.

Apache Spark

Apache Spark is a framework for scalable data processing. It was designed to be better than Hadoop: it tries to process data in memory and not to save intermediate results on disk. Additionally, it has more operations, not just map and reduce, and thus richer APIs.

The main unit of abstraction in Apache Spark is **Resilient Distributed Dataset** (RDD), which is a distributed collection of elements. The key difference from usual collections or streams is that RDDs can be processed in parallel across multiple machines, in the same way, Hadoop jobs are processed.

There are two types of operations we can apply to RDDs: transformations and actions.

- **Transformations**: As the name suggests, it only changes data from one form to another. As input, they receive an RDD, and they also output an RDD. Operations such as map, flatMap, or filter are examples of transformation operations.
- **Actions**: These take in an RDD and produce something else, for example, a value, a list, or a map, or save the results. Examples of actions are count and reduce.

Like in the Java Steam API, transformations are lazy: they are not performed right away, but instead they are chained together and computed in one go, without the need to save the intermediate results to disk. In the Steam API, the chain is triggered by collecting the stream, and it is the same in Spark: when we perform an action, all transformation that is needed for this particular action are executed. If on the other hand some transformations are not required, then they will never be executed, which is why they are called *lazy*.

So let's start with Spark by first including its dependency to the .pom file:

```
<dependency>
  <groupId>org.apache.spark</groupId>
  <artifactId>spark-core_2.11</artifactId>
  <version>2.1.0</version>
</dependency>
```

In this section, we will use it for computing TF-IDF: so we will try to reproduce the algorithm we just wrote for Hadoop.

The first step is to create the configuration and the context:

```
SparkConf conf = new SparkConf().setAppName("tfidf").setMaster("local[*]");
JavaSparkContext sc = new JavaSparkContext(conf);
```

Here, we specify the name of the Spark application and also the server URL to which it will connect. Since we are running Spark in a local mode, we put `local[*]`. This means that we set up a local server and create as many local workers as possible.

Spark relies on some Hadoop utilities, which makes it harder to run it on Windows. If you are running under Windows, you may have a problem with not being able to locate the `winutils.exe` file, which is needed by Spark and Hadoop. To solve this, do the following:

- Create a folder for Hadoop files, for example, `c:/tmp/hadoop` (make sure there are no spaces in the path)
- Download `winutils.exe` from `http://public-repo-1.hortonworks.com/hdp-win-alpha/winutils.exe`
- Put the file to the folder `c:/tmp/hadoop/bin`--note the `bin` subdirectory.
- Set the `HADOOP_HOME` environment variable to `c:/tmp/hadoop` and, alternatively, use the following code:

```
System.setProperty("hadoop.home.dir", "c:/tmp/hadoop");
```

This should solve the problem.

The next step is to read the text file, which we created with Hadoop after processing the Common Crawl files. Let's read it:

```
JavaRDD<String> textFile = sc.textFile("C:/tmp/warc");
```

To peek into the files, we can use the take function, which returns the top 10 elements from the RDD, and then we print each line to stdout:

```
textFile.take(10).forEach(System.out::println);
```

Now we can read the file line-by-line, and, for each document, output all the distinct tokens it has:

```
JavaPairRDD<String, Integer> dfRdd = textFile
    .flatMap(line -> distinctTokens(line))
    .mapToPair(t -> new Tuple2<>(t, 1))
    .reduceByKey((a, b) -> a + b)
    .filter(t -> t._2 >= 100);
```

Here, `distinctToken` is a function that splits the line and puts all the tokens into a set to keep only the distinct ones. Here is how it is implemented:

```
private static Iterator<String> distinctTokens(String line) {
    String[] split = line.split("t");
    Set<String> tokens = Sets.newHashSet(split[1].split(" "));
```

```
        return tokens.iterator();
    }
```

The `flatMap` function needs to return an iterator, so we invoke the iterator method on the set at the end.

Next, we convert each line to a tuple: this step is needed to tell Spark that we have key-value pairs, so functions such as `reduceByKey` and `groupByKey` are available. Finally, we call the `reduceByKey` method with the same implementation as we previously had in Hadoop. At the end of the transformation chain, we apply the filter to keep only frequent enough tokens.

You might have already noticed that this code is quite simple, compared to the Hadoop job we wrote previously.

Now we can put all the results into a `Map`: since we applied the filtering, we expect that the dictionary should easily fit into a memory even on modest hardware. We do it by using the `collectAsMap` function:

```
    Map<String, Integer> dfs = dfRdd.collectAsMap();
```

Lastly, we go over all the documents again, and this time apply the TF-IDF weighting scheme to all the tokens:

```
    JavaRDD<String> tfIdfRdd = textFile.map(line -> {
        String[] split = line.split("t");
        String url = split[0];
        List<String> tokens = Arrays.asList(split[1].split(" "));
        Multiset<String> counts = HashMultiset.create(tokens);

        String tfIdfTokens = counts.entrySet().stream()
                .map(e -> toTfIdf(dfs, e))
                .collect(Collectors.joining(" "));

        return url + "t" + tfIdfTokens;
    });
```

We parse the input as we did previously and use `Multiset` from Guava for calculating TF. The `toTfIdf` function is exactly the same as before: it takes in an entry from `Multiset`, weights it by IDF, and outputs a string in the `token:weight` format.

To have a look at the results, we can take the first 10 tokens from the RDD and print them to stdout:

```
    tfIdfRdd.take(10).forEach(System.out::println);
```

Finally, we save the results to a text file using the `saveAsTextFile` method:

```
tfIdfRdd.saveAsTextFile("c:/tmp/warc-tfidf");
```

As we see, we can do the same in Spark with significantly less code. What is more, it is also more efficient: it does not need to save the results to disk after each step and applies all the required transformations on-the-fly. This makes Spark a lot faster than Hadoop for many applications.

However, there are cases when Hadoop is better than Spark. Spark tries to keep everything in memory, and sometimes it fails with `OutOfMemoryException` because of this. Hadoop is a lot simpler: all it does is it writes to files, and then performa big distributed merge sort over the data. That being said, in general, you should prefer Apache Spark over Hadoop MapReduce, because Hadoop is slower and quite verbose.

In the next section, we will see how we can use Apache Spark and its Graph Processing and Machine Learning libraries for the Link Prediction problem.

Link prediction

Link Prediction is the problem of predicting which links will appear in a network. For example, we can have a friendship graph in Facebook or another social network, and functionality *like people you may know* is an application of Link Prediction. So, we can see Link Prediction is a recommendation system for social networks.

For this problem, we need to find a dataset that contains a graph evolving over time. Then, we can consider such a graph at some point in its evolution, calculate some characteristics between the existing links, and, based on that, predict which links are likely to appear next. Since for such graphs we know the future, we can use this knowledge for evaluating the performance of our models.

There are a number of interesting datasets available, but unfortunately, most of them do not have a time associated to the edges, so it is not possible to see how these graphs developed over time. This makes it harder to test the methods, but, of course, it is possible to do it without the time dimension.

Luckily, there are some datasets with timestamped edges. For this chapter, we will use the coauthorship graph based on the data from DBLP (`http://dblp.uni-trier.de/`) - a search engine that indexes computer science papers. The dataset is available from `http://project s.csail.mit.edu/dnd/DBLP/` (`dblp_coauthorship.json.gz` file) and it includes the papers from 1938 until 2015. It is already in the graph form: each edge is a pair of authors who published a paper together and each edge also contains the year when they did this.

This is what the first few lines of the file look like:

```
[
["Alin Deutsch", "Mary F. Fernandez", 1998],
["Alin Deutsch", "Daniela Florescu", 1998],
["Alin Deutsch", "Alon Y. Levy", 1998],
["Alin Deutsch", "Dan Suciu", 1998],
["Mary F. Fernandez", "Daniela Florescu", 1998],
```

Let's use this dataset to build a model that will predict who is very likely to become a coauthor in the future. One of the applications of such a model can be a recommender system: for each author, it may suggest the possible coauthors to cooperate with.

Reading the DBLP graph

To start with this project, we first need to read the graph data, and for this, we will use Apache Spark and a few of its libraries. The first library is Spark Data frames, it is similar to R data frames, pandas or joinery, except that they are distributed and based on RDDs.

Let's read this dataset. The first step is to create a special class `Edge` for storing the data:

```
public class Edge implements Serializable {
    private final String node1;
    private final String node2;
    private final int year;
    // constructor and setters omitted
}
```

Now, let's read the data:

```
SparkConf conf = new SparkConf().setAppName("graph").setMaster("local[*]");
JavaSparkContext sc = new JavaSparkContext(conf);
JavaRDD<String> edgeFile =
sc.textFile("/data/dblp/dblp_coauthorship.json.gz");

JavaRDD<Edge> edges = edgeFile.filter(s -> s.length() > 1).map(s -> {
    Object[] array = JSON.std.arrayFrom(s);

    String node1 = (String) array[0];
    String node2 = (String) array[1];
    Integer year = (Integer) array[2];

    if (year == null) {
        return new Edge(node1, node2, -1);
    }
```

```
            return new Edge(node1, node2, year);
    });
```

After setting up the context, we read the data from a text file, and then apply a map function to each line to convert it to `Edge`. For parsing JSON, we use the Jackson-Jr library as previously, so make sure you add this to the pom file.

Note that we also include a `filter` here: the first and the last line contain `[` and `]` respectively, so we need to skip them.

To check whether we managed to parse the data successfully, we can use the take method: it gets the head of the RDD and puts it into a `List`, which we can print to the console:

```
edges.take(5).forEach(System.out::println);
```

This should produce the following output:

```
Edge [node1=Alin Deutsch, node2=Mary F. Fernandez, year=1998]
Edge [node1=Alin Deutsch, node2=Daniela Florescu, year=1998]
Edge [node1=Alin Deutsch, node2=Alon Y. Levy, year=1998]
Edge [node1=Alin Deutsch, node2=Dan Suciu, year=1998]
Edge [node1=Mary F. Fernandez, node2=Daniela Florescu, year=1998]
```

After successfully converting the data, we will put it into a Data Frame. For that, we will use Spark DataFrame, which is a part of the Spark-SQL package. We can include it with the following dependency:

```
<dependency>
  <groupId>org.apache.spark</groupId>
  <artifactId>spark-sql_2.11</artifactId>
  <version>2.1.0</version>
</dependency>
```

To create a `DataFrame` from our `RDD`, we first create a SQL session, and then use its `createDataFrame` method:

```
SparkSession sql = new SparkSession(sc.sc());
Dataset<Row> df = sql.createDataFrame(edges, Edge.class);
```

There are quite a lot of papers in the dataset. We can make it smaller by restricting it to papers that were published only in 1990. For this we can use the `filter` method:

```
df = df.filter("year >= 1990");
```

Next, many authors can have multiple papers together, and we are interested in the earliest one. We can get it using the `min` function:

```
df = df.groupBy("node1", "node2")
        .min("year")
        .withColumnRenamed("min(year)", "year");
```

When we apply the min function, the column gets renamed to `min(year)`, so we fix it by renaming the column back to `year` with the `withColumnRenamed` function.

For building any machine learning model, we always need to specify a train/test split. This case is no exception, so let's take all the data before 2013 as the training part, and all the papers after as testing:

```
Dataset<Row> train = df.filter("year <= 2013");
Dataset<Row> test = df.filter("year >= 2014");
```

Now, we can start extracting some features that we will use for creating a model.

Extracting features from the graph

We need to extract some features that we will put to the Machine Learning model for training. For this dataset, all the information we have is the graph itself and nothing more: we do not have any external information such as author's affiliation. Of course, if we had it, it would be no problem to add it to the model. So let's discuss which features we can extract from the graph alone.

For graph models, there can be two kinds of features: node features (authors) and edge features (the coauthorship relation).

There are many possible features we can extract from graph nodes. For example, among others, we can consider the following:

- **Degree**: This is the number of coauthors this author has.
- **Page Rank**: This is the importance of a node.

Let's look at the following diagram:

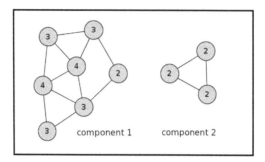

Here we have two connected components, and the number on the node specifies the degree of the node, or how many connections it has.

In some way, the degree measures the importance (or centrality) of a node: the more connections it has, the higher the importance. Page Rank (also called Eigenvector Centrality) is another measure of importance. You have probably heard about Page Rank - it is used by Google as one of the components of its ranking formula. The main idea behind Page Rank is that, if a page is linked to other important pages, it also must be important. Sometimes it also makes sense to use Chei Rank, the reverse of Page Rank-- which instead of looking at incoming edges, looks at outcoming ones.

However, our graph is not directed: if *A* and *B* are coauthors, then *B* and *A* are also coauthors. So, in our case Page Rank and Chei Rank are exactly the same.

There are other important measures such as Closeness Centrality or Betweenness Centrality, but we will not consider them in this chapter.

Also, we can look at the connected component of a node: if two nodes are from different connected components, it is often difficult to predict whether there is going to be a link between them. (Of course, it becomes possible if we include other features, not only the ones we can extract from the graph.)

Graphs also have edges, and we can extract a lot of information about them for building our models. For example, we may consider the following features:

- **Common Friends**: This is the number of common coauthors
- **Total Friends**: This is the total number of distinct coauthors both authors have
- **Jaccard Similarity**: This is the Jaccard similarity of the coauthor's sets
- **Node-based features** This is the difference in the Page Rank of each node, min and max degree, and so on

Of course there are a lot of other features we can include, for example, the length of the shortest path between two authors should be quite a strong predictor, but calculating it typically requires a lot of time.

Node features

Let's first concentrate on the features with which we can compute nodes of a graph. For that, we will need a graph library which lets us compute graph features such as degree or Page Rank easily. For Apache Spark, such a library is GraphX. However, at the moment, this library only supports Scala: it uses a lot of Scala-specific features, which makes it very hard (and often impossible) to use it from Java.

However, there is another library called GraphFrames, which tries to combine GraphX with DataFrames. Luckily for us, it supports Java. This package is not available on Maven Central, and to use it, we first need to add the following repository to our `pom.xml`:

```
<repository>
  <id>bintray-spark</id>
  <url>https://dl.bintray.com/spark-packages/maven/</url>
</repository>
```

Next, let's include the library:

```
<dependency>
  <groupId>graphframes</groupId>
  <artifactId>graphframes</artifactId>
  <version>0.3.0-spark2.0-s_2.11</version>
</dependency>
```

We also need to add the GraphX dependency, because GraphFrames relies on it:

```
<dependency>
  <groupId>org.apache.spark</groupId>
  <artifactId>spark-graphx_2.11</artifactId>
  <version>2.1.0</version>
</dependency>
```

 The GraphFrames library is under active development at the moment, and it is quite likely that some of the method names will change in the future. Refer to the official documentation from `http://graphframes.github.io/`, if, the examples from this chapter stop working.

However, before we can actually use GraphFrames, we need to prepare our data, as it expects the Data Frames to follow a specific convention. First, it assumes that the graph is directed, which is not the case for our example. To overcome this problem, we need to add the reverse links. That is, we have a record (A, B) in our dataset, we need to add its reverse (B, A).

We can do this by renaming the columns of a copy of our DataFrame and then use the union function with the original DataFrame:

```
Dataset<Row> dfReversed = df
        .withColumnRenamed("node1", "tmp")
        .withColumnRenamed("node2", "node1")
        .withColumnRenamed("tmp", "node2")
        .select("node1", "node2", "year")
Dataset<Row> edges = df.union(dfReversed);
```

Next, we need to create a special DataFrame for the nodes. We can do this by just selecting the node1 column of the edges dataset and then calling the distinct function:

```
Dataset<Row> nodes = edges.select("node1")
        .withColumnRenamed("node1", "node")
        .distinct();
```

GraphFrame, when taking in a DataFrame with nodes, expects it to have the id column, which we have to manually create. The first option is to just rename the node column to id and pass this to GraphFrame. Another option is to create surrogate IDs, which we will do here:

```
nodes = nodes.withColumn("id", functions.monotonicallyIncreasingId());
```

For the preceding code, we need to add the following import:

```
import org.apache.spark.sql.functions;
```

This functions is a utility class with a lot of useful DataFrame functions.

To see what our DataFrame looks like after all these transformations, we can use the show method:

```
nodes.show();
```

It will produce the following output (truncated to six first rows here and in all examples):

```
+--------------------+---+
|                node| id|
+--------------------+---+
|         Dan Olteanu|  0|
```

```
|       Manjit Borah|  1|
|   Christoph Elsner|  2|
|       Sagnika Sen|  3|
|       Jerome Yen|  4|
|     Anand Kudari|  5|
|           M. Pan|  6|
+-------------------+---+
```

Now, let's prepare the edges. GraphFrames requires the data frame to have two special columns: `src` and `dst` (*source* and *destination*, respectively). To get the values for these columns, let's join them with the nodes DataFrame and get the numerical IDs:

```
edges = edges.join(nodes, edges.col("node2").equalTo(nodes.col("node")));
edges = edges.drop("node").withColumnRenamed("id", "dst");
edges = edges.join(nodes, edges.col("node1").equalTo(nodes.col("node")));
edges = edges.drop("node").withColumnRenamed("id", "src");
```

It will create a DataFrame with the following content:

```
+-------------+-------------------+----+-------------+----+
|        node1|              node2|year|          dst| src|
+-------------+-------------------+----+-------------+----+
|A. A. Davydov| Eugene V. Shilnikov|2013|  51539612101|2471|
|A. A. Davydov|      S. V. Sinitsyn|2011| 326417520647|2471|
|A. A. Davydov|      N. Yu. Nalutin|2011| 335007452466|2471|
|A. A. Davydov|       A. V. Bataev|2011| 429496733302|2471|
|A. A. Davydov|Boris N. Chetveru...|2013|1486058685923|2471|
| A. A. Sawant|        M. K. Shah|2011| 231928238662|4514|
| A. A. Sawant|     A. V. Shingala|2011| 644245100670|4514|
+-------------+-------------------+----+-------------+----+
```

Finally, we can create `GraphFrame` from the nodes and edges dataframes:

```
GraphFrame gf = GraphFrame.apply(nodes, edges);
```

The `GraphFrame` class allows us to use a lot of graph algorithms. For example, computing Page Rank is as easy as follows:

```
GraphFrame pageRank = gf.pageRank().resetProbability(0.1).maxIter(7).run();
Dataset<Row> pageRankNodes = pageRank.vertices();
pageRankNodes.show();
```

It will create a `DataFrame` with the following columns:

```
+----+-------------------+
|  id|           pagerank|
+----+-------------------+
|  26| 1.4394843416065657|
```

```
|   29|  1.012233852957335|
|  474|  0.7774103396731716|
|  964|  0.4443614094552203|
|1677|   0.274044687604839|
|1697|   0.493174385163372|
+----+-------------------+
```

Calculating degrees is even simpler:

```
Dataset<Row> degrees = gf.degrees();
```

This line of code will create a `DataFrame` with the degree of each node:

```
+-------------+------+
|           id|degree|
+-------------+------+
|  901943134694|    86|
|  171798692537|     4|
|1589137900148|   114|
|    8589935298|    86|
|  901943133299|    74|
|  292057778121|    14|
+-------------+------+
```

The same is true for calculating connected components:

```
Dataset<Row> cc = gf.connectedComponents().run();
```

It will create a `DataFrame` where for each node we will have the ID of the connected component it belongs to:

```
+----+---------+
|  id|component|
+----+---------+
|  26|        0|
|  29|        0|
| 474|        0|
| 964|      964|
|1677|        0|
|1697|        0|
+----+---------+
```

As we see here 5 out of 6 first components are the 0th component. Let's look at the sizes of these components--maybe the 0th is the largest and includes almost everything?

To do it, we can count how many times each component occurs:

```
Dataset<Row> cc = connectedComponents.groupBy("component").count();
cc.orderBy(functions.desc("count")).show();
```

We use the `groupBy` function and then invoke the `count` method. After that, we order the DataFrame by the values of the count column in the decreasing order. Let's look at the output:

```
+------------+-------+
|   component|  count|
+------------+-------+
|           0|1173137|
| 60129546561|     32|
| 60129543093|     30|
|         722|     29|
| 77309412270|     28|
| 34359740786|     28|
+------------+-------+
```

As we see, most of the nodes are indeed from the same component. Thus, in this case, the information about the component is not very useful: almost always the component is 0.

Now, after computing the node features, we need to proceed to edge features. But before we can do that, we first need to sample edges for which we are going to compute these features.

Negative sampling

Before we compute another set of features, the edge features, we need to first specify which edges we would like to take for that. So we need to select a set of candidate edges, and then we will train a model on them for predicting whether an edge should belong to the graph or not. In other words, we first need to prepare a dataset where existent edges are treated as positive examples, and nonexistent ones as negative.

Getting positive examples is simple: we just take all the edges and assign them the label 1.

For negative examples, it is more complex: in any real-life graph, the number of positive examples is a lot smaller than the number of negative examples. So we need to find a way to sample the negative examples so that training a model becomes manageable.

Often, for the Link Prediction problems, we consider two types of negative candidates: simple and hard ones. The simple ones are just sampled from the same connected components, but the hard ones are one or two hops away. Since for our problem most of the authors are from the same component, we can relax it and sample the simple negatives from the entire graph, and not restrict ourselves to the same connected component:

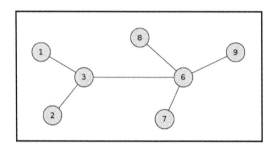

If we consider the preceding graph, positive examples are easy: we just get the existent edges (1, 3), (2, 3), (3, 6), and so on. For negative ones, there are two types: simple and hard. The simple ones are just sampled from the set of all possible nonexistent edges. Here, it can be (1, 8), (2, 7), or (1, 9). The hard negative edges are only one hop away: (1, 2), (1, 6), or (7, 9) are possible examples of hard negatives.

In our dataset, we have about 6 million positive examples. To keep the training data more or less balanced, we can sample about 12 million simple negatives and about 6 million hard ones. Then the proportion of positive to negative examples will be 1/4.

Creating positive examples is straightforward: we just take the edges from the graph and assign them the 1.0 target:

```
Dataset<Row> pos = df.drop("year");
pos = pos.join(nodes, pos.col("node1").equalTo(nodes.col("node")));
pos = pos.drop("node", "node1").withColumnRenamed("id", "node1");

pos = pos.join(nodes, pos.col("node2").equalTo(nodes.col("node")));
pos = pos.drop("node", "node2").withColumnRenamed("id", "node2");

pos = pos.withColumn("target", functions.lit(1.0));
```

Here we do a few joins to replace the author names with their IDs. The result is the following:

```
+-------------+-----+------+
|        node1|node2|target|
+-------------+-----+------+
|  51539612101| 2471|   1.0|
```

```
|  429496733302|  2471|    1.0|
|1486058685923|  2471|    1.0|
|1254130450702|  4514|    1.0|
|   94489280742|   913|    1.0|
|1176821039357|   913|    1.0|
+-------------+-----+------+
```

Next, we sample the easy negative ones. For that, we first sample with replacement from the node's DataFrame twice, once for `node1` and once - for `node2`. Then, put these columns together into one single data frame. We can take the samples this way:

```
Dataset<Row> nodeIds = nodes.select("id");
long nodesCount = nodeIds.count();
double fraction = 12_000_000.0 / nodesCount;

Dataset<Row> sample1 = nodeIds.sample(true, fraction, 1);
sample1 = sample1.withColumn("rnd", functions.rand(1))
                 .orderBy("rnd")
                 .drop("rnd");

Dataset<Row> sample2 = nodeIds.sample(true, fraction, 2);
sample2 = sample2.withColumn("rnd", functions.rand(2))
                 .orderBy("rnd")
                 .drop("rnd");
```

Here, the fraction parameter specifies what is the fraction of the DataFrame which the sample should contain. Since we want to get 12 million examples, we divide 12 million by the number of nodes we have. Then, we shuffle each sample by adding a column with random number to it and use it for ordering the DataFrames. We don't need this column after sorting is done, so it can be dropped.

It is possible that two samples have different sizes, so we need to select the minimal one, and then limit both samples to this size, so they become concatenable:

```
long sample1Count = sample1.count();
long sample2Count = sample2.count();

int minSize = (int) Math.min(sample1Count, sample2Count);

sample1 = sample1.limit(minSize);
sample2 = sample2.limit(minSize);
```

Next, we want to put these two samples together into one DataFrame. There is no easy way to do this with the DataFrame API, so we will need to use RDDs for that. To do it, we convert the DataFrames into JavaRDDs, zip them together, and then convert the result back to a single DataFrame:

```
JavaRDD<Row> sample1Rdd = sample1.toJavaRDD();
JavaRDD<Row> sample2Rdd = sample2.toJavaRDD();
JavaRDD<Row> concat = sample1Rdd.zip(sample2Rdd).map(t -> {
    long id1 = t._1.getLong(0);
    long id2 = t._2.getLong(0);
    return RowFactory.create(id1, id2);
});

StructField node1Field = DataTypes.createStructField("node1",
DataTypes.LongType, false);
StructField node2Field = DataTypes.createStructField("node2",
DataTypes.LongType, false);
StructType schema = DataTypes.createStructType(Arrays.asList(node1Field,
node2Field));
Dataset<Row> negSimple = sql.createDataFrame(concat, schema);
```

For converting the RDD into a DataFrame, we need to specify a schema, and the preceding code shows how to do it.

Finally, we add the target column to this DataFrame:

```
negSimple = negSimple.withColumn("target", functions.lit(0.0));
```

This will generate the following DataFrame:

```
+-------------+-------------+------+
|        node1|        node2|target|
+-------------+-------------+------+
| 652835034825|1056561960618|   0.0|
| 386547056678| 446676601330|   0.0|
| 824633725362|1477468756129|   0.0|
|1529008363870| 274877910417|   0.0|
| 395136992117| 944892811576|   0.0|
|1657857381212|1116691503444|   0.0|
+-------------+-------------+------+
```

 It is possible that by sampling this way we accidentally generate pairs that happen to be among positive examples. However, the probability of this is quite low and it can be discarded.

We also need to create hard negative examples - these are examples that are just one jump away from each other:

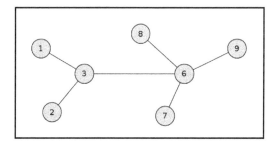

In this figure, as we already discussed, the (1, 2), (1, 6), or (7, 9) pairs are examples of hard negative examples.

To get such pairs, let's first formulate the idea logically. We need to sample all the possible pairs (B, C) such that there exist some node A and edges (A, B) and (A, C) both exist, but there is no edge (B, C).

When we phrase this sampling problem in such a way, it becomes easy to express this with SQL: all we need to do is a self-join and select edges with the same source, but a different destination. Consider the following example:

```
SELECT e1.dst as node1, e2.dst as node2
  FROM Edges e1, Edges e2
 WHERE e1.src = e2.src ANDe1.dst <> e2.dst;
```

Let's translate it to the Spark DataFrame API. To do a self-join, we first need to create two aliases of the edge `DataFrame` and rename the columns inside:

```
Dataset<Row> e1 = edges.drop("node1", "node2", "year")
        .withColumnRenamed("src", "e1_src")
        .withColumnRenamed("dst", "e1_dst")
        .as("e1");
Dataset<Row> e2 = edges.drop("node1", "node2", "year")
        .withColumnRenamed("src", "e2_src")
        .withColumnRenamed("dst", "e2_dst")
        .as("e2");
```

Now, we perform the join on condition that `dst` is different, but `src` is the same, and then rename the columns so they are consistent with the previous samples:

```
Column diffDest = e1.col("e1_dst").notEqual(e2.col("e2_dst"));
Column sameSrc = e1.col("e1_src").equalTo(e2.col("e2_src"));
Dataset<Row> hardNeg = e1.join(e2, diffDest.and(sameSrc));
```

```
hardNeg = hardNeg.select("e1_dst", "e2_dst")
        .withColumnRenamed("e1_dst", "node1")
        .withColumnRenamed("e2_dst", "node2");
```

Next, we need to take the first 6 million generated edges and call it the hard sample. However, Spark puts the values in this `DataFrame` in some particular order, which may introduce bias into our model. To make the bias less harmful, let's add some randomness to the sampling process: generate a column with random values and take only those edges where the value is greater than some number:

```
hardNeg = hardNeg.withColumn("rnd", functions.rand(0));
hardNeg = hardNeg.filter("rnd >= 0.95").drop("rnd");
hardNeg = hardNeg.limit(6_000_000);
hardNeg = hardNeg.withColumn("target", functions.lit(0.0));
```

After that, we just take the first 6m edges, and add the `target` column. The results follow the same schema as our previous samples:

```
+------------+------------+------+
|       node1|       node2|target|
+------------+------------+------+
| 34359740336| 970662610852|   0.0|
| 34359740336| 987842479409|   0.0|
| 34359740336|1494648621189|   0.0|
| 34359740336|1554778161775|   0.0|
| 42949673538| 326417515499|   0.0|
|266287973882| 781684049287|   0.0|
+------------+------------+------+
```

Putting them together is done with the `union` function:

```
Dataset<Row> trainEdges = pos.union(negSimple).union(hardNeg);
```

Finally, let's associate a ID with every edge:

```
trainEdges = trainEdges.withColumn("id",
functions.monotonicallyIncreasingId());
```

With this, we have prepared the edges for which we can compute the edge features.

Edge features

There are a number of edge features that we can compute: the number of common friends, the total number of distinct friends both people have, and so on.

Let us start with the common friend's feature, which for our problem is the number of common coauthors both authors have. To get them we need to join the edges we selected with all the edges (two times) and then group by the ID and count how many elements are there per group. In SQL, it looks like this:

```
SELECT train.id, COUNT(*)
  FROM Sample train, Edges e1, Edges e2
  WHERE train.node1 = e1.src AND
        train.node2 = e2.src AND
        e1.dst = e2.dst
GROUP BY train.id;
```

Let's translate this to DataFrame API. First, we use the joins:

```
Dataset<Row> join = train.join(e1,
        train.col("node1").equalTo(e1.col("e1_src")));
join = join.join(e2,
        join.col("node2").equalTo(e2.col("e2_src")).and(
        join.col("e1_dst").equalTo(e2.col("e2_dst"))));
```

Here, we reuse DataFrames e1 and e2 from the negative sampling subsection.

Then, we finally group by the id and count:

```
Dataset<Row> commonFriends = join.groupBy("id").count();
commonFriends = commonFriends.withColumnRenamed("count", "commonFriends");
```

The resulting DataFrame will contain the following:

```
+-------------+-------------+
|           id|commonFriends|
+-------------+-------------+
|1726578522049|          116|
|        15108|            1|
|1726581250424|          117|
|        17579|            4|
|         2669|           11|
|         3010|           73|
+-------------+-------------+
```

Now we calculate the Total Friends feature, which is the number of distinct coauthors both authors have. In SQL, it is a bit simpler than the previous feature:

```
SELECT train.id, COUNT DISTINCT (e.dst)
  FROM Sample train, Edges e
  WHERE train.node1 = e.src
GROUP BY train.id
```

Let's now translate it to Spark:

```
Dataset<Row> e = edges.drop("node1", "node2", "year", "target");
Dataset<Row> join = train.join(e,
        train.col("node1").equalTo(edges.col("src")));
totalFriends = join.select("id", "dst")
        .groupBy("id")

  .agg(functions.approxCountDistinct("dst").as("totalFriendsApprox"));
```

Here, we used the approximate count distinct because it is faster and typically gives quite accurate values. Of course, there is an option to use exact count distinct: for that, we need to use the `functions.countDistinct` function. The output of this step is the following table:

```
+-------------+------------------+
|           id|totalFriendsApprox|
+-------------+------------------+
|1726580872911|                 4|
|  601295447985|                 4|
|1726580879317|                 1|
|  858993461306|                11|
|1726578972367|               296|
|1726581766707|               296|
+-------------+------------------+
```

Next, we calculate the Jaccard Similarity between the two sets of coauthors. We first create a `DataFrame` with sets for each author, then join and calculate the jaccard. For this feature there's no direct way to express it in SQL, so we start from Spark API.

Creating the set of coauthors for each author is easy: we just use the `groupBy` function and then apply `functions.collect_set` to each group:

```
Dataset<Row> coAuthors = e.groupBy("src")
        .agg(functions.collect_set("dst").as("others"))
        .withColumnRenamed("src", "node");
```

Now we join it with our training data:

```
Dataset<Row> join = train.drop("target");

join = join.join(coAuthors,
join.col("node1").equalTo(coAuthors.col("node")));
join = join.drop("node").withColumnRenamed("others", "others1");

join = join.join(coAuthors,
join.col("node2").equalTo(coAuthors.col("node")));
```

```
join = join.drop("node").withColumnRenamed("others", "others2");

join = join.drop("node1", "node2");
```

At the end, the join column has the ID of the edge and the arrays of the coauthors for each edge. Next, we go over every record of this dataframe and compute the Jaccard similarity:

```
JavaRDD<Row> jaccardRdd = join.toJavaRDD().map(r -> {
    long id = r.getAs("id");
    WrappedArray<Long> others1 = r.getAs("others1");
    WrappedArray<Long> others2 = r.getAs("others2");

    Set<Long> set1 = Sets.newHashSet((Long[]) others1.array());
    Set<Long> set2 = Sets.newHashSet((Long[]) others2.array());

    int intersection = Sets.intersection(set1, set2).size();
    int union = Sets.union(set1, set2).size();

    double jaccard = intersection / (union + 1.0);
    return RowFactory.create(id, jaccard);
});
```

Here we use the **regularized Jaccard Similarity**: instead of just dividing intersection by union, we also add a small regularization factor to the denominator.

The reason for doing it is to give less score to very small sets: imagine that each set has the same element, then the Jaccard is 1.0. With regularization, the similarity of small lots is penalized, and for this example, it will be equal to 0.5.

Since we used RDDs here, we need to convert it back to a data frame:

```
StructField node1Field = DataTypes.createStructField("id",
DataTypes.LongType, false);
StructField node2Field = DataTypes.createStructField("jaccard",
DataTypes.DoubleType, false);
StructType schema = DataTypes.createStructType(Arrays.asList(node1Field,
node2Field));
Dataset<Row> jaccard = sql.createDataFrame(jaccardRdd, schema);
```

After executing it, we get a table like this:

```
+-------------+---------+
|           id|  jaccard|
+-------------+---------+
|1726581480054|    0.011|
|1726578955032|    0.058|
|1726581479913|    0.037|
|1726581479873|     0.05|
```

```
|1726581479976|        0.1|
|         1667|        0.1|
+-------------+---------+
```

Note that the preceding method is quite universal, and we could follow the same approach for calculating the *Common Friends* and *Total Friends* features: it would be the size of the intersection and union respectively. What is more, it could be computed in one pass along with Jaccard.

Our next step is to deprive edge features from the node features we already computed. Among others, we can include the following:

- Min degree, max degree
- Preferential attachment score: degree of node1 times degree of node2
- Product of page ranks
- Absolute difference of page ranks
- Same connected component

To do it we first join all the node features together:

```
Dataset<Row> nodeFeatures = pageRank.join(degrees, "id")
                                  .join(connectedComponents, "id");
nodeFeatures = nodeFeatures.withColumnRenamed("id", "node_id");
```

Next, we join the node features `DataFrame` we just created with the edges we prepared for training:

```
Dataset<Row> join = train.drop("target");

join = join.join(nodeFeatures,
            join.col("node1").equalTo(nodeFeatures.col("node_id")));
join = join.drop("node_id")
        .withColumnRenamed("pagerank", "pagerank_1")
        .withColumnRenamed("degree", "degree_1")
        .withColumnRenamed("component", "component_1");

join = join.join(nodeFeatures,
            join.col("node2").equalTo(nodeFeatures.col("node_id")));
join = join.drop("node_id")
        .withColumnRenamed("pagerank", "pagerank_2")
        .withColumnRenamed("degree", "degree_2")
        .withColumnRenamed("component", "component_2");

join = join.drop("node1", "node2");
```

Now, let's calculate the features:

```
join = join
    .withColumn("pagerank_mult",
join.col("pagerank_1").multiply(join.col("pagerank_2")))
    .withColumn("pagerank_max", functions.greatest("pagerank_1",
"pagerank_2"))
    .withColumn("pagerank_min", functions.least("pagerank_1",
"pagerank_2"))
    .withColumn("pref_attachm",
join.col("degree_1").multiply(join.col("degree_2")))
    .withColumn("degree_max", functions.greatest("degree_1", "degree_2"))
    .withColumn("degree_min", functions.least("degree_1", "degree_2"))
    .withColumn("same_comp",
join.col("component_1").equalTo(join.col("component_2")));
join = join.drop("pagerank_1", "pagerank_2");
join = join.drop("degree_1", "degree_2");
join = join.drop("component_1", "component_2");
```

This will create a `DataFrame` with edge ID and seven features: min and max Page Rank, a product of two Page Ranks, min and max degree, a product of two degrees (Preferential Attachment), and, finally, whether or not two nodes belong to the same component.

Now we have finished calculating all the features we wanted, so it's time we join them all together in a single `DataFrame`:

```
Dataset<Row> join = train.join(commonFriends, "id")
    .join(totalFriends, "id")
    .join(jaccard, "id")
    .join(nodeFeatures, "id");
```

So far we created the dataset with labels and computed a set of features. Now we are finally ready to train a machine learning model on it.

Link Prediction with MLlib and XGBoost

Now, when all the data is prepared and put into a suitable shape, we can train a model, which will predict whether two authors are likely to become coauthors or not. For that we will use a binary classifier model, which will be trained to predict what is the probability that this edge exists in a graph.

Apache Spark comes with a library which provides scalable implementation of several Machine Learning algorithms. This library is called MLlib. Let's add it to our `pom.xml`:

```
<dependency>
  <groupId>org.apache.spark</groupId>
  <artifactId>spark-mllib_2.11</artifactId>
  <version>2.1.0</version>
</dependency>
```

There are a number of models we can use, including logistic regression, random forest, and Gradient Boosted Trees. But before we train any model, let's split the training dataset into train and validation sets:

```
features = features.withColumn("rnd", functions.rand(1));
Dataset<Row> trainFeatures = features.filter("rnd < 0.8").drop("rnd");
Dataset<Row> valFeatures = features.filter("rnd >= 0.8").drop("rnd");
```

To be able to use it for training machine learning models, we need to convert our data to RDD of `LabeledPoint` objects. For that, we first convert the DataFrame to RDD, and then convert each row to `DenseVector`:

```
List<String> columns = Arrays.asList("commonFriends", "totalFriendsApprox",
        "jaccard", "pagerank_mult", "pagerank_max", "pagerank_min",
        "pref_attachm", "degree_max", "degree_min", "same_comp");

JavaRDD<LabeledPoint> trainRdd = trainFeatures.toJavaRDD().map(r -> {
    Vector vec = toDenseVector(columns, r);
    double label = r.getAs("target");
    return new LabeledPoint(label, vec);
});
```

The `columns`stores all the column names we want to use as features in the order we want to put them into `DenseVector`. The `toDenseVector` function has the following implementation:

```
private static DenseVector toDenseVector(List<String> columns, Row r) {
    int featureVecLen = columns.size();
    double[] values = new double[featureVecLen];
    for (int i = 0; i < featureVecLen; i++) {
        Object o = r.getAs(columns.get(i));
        values[i] = castToDouble(o);
    }
    return new DenseVector(values);
}
```

Since, in our DataFrame we have data of multiple types, including `int`, `double`, and `boolean`, we need to be able to convert all of them to double. This is what the `castToDouble` function does:

```
private static double castToDouble(Object o) {
    if (o instanceof Number) {
        Number number = (Number) o;
        return number.doubleValue();
    }

    if (o instanceof Boolean) {
        Boolean bool = (Boolean) o;
        if (bool) {
            return 1.0;
        } else {
            return 0.0;
        }
    }

    throw new IllegalArgumentException();
}
```

Now we finally can train the logistic regression model:

```
LogisticRegressionModel logreg = new LogisticRegressionWithLBFGS()
            .run(JavaRDD.toRDD(trainRdd));
```

After it finishes, we can evaluate how good the model is.

Let's go through the entire validation dataset and make a prediction for each element there:

```
logreg.clearThreshold();

JavaRDD<Pair<Double, Double>> predRdd = valFeatures.toJavaRDD().map(r -> {
    Vector v = toDenseVector(columns, r);
    double label = r.getAs("target");
    double predict = logreg.predict(v);
    return ImmutablePair.of(label, predict);
});
```

Note that we first need to invoke the `clearThreshold` method - if we don't do this, then the model will output hard predictions (only 0.0 and 1.0), which will make the evaluation more difficult.

Now we can put the predictions and the true labels into separate double arrays and use any of the binary classification evaluation functions, which we covered in Chapter 4, *Supervised Learning - Classification and Regression*. For example, we can use `logLoss`:

```
List<Pair<Double, Double>> pred = predRdd.collect();
double[] actual = pred.stream().mapToDouble(Pair::getLeft).toArray();
double[] predicted = pred.stream().mapToDouble(Pair::getRight).toArray();
double logLoss = Metrics.logLoss(actual, predicted);
System.out.printf("log loss: %.4f%n", logLoss);
```

This produces the following output:

```
log loss: 0.6528
```

This is not a very good performance: if we always output `0.5` as the prediction, the `logLoss` would be `0.7`, so our model is just a bit better than that. We can try other models available in MLlib such as linear SVM or random forest to see whether they give better performance.

But there is another option: if you remember from Chapter 7, *Extreme Gradient Boosting* XGBoost, can also run in parallel mode, and it can use Apache Spark for doing it. So let's try to use it for this problem. To see how to build XGBoost, refer to Chapter 7, *Extreme Gradient Boosting*.

To include the Spark version to our project, we add the following dependency declaration to the project:

```
<dependency>
  <groupId>ml.dmlc</groupId>
  <artifactId>xgboost4j-spark</artifactId>
  <version>0.7</version>
</dependency>
```

As input, XGBoost also takes RDDs of `Vector` objects. Apart from that, it takes the same parameters as XGBoost running on a single machine: model parameters, number of trees to build, and so on. This is how it looks in the code:

```
Map<String, Object> params = xgbParams();
int nRounds = 20;
int numWorkers = 4;
ObjectiveTrait objective = null;
EvalTrait eval = null;
boolean externalMemoryCache = false;
float nanValue = Float.NaN;
RDD<LabeledPoint> trainData = JavaRDD.toRDD(trainRdd);
```

```
XGBoostModel model = XGBoost.train(trainData, params,
        nRounds, numWorkers, objective, eval, externalMemoryCache,
        nanValue);
```

Here, the `xgbParams` function returns a `Map` of XGBoost model parameters we use for training.

Note that XGBoost Spark wrapper is written in Scala, not in Java, so the `Map` object is actually `scala.collection.immutable.Map`, not `java.util.Map`. Thus, we also need to convert a usual `HashMap` into the Scala `Map`:

```
HashMap<String, Object> params = new HashMap<String, Object>();
params.put("eta", 0.3);
params.put("gamma", 0);
params.put("max_depth", 6);
// ... other parameters
Map<String, Object> res = toScala(params);
```

Here, the `toScala` utility method is implemented in this way:

```
private static <K, V> Map<K, V> toScala(HashMap<K, V> params) {
    return JavaConversions.mapAsScalaMap(params)
            .toMap(Predef.<Tuple2<K, V>>conforms());
}
```

It looks a bit strange because it uses some Scala-specific features. But we don't need to go into details and can use it as is.

With this, we will be able to train a distributed XGBoost. However, for evaluation, we cannot follow the same approach as for logistic regression. That is, we cannot convert each row to a vector, and then run the model against this vector, and if you do so, XGBoost will throw an exception. The reason for this is that such an operation is quite costly, as it will try to build `DMatrix` for each vector, and it will result in a significant slowdown.

Since our validation dataset is not very large, we can just convert the entire `RDD` to a `DMatrix`:

```
JavaRDD<LabeledPoint> valRdd = valFeatures.toJavaRDD().map(r -> {
    float[] vec = rowToFloatArray(columns, r);
    double label = r.getAs("target");
    return LabeledPoint.fromDenseVector((float) label, vec);
});

List<LabeledPoint> valPoints = valRdd.collect();
DMatrix data = new DMatrix(valPoints.iterator(), null);
```

Here, we go through the rows of the `DataFrame`, and convert each row to a `LabeledPoint` class (from the `ml.dmlc.xgboost4j` package - not to be confused with `org.apache.spark.ml.feature.LabeledPoint`). Then, we collect everything to a list and create a `DMatrix` from it.

Next, we get the trained model and apply it to this `DMatrix`:

```
Booster xgb = model._booster();
float[][] xgbPred = xgb.predict(new ml.dmlc.xgboost4j.scala.DMatrix(data),
false, 20);
```

Then, our method for `logLoss` calculations expects to get doubles as input, so let us convert the results to arrays of doubles:

```
double[] actual = floatToDouble(data.getLabel());
double[] predicted = unwrapToDouble(xgbPred);
```

We have already used these functions in `Chapter 7`, *Extreme Gradient Boosting*, and they are pretty straightforward: `floatToDouble` just converts a float array to a double array, and `unwrapToDouble` converts two-dimensional float arrays with one column to 1-dimensional double array.

Finally, we can calculate the score:

```
double logLoss = Metrics.logLoss(actual, predicted);
System.out.printf("log loss: %.4f%n", logLoss);
```

It says that the score is 0.497, which is a huge improvement over what we had previously. Here, we used the model with default parameters, which are often not the most optimal. We can tune the model further, and you can find strategies on how to tune XGBoost in `Chapter 7`, *Extreme Gradient Boosting*.

`logLoss` was chosen here only for its simplicity and often it is hard to interpret when it comes to recommender systems. Choosing an evaluation metric is usually quite case-specific, and we can use scores such as F1 score, **MAP (Mean Average Precision)**, **NDCG (Normalized Discounted Cumulative Gain)**, and many others. In addition to that, we can use on-line evaluation metrics such as how many suggested links are accepted by the users.

Next, we will see how this model can be used for suggesting links and how we can evaluate it better.

Link suggestion

So far we have discussed in a lot of details about building features for Link Prediction models and training these models. Now we need to be able to use such models for making suggestions. Again, think about *people you may know* banner on Facebook - here we would like to have something similar, like *authors you should write a paper with*. In addition to that, we will see how to evaluate the model so the evaluation result is more intuitive and clear in this context.

The first step is to re-train the XGBoost model on the entire training set, without the train-validation split. This is easy to do: we just fit the model again on the data before making the split.

Next, we need to process the test dataset. If you remember, the test dataset contains all the papers published in 2014 and 2015. To make things simpler, we will select a subset of test users, and make recommendations to them only. This is how we can do it:

```
Dataset<Row> fullTest = df.filter("year >= 2014");
Dataset<Row> testNodes = fullTest.sample(true, 0.05, 1)
                                 .select("node1")
                                 .dropDuplicates();
Dataset<Row> testEdges = fullTest.join(testNodes, "node1");
```

Here we first select the test set, and then sample nodes from it - and this gives us a list of authors we selected for testing. In other words, only these authors will receive recommendations. Next, we perform the join of the full test set with the selected nodes to get all the actual links that were made during the testing period. We will use these links later for evaluation.

Next, we replace the names of the authors with IDs. We do it in the same way we did previously - by joining it with the nodes `DataFrame`:

```
Dataset<Row> join = testEdges.drop("year");
join = join.join(nodes, join.col("node1").equalTo(nodes.col("node")));
join = join.drop("node", "node1").withColumnRenamed("id", "node1");
join = join.join(nodes, join.col("node2").equalTo(nodes.col("node")));
join = join.drop("node", "node2").withColumnRenamed("id", "node2");
Dataset<Row> selected = join;
```

Next, we need to select candidates on who we will apply the model. The list of candidates should contain a list of authors who are most likely to become a potential coauthor (that is, form a link in the network). The most obvious way to select such candidates is to take the authors that are one jump away from each other - in the same way, we sampled hard negative links:

```
Dataset<Row> e1 = selected.select("node1").dropDuplicates();
Dataset<Row> e2 = edges.drop("node1", "node2", "year")
        .withColumnRenamed("src", "e2_src")
        .withColumnRenamed("dst", "e2_dst")
        .as("e2");
Column diffDest = e1.col("node1").notEqual(e2.col("e2_dst"));
Column sameSrc = e1.col("node1").equalTo(e2.col("e2_src"));
Dataset<Row> candidates = e1.join(e2, diffDest.and(sameSrc));
candidates = candidates.select("node1", "e2_dst")
                        .withColumnRenamed("e2_dst", "node2");
```

The code is almost the same except that we do not consider all possible hard negatives, but only those that are related to the nodes we have preselected.

We assume that these candidates did not become coauthors during testing period, so we add the target column with 0.0 in it:

```
candidates = candidates.withColumn("target", functions.lit(0.0));
```

While in general this assumption will not hold, because we look at the link obtained only from the training period, and it might be quite possible that some of these links were actually formed during the testing period.

Let us fix it by manually adding the positive candidates, and then removing duplicates:

```
selected = selected.withColumn("target", functions.lit(1.0));
candidates = selected.union(candidates).dropDuplicates("node1", "node2");
```

Now, as we did previously, we assign an ID to each candidate edge:

```
candidates = candidates.withColumn("id",
functions.monotonicallyIncreasingId());
```

To apply the model to these candidates, we need to calculate features. For that, we just reuse the code we previously wrote. First, we calculate the node features:

```
Dataset<Row> nodeFeatures = nodeFeatures(sql, pageRank,
connectedComponents, degrees, candidates);
```

Here, the `nodeFeatures` method takes in the `pageRank`, `connectedComponents` and `degree` `DataFrames`, which we computed on the train data, and calculates all the node-based features for the edges we pass in the `candidates` `DataFrame`.

Next, we compute the edge-based features for our candidates:

```
Dataset<Row> commonFriends = calculateCommonFriends(sql, edges,
candidates);
Dataset<Row> totalFriends = calculateTotalFriends(sql, edges, candidates);
Dataset<Row> jaccard = calculateJaccard(sql, edges, candidates);
```

We put the actual calculation of these features in utility methods, and just invoke them using a different set of edges.

Finally, we just join everything together:

```
Dataset<Row> features = candidates.join(commonFriends, "id")
        .join(totalFriends, "id")
        .join(jaccard, "id")
        .join(nodeFeatures, "id");
```

Now we are ready to apply the XGBoost model to these features. For that we will use the `mapPartition` function: it is similar to usual `map`, but instead of taking in just one item, it gets multiple at the same time. This way, we will build a `DMatrix` for multiple objects at the same time, and it will save time.

This is how we do it. First, we create a special class `ScoredEdge` for keeping the information about the nodes of the edge, the score it was assigned by the model as well as the actual label:

```
public class ScoredEdge implements Serializable {
    private long node1;
    private long node2;
    private double score;
    private double target;
    // constructor, getter and setters are omitted
}
```

Now we score the candidate edges:

```
JavaRDD<ScoredEdge> scoredRdd = features.toJavaRDD().mapPartitions(rows ->
{
    List<ScoredEdge> scoredEdges = new ArrayList<>();
    List<LabeledPoint> labeled = new ArrayList<>();

    while (rows.hasNext()) {
        Row r = rows.next();
```

```
        long node1 = r.getAs("node1");
        long node2 = r.getAs("node2");
        double target = r.getAs("target");
        scoredEdges.add(new ScoredEdge(node1, node2, target));

        float[] vec = rowToFloatArray(columns, r);
        labeled.add(LabeledPoint.fromDenseVector(0.0f, vec));
    }

    DMatrix data = new DMatrix(labeled.iterator(), null);
    float[][] xgbPred =
        xgb.predict(new ml.dmlc.xgboost4j.scala.DMatrix(data), false, 20);

    for (int i = 0; i < scoredEdges.size(); i++) {
        double pred = xgbPred[i][0];
        ScoredEdge edge = scoredEdges.get(i);
        edge.setScore(pred);
    }

    return scoredEdges.iterator();
});
```

The code inside the `mapPartition` function does the following: first, we go over all input rows, and create a `ScoredEdge` class for each row. In addition to that, we also extract features from each row (in exactly the same way we did it previously). Then we put everything into `DMatrix` and use the XGBoost model to score each row of this matrix. Finally, we put the score to the `ScoredEdge` objects. As a result of this step, we get an `RDD`, where each candidate edge is scored by the model.

Next, for each user we would like to recommend 10 potential coauthors. To do it we group by `node1` from our `ScoredEdge` class, then sort by score within each group and keep only the first 10:

```
JavaPairRDD<Long, List<ScoredEdge>> topSuggestions = scoredRdd
        .keyBy(s -> s.getNode1())
        .groupByKey()
        .mapValues(es -> takeFirst10(es));
```

Here, `takeFirst10` may be implemented this way:

```
private static List<ScoredEdge> takeFirst10(Iterable<ScoredEdge> es) {
    Ordering<ScoredEdge> byScore =
            Ordering.natural().onResultOf(ScoredEdge::getScore).reverse();
    return byScore.leastOf(es, 10);
}
```

If you remember, `Ordering` here is a class from Google Guava which does the sorting by score and then takes the first 10 edges.

Finally, let's see how good the suggestions are. For that we go over all the suggestions and count how many of these links were actually formed during the test period. And then we take the mean across all groups:

```
double mp10 = topSuggestions.mapToDouble(es -> {
    List<ScoredEdge> es2 = es._2();
    double correct = es2.stream().filter(e -> e.getTarget() ==
1.0).count();
    return correct / es2.size();
}).mean();

System.out.println(mp10);
```

What it does is it calculates `Precision@10` (the faction of correctly classified edges among the first 10) for each group and then takes a mean of it.

When we run it, we see that the score is about 30%. This is not a very bad result: it means that 30% of recommended edges were actually formed.

Still, this score is far from ideal, and there are a lot of ways to improve it. In real-life Social Networks, there often is additional information that we can use for building a model. For example, in case of the coauthors graph, we could use affiliation, titles, and texts from abstracts of the papers, conferences, and journals where the papers were published, and many other things. If the social graph comes from a web Social Network such as Facebook, we could use geographical information, groups and communities, and, finally, likes. By including this information, we should be able to achieve far better performance.

Summary

In this chapter, we looked at ways to handle very large amounts of data and special tools for doing this such as Apache Hadoop MapReduce and Apache Spark. We saw how to use them to process Common Crawl - the copy of the Internet, and calculate some useful statistics from it. Finally, we created a Link Prediction model for recommending coauthors and trained an XGBoost model in a distributed way.

In the next chapter, we will look at how Data Science models can be deployed to production systems.

10
Deploying Data Science Models

So far we have covered a lot of data science models, we talked about many supervised and unsupervised learning methods, including deep learning and XGBoost, and discussed how we can apply these models to text and graph data.

In terms of the CRISP-DM methodology, we mostly covered the *modeling* part so far. But there are other important parts we have not yet discussed: *evaluation* and *deployment*. These steps are quite important in the application lifecycle, because the models we create should be useful for the business and bring value, and the only way to achieve that is integrate them into the application (the deployment part) and make sure they indeed are useful (the evaluation part).

In this last chapter of the book we will cover exactly these missing parts--we will see how we can deploy data science models so they can be used by other services of the application. In addition to that, we will also see how to perform an online evaluation of already deployed models.

In particular, we will cover the following:

- Microservices in Java with Spring Boot
- Model evaluation with A/B tests and multi-armed bandits

By the end of this chapter you will learn how to create simple web services with data science models and how to design them in a way that is easy to test.

Microservices

Java is a very common platform choice for running production code for many applications across many domains. When data scientists create a model for existing applications, Java is a natural choice, since it can be seamlessly integrated into the code. This case is straightforward, you create a separate package, implement your models there, and make sure other packages use it. Another possible option is packaging the code into a separate JAR file, and include it as a Maven dependency.

But there is a different architectural approach for combining multiple components of a large system--the microservices architecture. The main idea is that a system should be composed of small independent units with their own lifecycle--their development, testing, and deployment cycles are independent of all other components.

These microservices typically communicate via REST API, which is based on HTTP. It is based on four HTTP methods--GET, POST, PUT and DELETE. The first two are most commonly used:

- GET: Get some information from the service
- POST: Submit some information to the service

There are quite a few libraries that allow creating a web service with a REST API in Java, and one of them is Spring Boot, which is based on the Spring Framework. Next, we will look into how we can use it for serving data science models.

Spring Boot

Spring is a very old and powerful Java library. The Core Spring module implements the **Dependency Injection** (**DI**) pattern, which allows developing loosely coupled, testable, and reliable applications. Spring has other modules which are built around the core, and one of them is Spring MVC, which is a module for creating web applications.

In simple terms, the DI pattern says that you should put the application logic in so-called *services* and then *inject* these services into web modules.

Spring MVC, as we already mentioned, is used for developing web services. It runs on top of the Servlet API, which is the Java way of dealing with processing web requests and producing web responses. Servlet containers implement the Servlet API. Thus, to be able to use your application as a web service, you need to deploy it to a servlet container. The most popular ones are Apache Tomcat and Eclipse Jetty. However, the API is quite cumbersome to use. Spring MVC is built on top of the Servlet API but hides all its complexity.

Additionally, the Spring Boot library allows us to quickly start developing a Spring application without going into a lot of configuration details such as, setting up Apache Tomcat, the Spring application context and so on. It comes with a good set of pre-defined parameters which are expected to work fine, so we can just start using it and concentrate on the application logic rather than configuring the servlet container.

Now let us see how we can use Spring Boot and Spring MVC for serving machine learning models.

Search engine service

Let us finally come back to our running example--building a search engine. In Chapter 7, *Extreme Gradient Boosting*, we created a ranking model, which we can use for reordering search engine results so that the most relevant content gets higher positions.

In the previous chapter, Chapter 9, *Scaling Data Science*, we extracted a lot of text data from Common Crawl. What we can do now is to put it all together--use Apache Lucene to index the data from Common Crawl, and then search its content and get the best results with the XGBoost ranking model.

We already know how to use Hadoop MapReduce to extract text information from Common Crawl. However, if you remember, our ranking model needs more than just text-- apart from just the body text, it needs to know the title and the headers. We can either modify existing MapReduce jobs to extract the parts we need, or process it without Hadoop and just index it with Lucene directly. Let us look at the second approach.

First, we will again use the HtmlDocument class, which has the following fields:

```
public class HtmlDocument implements Serializable {
    private final String url;
    private final String title;
    private final ArrayListMultimap<String, String> headers;
    private final String bodyText;
    // constructors and getters are omitted
}
```

Then we will also reuse the method for converting HTML to this HtmlDocument object, but will adapt it slightly so it can read the WARC record from Common Crawl:

```
private static HtmlDocument extractText(ArchiveRecord record) {
    String html = TextUtils.extractHtml(record);
    Document document = Jsoup.parse(html);
    String title = document.title();
    Element body = document.body();
```

```
    String bodyText = body.text();

    Elements headerElements = body.select("h1, h2, h3, h4, h5, h6");
    ArrayListMultimap<String, String> headers = ArrayListMultimap.create();
    for (Element htag : headerElements) {
        String tagName = htag.nodeName().toLowerCase();
        headers.put(tagName, htag.text());
    }

    return new HtmlDocument(url, title, headers, bodyText);
}
```

Here `extractHtml` is a method from the previous chapter that extracts HTML content from a WARC record, and the rest is the same as used in `Chapter 6`, *Working with Text - Natural Language Processing and Information Retrieval.*

Next, we need to go over each record of a WARC archive and convert it to an object of the `HtmlDocument` class. Since the archives are large enough, we do not want to keep the content of all the `HtmlDocument` objects in memory all the time. Instead, we can do this lazily on the fly: read the next WARC record, convert it to `HtmlDocument`, an index with Lucene. and do it again for the next record.

To be able to do it lazily, we will use the `AbstractIterator` class from Google Guava:

```
public static Iterator<HtmlDocument> iterator(File commonCrawlFile) {
    ArchiveReader archive = WARCReaderFactory.get(commonCrawlFile);
    Iterator<ArchiveRecord> records = archive.iterator();

    return new AbstractIterator<HtmlDocument>() {
        protected HtmlDocument computeNext() {
            while (records.hasNext()) {
                ArchiveRecord record = records.next();
                return extractText(record);
            }
            return endOfData();
        }
    };
}
```

First, we open the WARC archive and pass it to the instance of our `AbstractIterator` class. Inside, while there are still records, we convert them using our `extractText` function. Once we are done with processing, we signal about it by invoking the `endOfData` method.

Now we can index all the WARC files with Lucene:

```
FSDirectory directory = FSDirectory.open("lucene-index");
WhitespaceAnalyzer analyzer = new WhitespaceAnalyzer();
IndexWriter writer = new IndexWriter(directory, new
IndexWriterConfig(analyzer));

for (File warc : warcFolder.listFiles()) {
    Iterator<HtmlDocument> iterator = CommonCrawlReader.iterator(warc);

    while (iterator.hasNext()) {
        HtmlDocument htmlDoc = iterator.next();
        Document doc = toLuceneDocument(htmlDoc);
        writer.addDocument(doc);
    }
}
```

In this code, first we create a filesystem Lucene index, and then go over all WARC files from the `warcFolder` directory. For each such file we get the iterator using the method we just wrote, and then index each record of this WARC file with Lucene. The `toLuceneDocument` method should already be familiar to us from the Chapter 6, *Working with Text - Natural Language Processing and Information Retrieval;* it converts `HtmlDocument` to a Lucene document, and contains the following code:

```
String url = htmlDoc.getUrl();
String title = htmlDoc.getTitle();
String bodyText = htmlDoc.getBodyText();
ArrayListMultimap<String, String> headers = htmlDoc.getHeaders();

String allHeaders = String.join(" ", headers.values());
String h1 = String.join(" ", headers.get("h1"));
String h2 = String.join(" ", headers.get("h2"));
String h3 = String.join(" ", headers.get("h3"));

Document doc = new Document();
doc.add(new Field("url", url, URL_FIELD));
doc.add(new Field("title", title, TEXT_FIELD));
doc.add(new Field("bodyText", bodyText, TEXT_FIELD));
doc.add(new Field("allHeaders", allHeaders, TEXT_FIELD));
doc.add(new Field("h1", h1, TEXT_FIELD));
doc.add(new Field("h2", h2, TEXT_FIELD));
doc.add(new Field("h3", h3, TEXT_FIELD));
```

You can refer to Chapter 6, *Working with Text - Natural Language Processing and Information Retrieval* or more details.

With this code, we can quite quickly index a part of Common Crawl. For our experiment, we took only 3 WARC archives from December 2016, which contain about 0.5 million documents.

Now, after we indexed the data, we need to get our ranker. Let us reuse the models we created in Chapter 6, *Working with Text - Natural Language Processing and Information Retrieval* and Chapter 7, *Extreme Gradient Boosting:* the feature extractor and the XGBoost model.

If you remember, the feature extractor performs the following: tokenizes the query and the body, the title, and the headers of each document; puts them all into the TF-IDF vector space and computes the similarity between the query and all text features. In addition to that, we also looked at the similarity in the LSA space (the space reduced with SVD) and also a similarity between the query and the title in the GloVe space. Please refer to Chapter 6, *Working with Text - Natural Language Processing and Information Retrieval,* for more details about it.

So let us use these classes to implement our ranker. But first, we need to have a proper abstraction for all ranking functions, and for that, we can create the Ranker interface:

```
public interface Ranker {
    SearchResults rank(List<QueryDocumentPair> inputList);
}
```

 While creating the interface may seem redundant at this step, it will ensure the services we create are easily extensible and replaceable, and this is very important for being able for model evaluation.

Its only method rank takes in a list of QueryDocumentPair objects and produces a SearchResults object. We created the QueryDocumentPair class in Chapter 6, *Working with Text - Natural Language Processing and Information Retrieval,* and it contains the query along with the text features of the document:

```
public static class QueryDocumentPair {
    private final String query;
    private final String url;
    private final String title;
    private final String bodyText;
    private final String allHeaders;
    private final String h1;
    private final String h2;
    private final String h3;
    // constructor and getters are omitted
}
```

The `SearchResults` object just contains a reordered list of `SearchResult` objects:

```
public class SearchResults {
    private List<SearchResult> list;
    // constructor and getters are omitted
}
```

The `SearchResult` is another object that just holds the title and the URL of a page:

```
public class SearchResult {
    private String url;
    private String title;
    // constructor and getters are omitted
}
```

Now let us create an implementation of this interface and call it `XgbRanker`. First, we specify the constructor, which takes in the `FeatureExtractor` object and the path to the saved XGBoost model:

```
public XgbRanker(FeatureExtractor featureExtractor, String pathToModel) {
    this.featureExtractor = featureExtractor;
    this.booster = XGBoost.loadModel(pathToModel);
}
```

And the `rank` method is implemented the following way:

```
@Override
public SearchResults rank(List<QueryDocumentPair> inputList) {
    DataFrame<Double> featuresDf = featureExtractor.transform(inputList);
    double[][] matrix = featuresDf.toModelMatrix(0.0);

    double[] probs = XgbUtils.predict(booster, matrix);
    List<ScoredIndex> scored = ScoredIndex.wrap(probs);

    List<SearchResult> result = new ArrayList<>(inputList.size());

    for (ScoredIndex idx : scored) {
        QueryDocumentPair doc = inputList.get(idx.getIndex());
        result.add(new SearchResult(doc.getUrl(), doc.getTitle()));
    }

    return new SearchResutls(result);
}
```

Here we just took the code we wrote in `Chapter 6`, *Working with Text - Natural Language Processing and Information Retrieval* and `Chapter 7`, *Extreme Gradient Boosting* and put it inside, feature extractor creates a `DataFrame` with features. Then we use the utility class `XgbUtils` for applying the XGBoost model to the data from the `DataFrame`, and finally, we use the score from the model for reordering the input list. At the end, it just converts the `QueryDocumentPair` objects into `SearchResult` objects and returns it.

To create an instance of this class, we can first load the feature extracted we *trained* and saved previously as well as the model:

```
FeatureExtractor fe = FeatureExtractor.load("project/feature-
extractor.bin");
Ranker ranker = new XgbRanker(fe, "project/xgb_model.bin");
```

Here the `load` method is just a wrapper around `SerializationUtils` from Commons Lang.

Now we have the ranker, and we can use it to create a search engine service. Inside, it should take in Lucene's `IndexSearcher` for the Common Crawl index, and our ranker.

When we have a ranker, let us create a search service. It should take in Lucene's `IndexSearcher` and our `Ranker`.

Then we create the `search` method with the user query; it parses the query, gets the top 100 documents from the Lucene index, and reorders them with the ranker:

```
public SearchResults search(String userQuery) {
    Query query = parser.parse(userQuery);
    TopDocs result = searcher.search(query, 100);
    List<QueryDocumentPair> data = wrapResultsToObject(userQuery, searcher,
result)
    return ranker.rank(data);
}
```

Here we again reuse a function from `Chapter 6`, *Working with Text - Natural Language Processing and Information Retrieval:* the `wrapResultsToObject` which converts the Lucene results to `QueryDocumentPair` objects:

```
private static List<QueryDocumentPair> wrapResultsToObject(String
userQuery,
            IndexSearcher searcher, TopDocs result) throws IOException {
    List<QueryDocumentPair> data = new ArrayList<>();

    for (ScoreDoc scored : result.scoreDocs) {
        int docId = scored.doc;
        Document doc = searcher.doc(docId);
```

```
String url = doc.get("url");
String title = doc.get("title");
String bodyText = doc.get("bodyText");
String allHeaders = doc.get("allHeaders");
String h1 = doc.get("h1");
String h2 = doc.get("h2");
String h3 = doc.get("h3");

data.add(new QueryDocumentPair(userQuery, url, title,
        bodyText, allHeaders, h1, h2, h3));
}

return data;
}
```

Our search engine service is ready, so we can finally put it into a microservice. As discussed previously, a simple way to do it is via Spring Boot.

For that, the first step is including Spring Boot into our project. It is a bit unusual: instead of just specifying a dependency, we use the following snippet, which you need to put after your dependency section:

```
<dependencyManagement>
  <dependencies>
    <dependency>
      <groupId>org.springframework.boot</groupId>
      <artifactId>spring-boot-dependencies</artifactId>
      <version>1.3.0.RELEASE</version>
      <type>pom</type>
      <scope>import</scope>
    </dependency>
  </dependencies>
</dependencyManagement>
```

And then the following dependency in the usual place:

```
<dependency>
  <groupId>org.springframework.boot</groupId>
  <artifactId>spring-boot-starter-web</artifactId>
</dependency>
```

Note that the version part is missing here: Maven takes it from the dependency management section we just added. Our web service will respond with JSON objects, so we also need to add a JSON library. We will use Jackson, because Spring Boot already provides a built-in JSON handler that works with Jackson. Let us include it to our pom.xml:

```
<dependency>
  <artifactId>jackson-databind</artifactId>
  <groupId>com.fasterxml.jackson.core</groupId>
</dependency>
```

Now all the dependencies are added, so we can create a web service. In Spring terms, they are called Controller (or RestController). Let us create a SearchController class:

```
@RestController
@RequestMapping("/")
public class SearchController {
private final SearchEngineService service;

    @Autowired
    public SearchController(SearchEngineService service) {
        this.service = service;
    }

    @RequestMapping("q/{query}")
    public SearchResults contentOpt(@PathVariable("query") String query) {
        return service.search(query);
    }

}
```

Here we use a few of Spring's annotations:

- @RestController to tell Spring that this class is a REST controller
- @Autowired to tell Spring that it should inject the instance of the SearchEngineService into the controller
- @RequestMapping("q/{query}") to specify the URL for the service

Note that here we used the @Autowired annotation for injecting SearchEngineService. But Spring does not know how such a service should be instantiated, so we need to create a container where we do it ourselves. Let us do it:

```
@Configuration
public class Container {

    @Bean
    public XgbRanker xgbRanker() throws Exception {
```

```
            FeatureExtractor fe = load("project/feature-extractor.bin");
            return new XgbRanker(fe, "project/xgb_model.bin");
        }

        @Bean
        public SearchEngineService searchEngineService(XgbRanker ranker)
                throws IOException {
            File index = new File("project/lucene-rerank");
            FSDirectory directory = FSDirectory.open(index.toPath());
            DirectoryReader reader = DirectoryReader.open(directory);
            IndexSearcher searcher = new IndexSearcher(reader);
            return new SearchEngineService(searcher, ranker);
        }

        private static <E> E load(String filepath) throws IOException {
            Path path = Paths.get(filepath);
            try (InputStream is = Files.newInputStream(path)) {
                try (BufferedInputStream bis = new BufferedInputStream(is)) {
                    return SerializationUtils.deserialize(bis);
                }
            }
        }
    }
```

Here we first create an object of the XgbRanker class, and by using the @Bean annotation we tell Spring to put this class into the container. Next, we create the SearchEngineService which depends on XgbRanker, so the method where we initialize it takes it as a parameter. Spring treats this as a dependency and passes the XgbRanker object there so the dependency can be satisfied.

The final step is creating the application, which will listen to the 8080 port for incoming requests and respond with JSON:

```
@SpringBootApplication
public class SearchRestApp {
    public static void main(String[] args) {
        SpringApplication.run(SearchRestApp.class, args);
    }
}
```

Once we run this class, we can query our service by sending a GET request to http://localhost:8080/q/query, where query can be anything.

For example, if we want to find all the pages about *cheap used cars*, then we send a GET request to `http://localhost:8080/q/cheap%20used%20cars`. If we do this in a web browser, we should be able to see the JSON response:

As we see, it is possible to create a simple microservice serving data science models with a few easy steps. Next, we will see how the performance of our models can be evaluated online that is, after a model is deployed and users have started using it.

Online evaluation

When we do cross-validation, we perform offline evaluation of our model, we train the model on the past data, and then hold out some of it and use it only for testing. It is very important, but often not enough, to know if the model will perform well on actual users. This is why we need to constantly monitor the performance of our models online--when the users actually use it. It can happen that a model, which is very good during offline testing, does not actually perform very well during online evaluation. There could be many reasons for that--overfitting, poor cross-validation, using the test set too often for checking the performance, and so on.

Thus, when we come up with a new model, we cannot just assume it will be better because its offline performance is better, so we need to test it on real users.

For testing models online we usually need to come up with a sensible way of measuring performance. There are a lot of metrics we can capture, including simple ones such as the number of clicks, the time spent on the website and many others. These metrics are often called **Key Performance Indicators** (**KPIs**). Once we have decided which metrics to monitor, we can split all the users into two groups, and see where the metrics are better. This approach is called **A/B testing**, which is a popular approach to online model evaluation.

A/B testing

A/B testing is a way of performing a controlled experiment on users of your system. Typically, we have two systems--the original version of the system (the *control* system) and the new improved version (the *treatment* system).

A/B test is a way of performing controlled experiments on online users of the system. In these experiments, we have two systems--the original version (the *control*) and the new version (the *treatment*). To test whether the new version is better than the original one, we split the users of the system into two groups (*control* and *treatment*) and each group gets the output of its respective system. While the users interact with the system, we capture the KPI of our interest, and when the experiment is finished, we see if the KPI across the treatment group is significantly different from the control. If it is not (or it is worse), then the test suggests that the new version is not actually better than the existent one.

The comparison is typically performed using the *t*-**test**, we look at the mean of each group and perform a two-sided (or, sometimes, one-sided) test, which tells us whether the mean of one group is significantly better than the other one, or the difference can be attributed only to random fluctuations in the data.

Suppose we already have a search engine that uses the Lucene ranking formula and does not perform any re-ordering. Then we come up with the XGBoost model and would like to see if it is better or not. For that, we have decided to measure the number of clicks users made

This KPI was chosen because it is quite simple to implement and serves as a good illustration. But it is not a very good KPI for evaluating search engines: for example, if one algorithm gets more clicks than other, it may mean that the users weren't able to find what they were looking for. So, in reality, you should choose other evaluation metrics. For a good overview of existent options, you can consult the paper *Online Evaluation for Information Retrieval* by K. Hoffman.

Let us implement it for our example. First, we create a special class `ABRanker`, which implements the `Ranker` interface. In the constructor it takes two rankers and the random seed (for reproducibility):

```
public ABRanker(Ranker aRanker, Ranker bRanker, long seed) {
    this.aRanker = aRanker;
    this.bRanker = bRanker;
    this.random = new Random(seed);
}
```

Next, we implement the `rank` method, which should be quite straightforward; we just randomly select whether to use `aRanker` or the `bRanker`:

```
public SearchResults rank(List<QueryDocumentPair> inputList) {
    if (random.nextBoolean()) {
        return aRanker.rank(inputList);
    } else {
        return bRanker.rank(inputList);
    }
}
```

Let us also modify the `SearchResults` class and include two extra fields there, the ID of the result as well as the ID of the algorithm that generated it:

```
public class SearchResults {
    private String uuid = UUID.randomUUID().toString();
    private String generatedBy = "na";
    private List<SearchResult> list;
}
```

We will need that for tracking purposes. Next, we modify XGBRanker so it sets the
generatedBy field to xgb--this change is trivial, so we will omit it here. Additionally, we
need to create an implementation of the Lucene ranker. It is also trivial-- all this
implementation needs to do is returning the given list as is without reordering it, and
setting the generatedBy field to lucene.

Next, we modify our container. We need to create two rankers, assign each of them a name
(by using the name parameter of the @Bean annotation), and then finally create the
ABRanker:

```
@Bean(name = "luceneRanker")
public DefaultRanker luceneRanker() throws Exception {
    return new DefaultRanker();
}

@Bean(name = "xgbRanker")
public XgbRanker xgbRanker() throws Exception {
    FeatureExtractor fe = load("project/feature-extractor.bin");
    return new XgbRanker(fe, "project/xgb_model.bin");
}

@Bean(name = "abRanker")
public ABRanker abRanker(@Qualifier("luceneRanker") DefaultRanker lucene,
        @Qualifier("xgbRanker") XgbRanker xgb) {
    return new ABRanker(lucene, xgb, 0L);
}

@Bean
public SearchEngineService searchEngineService(@Qualifier("abRanker")
Ranker ranker)
        throws IOException {
    // content of this method stays the same
}
```

When we create ABRanker and SearchEngineService, in the parameters we provide the
@Qualifier - which is the name of the bean. Since we now have quite a few rankers, we
need to be able to distinguish between them, so they need to have names.

Once we have done it, we can restart our web service. From now on, half of the requests
will be handled by the Lucene default ranker with no reordering, and half--by the XGBoost
ranker with reordering by our model's score.

The next step is getting the user's feedback and storing it. In our case the feedback is the clicks, so we can create the following HTTP endpoint in `SearchController` for capturing this information:

```
@RequestMapping("click/{algorithm}/{uuid}")
public void click(@PathVariable("algorithm") String algorithm,
        @PathVariable("uuid") String uuid) throws Exception {
    service.registerClick(algorithm, uuid);
}
```

This method will be invoked when we receive a GET request to the `click/{algorithm}/{uuid}` path, where both `{algorithm}` and `{uuid}` are placeholders. Inside this method, we forward the call to the `SearchEngineService` class.

Now let us re-organize our abstractions a bit and create another interface `FeedbackRanker`, which extends the `Ranker` interface and provides the `registerClick` method:

```
public interface FeedbackRanker extends Ranker {
    void registerClick(String algorithm, String uuid);
}
```

We can make `SearchEngineService` dependent on it instead of a simple `Ranker`, so we can collect the feedback. In addition to that, we can also forward the call to the actual ranker:

```
public class SearchEngineService {
    private final FeedbackRanker ranker;

    public SearchEngineService(IndexSearcher searcher, FeedbackRanker
ranker) {
        this.searcher = searcher;
        this.ranker = ranker;
    }

    public void registerClick(String algorithm, String uuid) {
        ranker.registerClick(algorithm, uuid);
    }

    // other fields and methods are omitted
}
```

Finally, we make our `ABRanker` implement this interface, and put the capturing logic in the `registerClick` method.

For example, we can make the following modifications:

```
public class ABRanker implements FeedbackRanker {
    private final List<String> aResults = new ArrayList<>();
    private final List<String> bResults = new ArrayList<>();
    private final Multiset<String> clicksCount =
ConcurrentHashMultiset.create();

    @Override
    public SearchResults rank(List<QueryDocumentPair> inputList)
                    throws Exception {
        if (random.nextBoolean()) {
            SearchResults results = aRanker.rank(inputList);
            aResults.add(results.getUuid());
            return results;
        } else {
            SearchResults results = bRanker.rank(inputList);
            bResults.add(results.getUuid());
            return results;
        }
    }

    @Override
    public void registerClick(String algorithm, String uuid) {
        clicksCount.add(uuid);
    }

    // constructor and other fields are omitted
}
```

Here we create two array lists, which we populate with UUIDs of created results and one Multiset from Guava, which counts how many clicks each of the algorithms received. We use collections here only for illustration purposes, and in reality, you should write the results to a database or some log.

Finally, let us imagine that the system was running for a while and we were able to collect some feedback from the users. Now it's time to check if the new algorithm is better than the old one. This is done with the *t*-test, which we can take from Apache Commons Math.

The simplest way of implementing it is the following:

```
public void tTest() {
    double[] sampleA = aResults.stream().mapToDouble(u ->
clicksCount.count(u)).toArray();
    double[] sampleB = bResults.stream().mapToDouble(u ->
clicksCount.count(u)).toArray();

    TTest tTest = new TTest();
    double p = tTest.tTest(sampleA, sampleB);

    System.out.printf("P(sample means are same) = %.3f%n", p);
}
```

After executing it, this will report the *p*-**value** of the *t*-test, or, the probability of rejecting the null hypothesis that two samples have the same mean. If this number is very small, then the difference is significant, or, in other words, there is strong evidence that one algorithm is better than another.

With this simple idea, we can perform online evaluation of our machine learning algorithm and make sure that the offline improvements indeed led to online improvements. In the next section, we will talk about a similar idea, multi-armed bandits, which allow us to select the best performing algorithm at runtime.

Multi-armed bandits

A/B testing is a great tool for evaluating some ideas. But sometimes there is no better model, for one particular case sometimes one is better, and sometimes another is better. To select the one which is better at this particular moment we can use on-line learning.

We can formulate this problem as a Reinforcement Learning problem--we have the **agents** (our search engine and the rankers), they interact with the **environment** (the users of the search engine), and get some **reward** (clicks). Then our systems learn from the interaction by taking **actions** (selecting the ranker), observing the feedback and selecting the best strategy based on it.

If we try to formulate A/B tests in this framework, then the action of the A/B test is choosing the ranker at random, and the reward is clicks. But for A/B tests, when we set up the experiment, we wait till it finishes. In online learning settings, however, we do not need to wait till the end and can already select the best ranker based on the feedback we received so far.

This problem is called the **bandit problem** and the algorithm called multi-armed bandit helps us solve it--it can select the best model while performing the experiment. The main idea is to have two kinds of actions--exploration, where you try to take actions of unknown performance, and exploitation, where you use the best performing model.

The way it is implemented is following: we pre-define some probability *e* (epsilon), with which we choose between exploration and exploitation. With probability *e* we randomly select any available action, and with probability *1 - e* we exploit the empirically best action. For our problem, it means that if we have several rankers, we use the best one with probability *1 - e*, and with probability e we use a randomly selected ranker for re-ordering the results. During the runtime, we monitor the KPIs to know which ranker is currently the best one, and update the statistics as we get more feedback.

This idea has a small drawback, when we just start running the bandit, we do not have enough data to choose which algorithm is the best one. This can be solved with a series of warm-ups, for example, the first 1000 results may be obtained exclusively in the exploration mode. That is, for the first 1000 results we just choose the ranker at random. After that we should collect enough data, and then select between exploitation and exploration with probability *e* as discussed above.

So let us create a new class for this, which we will call `BanditRanker`, which will implement the `FeedbackRanker` interface we defined for our `ABRanker`.

The constructor will take a map of `Ranker` with names associated to each ranker, the `epsilon` parameter, and the random `seed`:

```
public BanditRanker(Map<String, Ranker> rankers, double epsilon, long seed)
{
    this.rankers = rankers;
    this.rankerNames = new ArrayList<>(rankers.keySet());
    this.epsilon = epsilon;
    this.random = new Random(seed);
}
```

Inside, we will also keep a list of ranker names for internal use.

Next, we implement the `rank` function:

```
@Override
public SearchResults rank(List<QueryDocumentPair> inputList) throws
Exception {
    if (count.getAndIncrement() < WARM_UP_ROUNDS) {
        return rankByRandomRanker(inputList);
    }
```

```
        double rnd = random.nextDouble();
        if (rnd > epsilon) {
            return rankByBestRanker(inputList);
        }

        return rankByRandomRanker(inputList);
    }
```

Here we always select the ranker at random at first, and then either explore (select the ranker at random via the `rankByRandomRanker` method) or exploit (select the best ranker via the `rankByBestRanker` method).

Now let us see how to implement these methods, First, the `rankByRandomRanker` method is implemented in the following way:

```
    private SearchResults rankByRandomRanker(List<QueryDocumentPair> inputList)
    {
        int idx = random.nextInt(rankerNames.size());
        String rankerName = rankerNames.get(idx);
        Ranker ranker = rankers.get(rankerName);
        SearchResults results = ranker.rank(inputList);
        explorationResults.add(results.getUuid().hashCode());
        return results;
    }
```

This is pretty simple: we randomly select a name from the `rankerName` list, then get the ranker by the name and use it for re-arranging the results. Finally, we also have the UUID of the generated result to a `HashSet` (or, rather, its hash to save the RAM).

The `rankByBestRanker` method has the following implementation:

```
    private SearchResults rankByBestRanker(List<QueryDocumentPair> inputList)
    {
        String rankerName = bestRanker();
        Ranker ranker = rankers.get(rankerName);
        return ranker.rank(inputList);
    }

    private String bestRanker() {
        Comparator<Multiset.Entry<String>> cnp =
                (e1, e2) -> Integer.compare(e1.getCount(), e2.getCount());
        Multiset.Entry<String> entry =
    counts.entrySet().stream().max(cnp).get();
        return entry.getElement();
    }
```

Here we keep `Multiset<String>`, which stores the number of clicks each algorithm has received. Then we select the algorithm based on this number and use it for re-arranging the results.

Finally, this is how we can implement the `registerClick` function:

```
@Override
public void registerClick(String algorithm, String uuid) {
    if (explorationResults.contains(uuid.hashCode())) {
        counts.add(algorithm);
    }
}
```

Instead of just counting the number of clicks, we first filter out the clicks for results generated at the exploitation phase, so they do not skew the statistics.

With this, we implemented the simplest possible version of multi-armed bandits, and you can use this for selecting the best-deployed model. To include this to our working web service, we need to modify the `container` class, but the modification is trivial, so we omit it here.

Summary

In this book we have covered a lot of material, starting from data science libraries available in data, then exploring supervised and unsupervised learning models, and discussing text, images, and graphs. In this last chapter we spoke about a very important step: how these models can be deployed to production and evaluated on real users.

Index

A

A/B testing 333, 338
AOL Cyclops React
  about 38
  reference 39
AOL Cyclops-React
  reference 18
Apache Common Collections
  reference 17
Apache Commons IO
  reference 18
Apache Commons Math
  reference 19
Apache Commons
  Apache Commons Lang 31
  common modules 33
  Commons Collections 33
  Commons IO 32
  reference 32, 34
Apache Flink
  reference 19
Apache Hadoop
  about 276, 279
  Common Crawl 277, 282, 285
  Hadoop MapReduce 276
  reference 19
  YARN 276
Apache HttpComponents
  reference 46
Apache Lucene
  about 171
  customizing 175, 176
  reference 20
  using 167, 169
Apache Mahout
  reference 19, 20

Apache OpenNLP
  reference 20
Apache Spark DataFrames
  reference 18
Apache Spark
  about 287
  reference 19
Apache Tika
  reference 41

B

Bag of Words 158
bandit problem 339
Bayesian Information Criterion (BIC) 146
binary classification models 74
bottom-up approach 137

C

cats, versus dogs
  data augmentation 266, 269
  data, reading 252, 255
  deep learning, URL 252
  DeepLearning4J, running on GPU 270, 274
  model, creating 255, 259
  performance, monitoring 259, 265
classification models
  about 75, 85
  Encog 86
  Java Statistical Analysis Tool (JSAT) 77
  LIBLINEAR 79
  LIBSVM 79
  Statistical Machine Intelligence and Learning
    Engine (Smile) 75
classification problem
  binary 10
  multi-class 10
classification

about 74
binary classification 74
binary classification models 74
evaluation 87
multi-class classification 74
cluster analysis
about 11, 136
additional set of features, adding 148
as dimensionality reduction 148, 150
density-based 136
graph-based 136
hierarchical methods 136, 138, 139, 141
K-means 143
partitioning 136
using, in supervised learning 147
versus supervised learning 151
clustering 11
Common Crawl
about 277, 278, 279, 284
download link 277
compressed row storage (CRS) 135
Convolutional Neural Networks
about 250
using 245, 251
Cross Industry Standard Process for Data Mining
(CRISP-DM)
about 7, 13
business understanding 14
data preparation 14
data understanding 14
evaluation 15
feature engineering 15
model development 15
modeling 15
curve of dimensionality 131
customer segmentation 11

D

data accessing
about 39
Comma Separated Values (CSV) 39
databases, using 46
DataFrames 49
HTML, using 41
JSON, using 44

text data, reading 39
web, using 41
data augmentation 266
data mining 8
data science libraries
about 17
categories 17
data mining 19
data processing libraries 17
machine learning 19
math and stats libraries 19
text processing 20
data science
about 8, 16
libraries 17
machine learning 9
process models 13
uses 8
DeepLearning4J
in neural network 242
neural network 235
neural networks 238
reference 20
density-based spatial clustering of applications with
noise (DBSCAN) 11, 146
Dependency Injection (DI) 322
dimensionality reduction
shortcomings 118
supervised dimensionality reduction 118
truncated SVD 126
unsupervised dimensionality 118
unsupervised dimensionality reduction 119
distortion 143
Dual Coordinate Descent (DCD) 79
dummy-coding 127
dying ReLU 241

E

Eigenvalue Decomposition (EVD) 120
elbow method 145
Encog
reference 20
epoch 238
evaluation metrics, classification
about 87

accuracy 88
F1 89
k-fold cross-validation 97
precision 89
recall 89
result validation 94, 95
ROC 91, 94
ROC (AUC) 91, 94
testing 99
training 96, 99
validation 99
evaluation metrics, regression
  Mean Absolute Error (MAE) 109
  Mean Squared Error (MSE) 108
evaluation, cluster analysis
  about 152
  manual evaluation 152
  supervised evaluation 153
  unsupervised evaluation 156
Exploratory Data Analysis (EDA)
  about 14, 57
  Apache Commons Math 59, 61
  in Java 57
  joinery 62, 63
  search engine dataset 58
extensions, to standard Java library
  about 31
  AOL Cyclops React 38
  Apache Commons 31
  Google Guava 34
Extreme Gradient Boosting (XGBoost) 206, 231

F

F1 score 90
feature extraction algorithms, dimensionality
    reduction
  Locally Linear Embedding (LLE) 119
  Non-Negative Matrix Factorization (NNMF) 119
  Principal Component Analysis (PCA) 119
  random projection 132, 134, 135
  random projections 119
  Singular Value Decomposition (SVD) 119
  t-SNE 119
  truncated SVD 123, 124, 125
  truncated SVD for categorical and sparse data
    126, 130, 131
features, extracting from graph
  node feature 296
flow
  reference 51
FScore 219

G

GATE
  reference 20
Google Guava
  about 34, 35, 37
  reference 17
Gradient Boosted Classification Trees 206
Gradient Boosted Regression Trees 206
Gradient Boosted Trees 206
Gradient Boosting Machines (GBM) 205
Graphics Processing Unit (GPU) 270

H

H2O
  reference 20
hardware performance project 109, 111, 113, 114
hold out technique 94

I

indexing 167
information retrieval (IR)
  about 158
  ranking 196, 198, 200
  reranking, with Apache Lucene 201, 204
Interactive Exploratory Analysis Data
  about 64
  joinery shell 66, 71
  JVM languages 64
issues, text classification
  about 194
  language detection 193
  sentiment analysis 193
  spam detection 193
iteration 238

J

Java 9

download link 65
Java Database Connectivity (JDBC) 18, 46
Java Native Interface (JNI) 206
Java Statistical Analysis Tool (JSAT)
  reference 77
Java Virtual Machine (JVM) 64
Java
  data frame libraries 18
  data science 16
  Exploratory Data Analysis (EDA) 57
JavaML
  reference 20
JBlas
  reference 19
joinery
  reference 18, 51, 66
JSAT
  reference 20
JSON
  reference 45
JVM languages
  about 64
  interactive Java 65

K

k-fold cross-validation 97
K-means
  DBSCAN 146
  implementing 143
  K, selecting 144
Kaggle
  customer complaints, URL 126
Key Performance Indicators (KPIs) 333

L

Latent Semantic Indexing (LSI) 177
Launch Instance button 272
LIBLINEAR
  reference 79, 83
LIBSVM
  reference 79
LingPipe 20
Link Prediction
  about 290
  DBLP graph, reading 291, 293

edge feature 307, 309
edge features 304
features, extracting from graph 293, 294
link suggestions 315, 316, 318
MLlib, using 309, 311
negative sampling 299, 300, 303
node feature 295, 299
XGBoost, using 310, 312
linkages
  about 137
  average linkages (UPGMA linkage) 137
  complete linkages 137
  single linkages 137
linking 137

M

machine learning libraries, for regression
  JSAT 107
  LIBSVM 108
  Smile 106
machine learning
  for texts 177
MALLET
  reference 20
Matrix Java Toolkit (MTJ) 130, 165
Maven Central repository
  reference 18
Mean Absolute Error (MAE) 109
Mean Average Precision (MAP) 201, 314
Mean Squared Error (MSE) 108
microservices
  about 322
  search engine service 323
  Spring Boot, using 322
multi-armed bandits 338
multimap 36
Multiple Additive Regression Trees
  (LambdaMART) 225
multisets 35

N

N-dimensional arrays for Java (ND4J) 232, 235
Natural Language Processing (NLP) tools
  lemmatization 171
  Named Entity Recognition (NER) 171

Part-of-Speech tagging (POS) Tagging 171
sentence splitting 171
Stanford CoreNLP 172, 175
tokenization 171
Natural Language Processing (NLP)
  about 12, 158
  tools 171
neural networks
  about 232
  in DeepLearning4J 235, 238
Normalized Discounted Cumulative Gain (NDCG)
  201, 314

O

Obtain, Scrub, Explore, Model, and iNterpret
    (OSEMN) 13
online evaluation
  A/B testing 333
  about 333
Ordinary Least Squares (OLS) 106, 118

P

page prediction 101, 102, 103, 105
Pointwise Mutual Information (PMI) 184
predictive analytics 8
Principal Component Analysis (PCA) 12, 119, 122
problem solution categories, with machine learning
  Natural Language Processing (NLP) 12
  reinforcement learning 9
  semi-supervised learning 9
  supervised learning 9, 10
  unsupervised learning 9, 11
process models, data science
  about 13
  Cross Industry Standard Process for Data Mining
    (CRISP-DM) 13
  example 15
proximity matrix 138

R

Radial Basis Function (RBF) 80
ranking classifier 91
Read-Evaluate-Print Loop (REPL) 64
regression problem 10
regression

about 105
evaluation 108
machine learning libraries 106
regularized Jaccard Similarity 307
Resilient Distributed Dataset (RDD)
  about 287
  actions 287
  transformations 287
Rhino 66
Root Mean Squared Error (RMSE) 109

S

Saddle
  reference 18
sbt tool
  reference 76
Search engine service
  multi-arm bandits 341
  multi-armed bandits 338
search engine
  building 51, 323
Singular Value Decomposition (SVD) 114, 120,
    178
Spring Batch
  reference 19
Spring Boot 322
standard Java library
  about 23, 24
  collections 24, 25
  extensions 31
  input data, reading 25
  input/output 25
  output data, writing 27
  streaming API 28
Stanford CoreNLP
  reference 20
Statistical Machine Intelligence and Learning
    Engine (Smile)
  reference 20, 75, 106, 107
supervised dimensionality reduction
  feature selection 118
supervised learning
  about 10
  for texts 192
Support Vector Machine (SVM) 10

Support Vector Regression (SVR) 10

T

Tablesaw
  reference 18
tensor 232
text categorization 11
tokens 158
top-down clustering 136

U

unstructured data 158
unsupervised dimensionality reduction
  feature extraction 118
unsupervised learning, for texts
  Latent Semantic Analysis (LSA) 177, 178, 179
  text clustering 181
  word embeddings 183, 185, 186, 190, 192
unsupervised learning
  about 11, 117
  clustering 11
  dimensionality reduction 11
  for texts 177

V

vanishing activation problem 265
vanishing gradient problem 241, 265
variables, not using in cluster analysis
  company response to customer 154
  consumer disputed 154

timely response 154
Vector Space Model
  about 158, 159
  implementing 161, 163, 165, 167

W

Weka
  reference 19
winutils.exe file
  reference 288
word embeddings
  about 191
  download link 190
Word2Vec 183

X

XGBFI
  reference 220
XGBoost4j 206
XGBoost
  features, importance 219
  for Learning to Rank 224, 228
  for regression 223
  installing 207
  of regression 221
  parameter tuning 216
  parameter tuning, algorithm 217
  r Learning to Rank 226
  text features 218
  used, for classification 209, 213, 216
  using 209